Order without Government

ORDER WITHOUT GOVERNMENT

The Society of the Pemon Indians of Venezuela

DAVID JOHN THOMAS

Illinois Studies in Anthropology
No. 13

UNIVERSITY OF ILLINOIS PRESS

Urbana   Chicago   London

© 1982 by the Board of Trustees of the University of Illinois
Manufactured in the United States of America

Library of Congress Cataloging in Publication Data

Thomas, David John, 1945-
   Order without government.

   (Illinois studies in anthropology; no. 13)
   Bibliography: p.
   Includes index.
   1. Arecuna Indians.   I. Title.   II. Series.
F2380.1.A7T48   980' .004'98   81-1818
ISBN O-252-00888-X   AACR2

Dedicated
to
J.A.F.
uruiko echikaijarɨ
and
to the memory of
Theodor Koch-Grunberg (1872–1924)

Preface

This book was written at intervals between the summer of 1977 and Christmas of 1979, though it first took shape in my mind in Uonken in July, 1975. I have changed all actual names of individuals in the account, to protect the privacy of the Pemon, with one exception, that of Alejo Calcaño, former regional leader in Kamarata, now deceased. I have endeavored wherever possible to use names which are not common among the Pemon today (names were selected at random from Conto and Isaza, 1895).

Fieldwork was carried out from May, 1970, through June, 1971, and in June-July, 1975. An account of fieldwork among the Pemon will be found in the Appendix. Unless specifically stated to the contrary, the "ethnographic present" is 1970. In some cases the reader is referred to prior work (Thomas, 1971, 1972, 1973, 1979a) for tabular representations of data. By and large, I have meant this to be read as a book, not as a print-out of data, hypotheses, and tests. The Pemon would probably say to the reader *etamen waki* (roughly, "may you walk well").

My debt to the Pemon cannot be paid in kind and must remain part of our mutual experience.

Professor Ken Kensinger and Dr. Kathleen Adams have provided support, encouragement, and excellent advice during the preparation of this work, though they are responsible for none of its deficiencies. Dr. Audrey Butt Colson has provided encouragement and advice over many years. Anna V. Thomas has done extensive editorial and critical work on numerous sections of this book, and her command of the English language has helped it immeasurably.

I would also like to thank Dr. J. V. Neel, chairman of the Department of Human Genetics, University of Michigan Medical School, and Dr. N. A. Chagnon, then research associate there, for support of my 1970–71 fieldwork under an AEC contract, and the University Research Council, Vanderbilt University, for a grant which enabled me to return to the field in the summer of 1975.

Many Venezuelan friends have given help, kindness, and hospitality. These include Dr. Miguel Layrisse, Fisiopatologia, IVIC; Walter Coppens, Fundacion La Salle; Dra. Nelly Arvelo-Jimenez, Antropologia, IVIC; Professor Roberto Lizarralde, Universidad Central de Venezuela; Dr. F. Rubens Coronil and Dra. Lya Imber de Coronil and their family.

My thanks to three men who have been teachers, friends, and colleagues for many years: Dr. Aram Yengoyan, Dr. Roy Rappaport, and Dr. Joseph Jorgensen. Dr. George G. Simpson kindly gave permission for me to consult a portion of the English version of his work on the Kamarakoto.

My thanks to Marlene Windsor for typing numerous drafts, and for much patience. Responsibility for the facts, inferences, and opinions in this book is solely my own.

Contents

Figures

Tables

Orthography of Pemon words

It is assumed that the reader's interest is not primarily linguistic; for convenience, the following representation of Pemon phonemes has been adopted.

All consonantal phonemes have the same value as their corresponding English representations, with the following exceptions:

1) The sounds *ch* and *sh* are allophones of the *s* phoneme in Pemon. Nevertheless, I have included *ch* and *sh* because certain words (e.g. *cachiri*, the Pemon word for fermented manioc beer) have already customarily come to be transcribed using the *ch* and *sh* representation.

2) The glottal stop is represented by ʔ.

3) Word-final *n* is pronounced *ng*.

4) Nasalization is represented by ˜.

5) The phoneme *d* is pronounced *th* (interdental, voiced fricative) before the vowel *a*. It is here represented by *d* for all occurrences.

6) The flapped *l* or *r* (flapped, voiced, alveolar, liquid) is a single phoneme, represented here by *r*.

Vocalic phonemes (correspondences with English sounds)

a = *a* as in father ɨ = *e* as in ros*e*s (high, central, unrounded vowel)
e = *ay* as in b*ay* o = *o* as in n*o*te
i = *ee* as in b*ee*t u = *oo* as in b*oo*t

Genealogical Notation

The system currently in use by British social anthropologists to represent genealogical connections between individuals has been adopted here. The following symbols are put together in the form of a relative product to specify a genealogical designation: F = father, M = mother, B = brother, Z = sister, S = son, D = daughter, C = child, H = husband, W = wife. They are put together in accordance with English usage, as illustrated by the following examples: WB = wife's brother; MB = mother's brother; MBD = mother's brother's daughter; MMBDD = mother's mother's brother's daughter's daughter, and so on. In this book "genealogical" refers to a relationship which can be defined by one of these relative product strings in which all links are through known, named individuals, living or dead.

The following shorthand expressions have also been used: f-i-l = father-in-law (spouse's father), s-i-l = son-in-law (daughter's husband), b-i-l = brother-in-law (wife's brother or sister's husband).

The letter *e* in front of a genealogical symbol means *elder* and the letter *y* in front of a genealogical symbol means *younger*; thus eB = elder brother, yZ = younger sister, etc. The *e* or *y* modifies only the symbol immediately following it, and no others.

CHAPTER I

Introduction

Order without Government is a study of an egalitarian people who live in a vast expanse of savanna and tropical forest in southeastern Venezuela. They are Carib-speaking American Indians who first appear in the Western historical record in the eighteenth century. At the time of my first stay with them (1970) there were about 4,000 Pemon in Venezuela, though now (1980) there are substantially more. The vast majority of Pemon support themselves by slash-and-burn cultivation and by fishing and hunting in the rivers and forests of the Gran Sabana and nearby areas. Their society, though it shows many features in common with other South American native peoples, may be singular in its degree of dispersion, its far-flung relations with neighboring peoples, and the general informality of social life, even in its ritual aspects.

A society like that of the Pemon holds special appeal for Americans, who like to think of their own social order as egalitarian. Here the term "egalitarian society" means a society whose members have equal access to the benefits of that society. Pemon society is but one example of a whole range of societies which could conceivably fall under this rubric, though it is more amorphous than many such. The purpose here is to show how this particular people has maintained an egalitarian way of life in a particular setting. Certain Pemon notions and ways of doing things shed light on other, similar societies. I shall point these out, without trying to generalize where it is not appropriate.

Since the remainder of this Introduction is concerned mostly with the "how" of this book, its assumptions and underpinnings, a word about the "why" is appropriate. The job of anyone who delves into another culture is one of translation, yet few inquiries are made as to why people are moved to undertake such an effort. Like any endeavor, anthropology is many things to many people. Yet it alone, of all approaches to the study of humankind, starts out with the attempt to come to grips with "otherness," with that which is outside of oneself, beyond one's ken, and far from one's kin. It goes without saying that an apprehension of "otherness," and its rendering into our own terms, are always undertaken from a particular point of view. While it is seldom possible to get to rock bottom where motives are concerned, my desire to work and live among indigenous South Americans stemmed from a combination of influences. These included a rather long-term familiarity with the continent (I had lived in both Brazil and Venezuela prior to my fieldwork), some disaffection with aspects of advanced industrial society (shared with many members of my own society), and intense curiosity about societies which operate at the scale of the human stride. Anthropologists are often beset with accusations of romanticization, and it would be naive to think that they do not identify to some extent with those they live among. Nevertheless, I have not attempted to hide the warts. I have also attempted to keep my own concepts separate from those of the Pemon, insofar as it is possible while writing in English. Fieldwork, as it is lived, is partly the intersection of two sets of abstractions (ours and theirs), but the attempt must be made to sort them out in the process of translation. The translation of culture, then, is an ethnographer's effort to sort things out.

Some sections (particularly Chapter III, "Relatives, Residents, and Neighborhoods") may be rough going for those unfamiliar with anthropological discussions of social organization. I can only assure the reader that, just as the dry season and easy walking follow the "rain time" when feet sink in the mushy soil of forest and savanna, the intricacies of kinship are balanced by what comes after.

Plan of the Book

A brief chapter on setting and history presents the land itself, outside influences on the Pemon, and aspects of subsistence. The bulk of the book centers on four topical areas: the basic idiom of everyday life, the kinship domain; leadership and statuses outside the kinship domain; forces of disharmony, i.e. conflicts, conflict situations, and outcomes, and means of avoiding or defusing conflicts; and ideology as manifested in Pemon tales. A concluding chapter focuses on the basic premises of Pemon society, which can be summarized in the words "separation," "equality," and "autonomy." The Epilogue is a note on the passing of Pemon society as an egalitarian social order.

To those who live in our own society it is often difficult to convey the experience of life in a society in which daily activities are dealt with in the context of who one's relatives are, how to determine one's obligations to them as well as defend oneself from their importuning if need be, how to separate relatives and nonrelatives, how to absorb new people into already existing categories of relatives, and so on. Dealing with this fundamental aspect of life in Pemon society necessitates talking about rules of classification and their application, patterns of residence and interaction both within and between settlements, and the verbal statements Pemon make about whom one should marry, whom one should aid and why, and what kinds of people are praiseworthy and blameworthy. Kinship in Pemon society is an area of binding obligations, but it is not an inflexible or ascribed domain. The concepts of siblingship, filiation, and affinity are used to elucidate the operation of Pemon ideas and practice regarding relatives. Special emphasis is placed on the sibling set (set of brothers and sisters) as a unit which, while internally containing elements of hierarchy, is seen as a whole by members of other such units. Also, emphasis is placed on the positive marriage rule of the Pemon (a rule which enjoins marriage with a specific category of relative) and on its manipulation. The complexity of actual marriage patterns is examined in the light of manipulation and different interpretations of the marriage rule, as well as in light of lack of conformity with it. Throughout, the limits which Pemon kinship concepts and practices place on the development of specific settlements and leaders are stressed.

Though kinship looms large in this account, other integrative aspects of Pemon society must be considered in portraying adequately the forces which keep Pemon society egalitarian. Subsistence, for example, depends on access to certain tools and implements which come from outside the tribe or from a particular area within it. There is an essential "openness" of access to traded items, and that openness is ensured by the rules governing trade and their application (Thomas, 1972). There are of course persons — big traders — who participate most avidly in the workings of the trade system, ranging far and wide on trading expeditions and manipulating their kin networks to provide outlets for goods in distant parts of Pemon territory. They are leaders in the realm of trade, though their renown does not carry over into a generalized position of pre-eminence.

A leader in Pemon society can be a person who achieves prominence in any one of a number of areas, but a leader is not a person who gives orders. Even in a conflict situation or a situation in which he or she is trying to move people toward a certain course of action, the function of a leader in any realm is to exhort, remind, and persuade (and sometimes to threaten). Most Pemon leadership statuses are based to some extent on expertise, and one outstanding status in this regard — that of warfare chief or leader — has not existed during the past 100 years (see Koch-Grunberg, 1916–28, III: 101–7, for a discussion of accounts of warfare and warfare leaders by his informants).

The various kinds of leaders in Pemon society today reflect expertise in some area and a more general standing based on their personality, their generosity, and the size of their personal kindred. The standing of a particular shaman, for example, rests upon his reputation as a curer (or as a malevolent sorcerer), his knowledge of esoteric ritual formulae, and his actual effectiveness with his patients (clients), and also on how isolated his residence and activities are with respect to his own kinsmen and neighbors. If he is relatively accessible, charges of malfeasance and sorcery will tend to be mitigated, and his reputation as a "good" or curing shaman will be enhanced. The capitan, or local political leader, must display some skill and enough Spanish to be credible in his negotiations with outsiders (e.g. miners, missionaries, anthropologists, members of non-Pemon indigenous peoples), and must display the proverbial (in South America) rhetorical flair of the good talker. The rezadora who leads Hallelujah ceremonies must have expert knowledge of the chants, songs, and stories of the Hallelujah religion, and must also be an older woman who conveys decorum and propriety in her personal life. The expertise of the prophet is limited to the validation of his or her status by knowledge of "heaven" obtained in visions, and prophetic leadership depends heavily on spatial mobility (to recruit followers), right conduct ("purer" than that of the average person), and the size of one's personal kindred. Expertise, then, is a necessary but not sufficient condition for leadership, and is always accompanied by other factors in a given case.

The analysis of Pemon leadership patterns centers on the degree of permanence and of heritability in these statuses, on the situational determinants of leadership (how leaders are brought into being), and most importantly on the ways in which leaders are constrained from overstepping the bounds of their role (and of their area of expertise) and from concentrating power in more than one domain. The interactions between different types of leaders — particularly the conflicts between capitanes and shamans — form a portion of the set of constraints which keep them in their places. An important aspect of Pemon egalitarianism is the separation of realms of expertise (and hence leadership) into only partially overlapping domains. This separation tends to prevent the rise of a single leader who is simultaneously dominant in political, religious, and economic areas of Pemon life. If Pemon society cannot be said to have abolished power (though much of it is found only in the supernatural form), it can at least be said to have dispersed and separated centers of personal and group power to a remarkable extent. Since the possibilities of the exercise of power through economic coercion are so limited in Pemon society, a leader of any type must maintain "an estate in persons" (K. Adams, 1976) which must be continually managed and renewed.

Chapter V, "Forces of Disharmony," focuses on cases of conflict — between neighbors, between spouses, between and within aggregates of cognatic kin, and between leaders of various kinds — and their outcomes. Prominent in the discussion is the fact that there are sometimes no direct sanctions against offenses which are considered serious by the Pemon (and would be considered very serious in our own society as well, e.g. incest between brother and sister) (see Dole, 1964, 1966, on situations among the Kuikuru where certain offenses go unpunished). One particular case of alleged sorcery, which had wide ramifications over a span of four years in the whole of the central portion of the tribal territory, is treated extensively. The relationship of conflicts to Pemon thinking about harmony — personal, social, and supernatural — is discussed in detail, with particular attention to the concept of being angry (Pemon *sakorope*) or a "fighter" (a strongly reproved trait). Finally, cases of conflict are linked to the operation of the marriage system, the abuse of supernatural power, and conceptions of the welfare of the community at large.

A brief consideration of Pemon tales shows that fundamental notions of kinds of hierarchy, balanced reciprocity, and the disruptiveness of certain kinds of demands on individuals are embodied in them. The analysis combines considerations of both structure and content of the tales to show their functions as warnings, injunctions, and rationalizations regarding Pemon social relations, as well as their function as means of resolving or attenuating logical conflicts in Pemon thinking.

The concluding chapter links the discussions of kinship, leadership, disharmony, and ideology. It centers on the kinds of hierarchy which are disallowed in Pemon society and the various ways in which this amorphous society has kept people apart while providing means of inclusion when the occasion demands. Order is seen to be a result, paradoxically, of the minimization of hierarchy and the emphasis on personal autonomy which characterize Pemon life.

Assumptions and Underpinnings

Life in so-called "primitive" societies is neither "poor, nasty, brutish, and short" nor idyllic. However, life in a horticultural, low-density, egalitarian society like that of the Pemon is radically different from life in our own society. Several assumptions commonly made about life in society by members of our own culture do not apply there. Among these are:

1) The assumption of perpetual scarcity. Pemon society, even today in the face of massive influx of goods from the Venezuelan national economy, is a society of relatively finite material needs. Pemon, when comparing themselves with criollos, will say *Pemonton, tuariton* ("We Pemon are poor people"). They do not make such comparisons when talking about their Pemon neighbors. They will also often remind one that "though we don't eat so well sometimes, no one starves here." There are complaints about the paucity of fish and game nowadays as com-

pared with past time, but no Pemon is involved in competitive accumulation of material goods in order to "beat out" or "keep up with" his neighbors. Pemon attitudes toward work, and actual work regimes, show that the regularized and rigid work regime which would be associated with a system of competitive material accumulation and the assumption of perpetual scarcity simply does not exist.

2) The assumption that violence is an inevitable part of social life.

3) The assumption that hierarchy (outside the domestic unit) is universal.

4) The assumption that concentration of power (centralization) is inevitable.

The rubric "egalitarian" is rather broad, and Pemon society can be thought of as one type or variety under this broad term. It is my feeling that a range of types of egalitarian societies can be defined and exemplified in the "primitive" world. The relative absence of hierarchy outside the domestic unit cannot be assumed merely from poverty of material possessions, dispersion over the land, and other conventional techno-economic and ecological explanations. While certain techno-economic factors may in effect set outer limits on the possibility for an egalitarian social system, the variations in density and population distribution among egalitarian societies make it clear that there is considerable latitude in this respect. As Stauder (1972) has pointed out, the equation of egalitarian political type with a specific level of techno-economic development is untenable, as there are many societies practicing slash-and-burn or intensive horticulture that qualify as egalitarian (as well as many hunting and gathering societies).

Of major importance in a consideration of egalitarian social systems are the procedures for maintaining order, in the absence of authority-bearing elites. The problem thus becomes twofold: to discuss those features that produce a relative absence of hierarchy (outside the domestic unit), and those features that maintain order in the absence of hierarchy. The problem of order has come in for detailed treatment by anthropologists, and characteristics of egalitarian societies related to the problem of order can be summed up as follows:

1) People live in dense social networks, in which each individual appears to his fellows in multiple roles; their interaction, therefore, often tends to be in terms of a concept of "person" rather than simply role, and reputation is of paramount importance (see E. Colson, 1974: 5–6).

2) People expect to interact with pretty much the same people over the course of their lives (though some of these societies have high spatial mobility, and in such cases this characteristic does not hold, e.g. the pastoral Jie and Turkana of East Africa [Gulliver, 1955]).

3) These societies have strongly internalized norms (in the absence of many formalized institutions of social control). This proposition is more

often affirmed than demonstrated by anthropologists and requires some examination.

4) These societies are characterized by the norm of reciprocity, and the threat of withdrawal of reciprocity is a severe sanction encouraging right conduct (see Sahlins, 1965).

5) Fears of various kinds keep people in line. Notable among these are fear of sorcery and fear of ostracism (an ultimate sanction).

6) Norms to the effect that each man is his own master are likewise strong in these societies (see E. Colson, 1974:3, speaking of the Tonga of Rhodesia after decades of colonial rule: " . . . the Tonga still have little respect for hierarchy. Instead they stress personal independence, the equality of all men, and the right of each man to make his own law").

7) Virtually all anthropologists (see Gluckman, 1965) are agreed that the social order in these societies is sacralized, that it operates in close coordination with supernatural sanctions that have marked influences on individual behavior.

Previous approaches to the problems of "ordered anarchy" (the phrase is Evans-Pritchard's, as applied to the type case, the Nuer of the Sudan) have emphasized the structure of interaction between corporate groups (lineages, clans, clan-parishes, etc.). Many studies were done by British social anthropologists, largely in East and Central Africa. They produced the concept of "segmentary lineage organization" in which segments of different genealogical levels both opposed one another and were welded into larger units under pressures from outside. The focus was on the place of corporate groups in the resolution of disputes and the maintenance of order.

The connection of concepts of self-help and redress to the context of corporate groupings was an important step, but one that to a certain extent impeded examination of societies in which self-help, redress, and other processes related to order might not be linked to corporate groups. In some societies self-help is linked to ad hoc groups of kinsmen or friends and associates (see Moore, 1972). As Burridge has made clear in his section entitled "The Moral and Divine" in his masterful work *Tangu Traditions* (1969a), societies in which corporate groups beyond the household are shifting or ill-defined or nonexistent make it incumbent on the investigator to understand in detail the moral universe and the ethical precepts held by individual members of such societies. Burridge focuses on the ways in which the idiom of reciprocity is modulated in Tangu to allow its expression in different social contexts.

Pemon society can be classed as egalitarian, anarchic (without government, political functions being diffused throughout the society), and to a certain extent amorphous (lacking corporate groups beyond the household). Hierarchy usually implies control, or the potential for control, of a subordinate. The problem of egalitarianism then is linked to means of preventing the formation of enduring centers or loci of control, of subordination. In Pemon society, fundamental contradictions at the level of norms work to prevent the building up of concentrations of power in the hands of specific individuals. These conflicts of norms (particularly of norms of obligation to specific categories of persons) counteract tendencies toward assumption of personal power by individuals (heads of settlement) and also work to prevent group formation over a time span long enough to concentrate power in group terms. Contradictions at the normative level not only provide mechanisms that prevent loci of power from building up but also, in concert with the specific obligations of the kinship domain, serve to maintain order.

The notion of power used here is rather broad, and simply refers to the ability to affect the environment and behavior of an individual or group regardless of the will of that individual or group (for a different, narrower usage, see R. Adams, 1970, 1975). Power in this sense is very limited in Pemon life, and the term "influence" will be much more prominent below. I use this term to mean the moving of an individual or group into a desired situation or toward a desired action by means — usually persuasion, sometimes veiled threats — that attempt to take into account the will of the individual or group. Influence in this sense shades off into power on the one hand and into simple convergence of interests on the other. I do not consider that all aspects of Pemon life are political, or that all the institutions of Pemon society are colored by a political component.

My description and analysis of Pemon life focuses on the level of social relations. This aspect of Pemon life has exhibited the most continuity over the past hundred years or so. While the Pemon have gone through numerous ideological and technological changes during that time (the Hallelujah and Chochiman religious movements, the missionary incursions and presence, the advent of the shotgun, clothing, and air travel, to mention but a few), the level of social organization has remained remarkably stable. Exactly why this should be so cannot be fully explained at present, but it draws the eye of the ethnographer to the often contradictory norms and practices which sustain Pemon social organization.

Levi-Strauss's statement (1963: 13–14) "that a society functions is a truism, that everything in a society functions is an absurdity" seems relevant here. When I speak of mechanisms in Pemon social organization, I do not mean to imply that these are reciprocally interacting parts of some homeostatic machine (or organism) that is Pemon society. I do not believe that Pemon society, or any other, is well served by either a machine analogy or an organismic analogy. As Evans-Pritchard (1964) reminds us, societies are neither organisms nor machines, but moral orders. They may well be systems, but they are systems of a different kind from those embodied in machines or in organisms.

An argument is made not for the value of any single systemic model in interpreting Pemon society but for the connection of kinship and non-kinship domains of social relations by contradiction and separation of elements within and between domains. Ultimately, Pemon society continues to be egalitarian because the Pemon can keep domains of power and influence apart. Pemon measures of social control seem diffuse and potentially ineffective by our standards. But for the Pemon, social control is directly connected with its obverse, personal autonomy. Control measures which are explicit and involve extended group action are foreign to the Pemon in many instances because the desire for personal autonomy is extended to the "other" as much as to oneself. Personal autonomy, of high value to the Pemon, is a subject seldom dealt with by contemporary students of society, who prefer to speak of social control largely in terms of sanctions. Pemon society reveals that in an egalitarian society there is also a marked desire to "bring someone around" by indirect means which maintain autonomy largely intact. Measures that prevent conflicts from breaking out are often as important as self-help or redress in such a society, since they may preclude the use of sanctions and, on the surface at least, preserve personal autonomy (see Nadel, 1953).

This book, then, is an exploration of the themes of personal autonomy, the exercise and dispersion of power, and the social practices that maintain an egalitarian society. I move across Pemon behavior, norms, and ideas to develop these themes, and the principal assumption I use is that Pemon society is a meaningful order, a moral order, and an order by which power is mediated (and contained). There is at present no single theoretical framework in the social studies for treating these three "orders" simultaneously, and this account cuts across them. It therefore draws on several different theoretical traditions in dealing with different parts of the Pemon material. Included are several, sometimes conflicting, approaches to kinship (Fortes, Levi-Strauss) and an interpretation of Pemon tales which draws most heavily on Burridge's (1967, 1969a) adaptation of Levi-Strauss's work. My own background (structural engineering, in the first instance) moves me toward fitting methods and models to problems, not the other way around.

A word about what seems to be a current concern, epistemology. My rule of thumb in the field was: "If they have a word for it or if I have a word for it, it's real enough." In other words, if I could formulate it or if the Pemon could formulate it, it found its way into my notebooks. We have no way of knowing how adequately an individual can enter an alien social world, and can only judge the results. To develop an adequate anthropological epistemology would mean following out all the behavioral cues and internal processes by which the ethnographer comes to understand what is around him. I am enough of an empiricist to recognize the empirical reality of subjectivity, both my own and that of the Pemon. One can talk about what they do, what they say, and what they say they do, and one can and does infer what they mean and feel. All of these go into an account of a given social reality. Because they are all included, social anthropology is and must be a systematic art, not a science of systems.

Problems and assumptions thus stated, on to the Pemon.

CHAPTER II

Setting and History

The Guiana Shield and the Guiana Highlands Culture Area

In the area between the Atlantic Coast of South America, the Amazon, and the Orinoco lies the Guiana Shield, a geological formation of prepaleozoic age and of great geological stability. The gneiss which forms the base of the shield has its origin in prepaleozoic igneous rock. The erosion of the metamorphic rocks of the shield formed a great part of the savanna soils found to the south of Cd. Bolivar on the lower Orinoco. Erosion has left bare the more resistant quartz-iron rocks, and in many places waterfalls are formed by resistant granites and basalts found in the gneiss complex (Vila, 1951: 21). Along the riverbeds there have formed soils of Quaternary age, some of them of relatively high fertility. Intrusions of quartz in the gneiss complex are in some places quite rich in gold, and alluvial formations in the Caroni drainage are often rich in diamonds. In the north-central part of Estado Bolivar, Venezuela, there are extensive deposits of high-grade iron ore (e.g. Cerro Bolivar).

Moving southward from the Orinoco, there are two divisions to the terrain. From the Orinoco to about 6°15' N latitude the countryside is dominated by lowlands with an average altitude of about 250 meters; farther south, extending well into the Amazon drainage, is a more mountainous terrain whose mean altitude is between 700 and 800 meters (Vila, 1951: 47). As late as 1965 (date of issue), Operational Navigation Chart (ONC) L-27, covering much of the Guiana Shield from 0° N latitude to 8°N latitude, showed vast areas of incomplete relief data on the Venezuelan side of the highlands area.

The aboriginal inhabitants of the Guiana Highlands are characterized by many cultural elements which place them in the broad category of lowland tropical forest cultures: they sustain themselves on manioc, use tobacco, employ blowguns and poisoned darts in hunting, fish with fish poisons, construct semipermanent dwellings, and generally sleep in

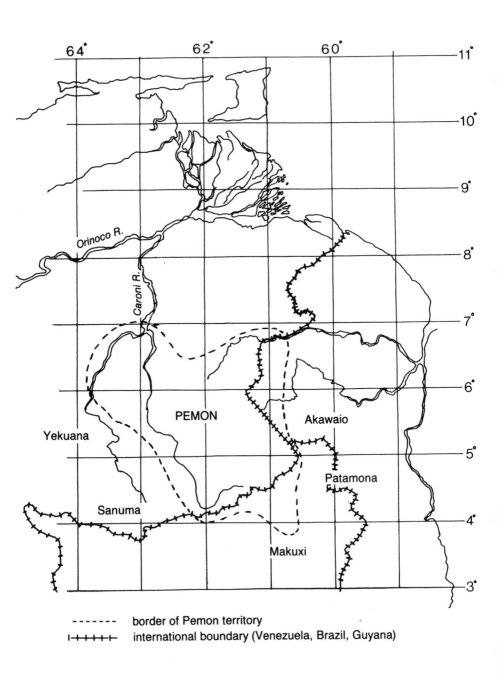

Figure 1. Map of Pemon tribal territory (1970).

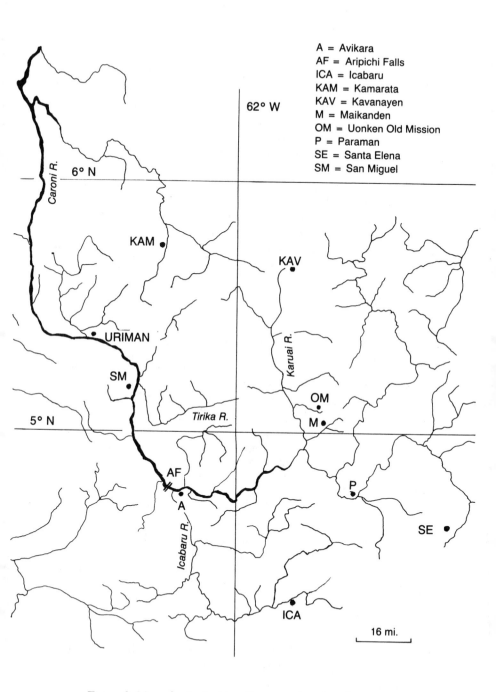

Figure 2. Map of principal locations mentioned in the text.

hammocks. Formerly they went naked or used only a loincloth; they have a long pottery-making tradition, and they use canoes for river travel.

Within the broad category of tropical forest cultures, the cultures of the Guiana Highlands distinguish themselves by a number of characteristics: they use no narcotics other than tobacco; they cultivate and spin cotton and have a rather advanced weaving technology; they squeeze manioc in a particular type of tube-like fiber press; they have an extensive repertory of finely made fiber basketwork. In the area of social organization, the cultures of the Guiana Highlands show an emphasis on the nuclear family, matrilocal residence, and bilateral cross-cousin marriage as expressed norms, and an emphasis on cognatic descent and the personal kindred.

Gillin (1948: 800) divides the whole of the Guiana area (high- and lowlands) into three subareas: "(1) the coastal area, (2) the inland mountain savanna area, and (3) the Amazonian area. Not only have migration and mixing of culture elements blurred the distinctions which may have been clearer at one time, but lack of information may also lead us astray." Gillin (ibid.:801) continues, remarking on the area which is the focus of this book:

> Characteristic traits of the inland mountain-savanna region are the lance, blowgun, tobacco-chewing, use of parica, circular houses with walls, sandals, discoid paddle blades, possibly cremation as an earlier trait, nose flutes, dance sticks, turtle-shell friction drums, and more elaborate ceremonial costumes, star lore, and puberty and mourning ceremonies than those of the coastal region. These traits are not all common to all the inland tribes, and, although they are found with greater frequency in the inland area, they are not unknown to all the coastal tribes. . . .
>
> Thus, no clear-cut lines of culture dissimilarities are discernible among the various regions of the Guiana area; rather the culture area must be distinguished on the basis of tendencies, emphasis, and statistical averages. Even the Guiana area as a whole is not strikingly distinctive, for it shares many traits and configurations in common with the other tropical regions of South America.

The Pemon, while similar to all the Carib-speakers who surround them to the east, south, and west, differ in the extent of expanse of their tribal territory (they are the most far-flung of the central Guiana Highlands peoples) and in the degree to which the autonomy of the nuclear family is emphasized. Pemon life is much less centered around the focus of a "village" than is Yekuana life as described by Arvelo-Jimenez (1971). Likewise, the Akawaio and Patamona to the east of the Pemon seem to be more centered on a cultural pattern which emphasizes the village as a coherent unit than do the Pemon.

In general, while the similarities in material culture and social organization among all the people of the central Guiana Highlands are striking, the Pemon seem to have gone furthest among these peoples in the direction of the autonomy of the minimal units (the individual, nuclear family, and sibling set) of the society. Unlike the Barama River Carib (Gillin, 1936), the Pemon have not been an involuted, isolated social system but rather a social system which has established important connecting links (principally trade; see Thomas, 1972, 1973) with surrounding indigenous peoples and which has looked outward from its geographical redoubt. The Pemon are the largest in population of all the central Guiana Highlands peoples, and their spatial mobility has been almost equal to that of their voyaging Yekuana neighbors to the west. For a complete picture of the similarities and differences among the peoples of the central Guiana Highlands, the reader is referred to A. Colson (1971b).

The Gran Sabana and Neighboring Areas

In the central part of the Guiana Highlands, within the boundaries of Estado Bolivar, Venezuela, is a broad expanse of savanna and mountains known as the Gran Sabana. It is an area bounded by the Serrania de Lema and the valley of the Carrao River on the north, by the Guyana border on the east, by the Serra Parima along the Brazilian-Venezuelan frontier, and by the valley of the Caroni on the west. Comprising about 30,000 square kilometers, the Gran Sabana forms the greater part of the tribal territory of those aborigines who call themselves Pemon. Known in the literature as Arecuna, Kamarakoto, and Taurepan, the Pemon are roughly divisible into three subgroups with those names.

In 1970 the Pemon inhabited not only the Gran Sabana and the drainage of the Caroni as far north as San Pedro de las Bocas but also portions of the middle and lower Paragua. There are Pemon settlements on the Carun and Antabari and other tributaries of the middle Paragua, and downstream from Auraima Falls on the Oris River and Isla Casabe, as well as farther downstream all the way to the mouth of the Paragua. Outside the boundaries of Venezuela, there are 300 Taurepan (southern Pemon) in 15 settlements in the Brazilian Territorio de Roraima (see Migliazza, 1970). There are also Arekuna (northern Pemon) on the Guyana side of the Venezuela-Guyana border, but I know of no recent estimates as to how many Pemon are actually living on the Guyana side. There are also Pemon settlements on the upper Cuyuni, upstream from El Dorado, and between El Dorado and Kavanayen along and at some distance from the road which (as of 1973) extends through the easternmost part of Pemon territory to Santa Elena de Uairen.

Pemon within the boundaries of Venezuela but within the tribal territory outlined above numbered 4,000 in 1970 (Thomas, 1971: 3). This figure does not include Pemon living in Venezuelan towns and cities outside the tribal territory. The tribal territory in 1970 was as found in Figure 1, and includes the valley of the Carrao and part of the upper Cuyuni, as well as the Caroni drainage above San Pedro de las Bocas and the indicated parts of the Paragua drainage.

A map provided by the Division de Marlariologia y Saneamiento Ambiental in Cd. Bolivar in 1970 showed over 600 named settlements in Municipio Santa Elena, which comprises the Gran Sabana plus the Icabaru drainage and the right bank of the Caroni as far downstream as the mouth of the Carrao. Of the 617 named settlements on the map, 309 had Pemon names and 308 had Spanish names. Though not all of the named settlements were occupied in 1970, the approximate ratio of about 300 named Pemon settlements to the roughly 30,000 square kilometers of the Gran Sabana shows an average of one settlement per 100 square kilometers. This is an extremely low average density, which of course does not reflect the clustering of settlements in river valleys and the general lack of settlements in the highest elevations.

Tribal Names and Ethnic Boundaries

What people call themselves and what they are called by others seldom coincide; this has given rise to innumerable confusions in the ethnographic record, no less so in the case of the Pemon than in other instances.

The term "Arekuna" (Arecuna), which became the common term of reference for the northern Pemon in the nineteenth-century accounts of R. H. Schomburgk (1854:50) and others, does not appear on Surville's map of 1778 (see Caulin, 1966: facing p. 2). On that map the area of the Gran Sabana bears the designation "N. [Nacion] Barinagotos," and the area between the Caroni and Paragua bears the labels "N. Purugotos" and "N. Achirigotos." The term "Arecuna" was not used by the late eighteenth-century Capuchin missionaries of the Caroni Prefectura, who used the term "Camaragoto" to refer to the aboriginal inhabitants of the middle reaches of the Caroni, from the mouth of the Carrao to the area of Uriman, and the term "Hipurugoto" to refer to the aborigines of the Icabaru River area (see Armellada, 1960: 117–60).

Simpson (1940: 356) states the following about the use of the word "Arekuna" by the inhabitants of Kamarata in 1939:

> Actually, the name "Arekunas" is applied by all these Indians to their neighbors and frequently to themselves. The Kamarakotos, for example, use that name for themselves, but call the people neighboring the Caroni Arekunas, although they are of Kamarakoto descent or have close relationship with them and call themselves Kamarakotos. The Kamarakotos also call all the Indians of the Gran Sabana and all the more distant ones of the Upper Caroni, Arekunas.

> I see no reason why we should not return to the usages of the ancient travelers, sanctioned by the Indians themselves, of naming all this incoherent mass of Indians and their common language Arekunas. Here and there appear a better known or defined center or group, and these can bear the name of their respective locality or region.

The term "Arekuna" is that used by the Akawaio of the upper Mazaruni District in Guyana to refer to the inhabitants of the Gran Sabana: "From the centre of their homeland, the upper Mazaruni District, the Akawaio look out to their immediate neighbors, the Patamona to the south and the 'Arekuna' (that is, the Arekuna and Taulepang) on the Gran Sabana, with whom they have long had some degree of inter-marriage and direct trading contacts. Beyond the 'Arekuna' are the Kamarakoto . . . " (A. Colson, 1973: 6).

Since the suffixes -*koto* and -*goto* in the Pemon language mean "inhabitant of," it is easy to see the proliferation of place names plus suffixes in the designation of various local groupings on Surville's map and in the usages of the Pemon themselves and neighboring groups. Confusion only intensifies when one tries to put down hard and fast meanings and explicit boundaries for vague terms in travelers' accounts and the indigenous lexicon. By the early nineteenth century the term "Arekuna" had come into general use in British Guiana to refer to the indigenous population of the Gran Sabana: " . . . the Arecunas, who inhabit the mountainous regions at the headwaters of the Caroni and Cuyuni. They are a powerful tribe, but are more properly the inhabitants of the Venezuelan territory . . . " (Schomburgk, 1840: 50).

The word "Taurepan," now used (see Layrisse and Wilbert, 1966: 80) to refer to the southern Pemon of the Roraima area and farther south, was introduced by Koch-Grunberg (1916–28). Armellada (1943–44, I: 15) states that the Capuchin missionaries of the Santa Elena area continued to use the word in the same sense but that " . . . it is true that the word Taurepan, in spite of our familiarity with the Indians and the questions, some direct and some captious, that the other missionaries and I asked them has never come spontaneously from the mouths of these natives, and, when we said the word, they were never able to give us its meaning."

Armellada (1943–44, I: 13–14) objects to the conventional (after the time of Koch-Grunberg) division of the Pemon into the three subgroups, Arekuna, Kamarakoto, and Taurepan:

> Frankly, I do not see sufficient somatological, ethnic, or glottological differences to denominate the inhabitants of the south of the Gran Sabana Taurepanes, those of the north Arekunas, and those of Kamarata, Kamarakotos; but all of these, and the inhabitants of Tirika, Uriman and the lower part of the Paragua River form a single lexical and grammatical unit, although the phonetics are different enough.

What is certain (as Armellada notes) is that all of the aboriginal inhabitants of the Gran Sabana and the neighboring areas referred to above as falling within the tribal territory, refer to themselves as "Pemon" (meaning people, or people who speak the Pemon language) and *by this term distinguish themselves from named groups of neighboring peoples.* Pemon distinguish from themselves the Akawaio to the east, whom the Pemon call Waika; the Patamona to the southeast, whom the Pemon call Ingariko; the Makuxi to the south; and the Sape, Yekuana (Pemon Mayongong: Venezuelan designation Maquiritare), and Shiriana to the west. Some Sape-speakers survive incorporated into Pemon communities in the lower Paragua, but the Sape as an ethnic unit are now extinct. The Makuxi, neighbors of the Pemon to the south, also refer to themselves as Pemon, though all neighboring groups refer to them as Makuxi. The Yekuana located at Parupa and Isla Casabe on the Paragua in 1970 referred to the Pemon, and to the Pemon language, as Makuxi, indicating that at least some Yekuana lump the Pemon and Makuxi into a single category.

Taking the Gran Sabana as the center of our universe for the moment, we can visualize the Pemon classification of non-Pemon via Figure 3.

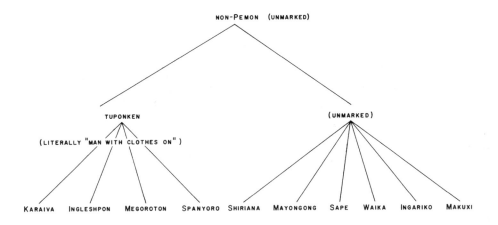

Figure 3. Pemon classification of non-Pemon.

A word which deserves mention is *paranakiri.* Armellada (1960: 118) states: "Centuries later our Indians continue using this word *paranakiri* for Europeans of the Guianas (English, French and Dutch), distinguishing them from the "Españoro' (Spanish-Venezuelan) and from the 'Karaiva' (Portuguese-Brazilian)." In his dictionary (1934–44,

II: 112) Armellada notes the following definition: "English (person)/ probable etymology: *Parana kiri*. That likes the coast, coastal, maritime; the Pemon and Akawaio believe them all to be the residents of the coasts of Guiana." Armellada (1960: 118) indicates that the word originally referred to the Dutch. The word was not current in the central part of the Gran Sabana by 1970, apparently having been replaced by the term *ingleshpon* to refer to English-speakers. As can be seen from these examples, the Pemon have incorporated into their language not only terms for neighboring indigenous peoples but also for aliens from European colonizing powers.

When discussing ethnic units, the question of exact boundaries is often a troubled one. Pemon are intermarried to some extent with the Akawaio to the east and with the Makuxi to the south. Exact demarcations along these parts of the tribal territory would be difficult to draw, notwithstanding the fact that Pemon would unhesitatingly differentiate themselves from both Akawaio and Makuxi on the basis of their linguistic differences. In fact, language is the major identifying emblem which the Pemon use to separate themselves from others — even their designations for Europeans are based primarily on the recognition of speakers of different languages. That language should be the major "marker" of ethnic identity for the Pemon is not at all surprising, particularly in view of the degree of technological and cultural similarity among the Pemon and their indigenous neighbors. The Pemon and their Carib-speaking neighbors share marked similarities in material culture, social organization, and mythical and religious concepts. Given the absence of any major visible differences in physical types among the aboriginal populations of the Guiana Highlands, language is a convenient point of difference. In fact, dialectical differences within the Pemon language, particularly between Kamarakoto- and non-Kamarakoto-speakers, are used as markers of provenience within Pemon society as a whole.

Language

Loukotka (1968: 209–11) classifies Pemon as the principal language of the Pemon or Taurepan group of languages of the Carib stock, in the northeastern division of the languages of tropical forest tribes. He recognizes Taurepan, Arecuna, and Kamarakoto, along with Ingarico, Uaica, and Acawai as the languages of this group. In the adjacent Makuxi group (1968: 208–9) he places Makuxi, Keseruma, Purucoto, Wayumara, Paraviyana, and Zapara, all of which are or were spoken by groups in the Brazilian Territorio de Roraima.

The three dialects of the Pemon language and the Akawaio, Ingariko (Patamona), and Makuxi languages are all closely related and, according to some sources, mutually intelligible. Im Thurn (1883: 165) commented as follows: "The Makuxi dialect is very closely similar to the Arecuna, from which it differs chiefly in the mode of pronunciation; and a similar dialect, with a few exceptional differences, principally in the lower numerals, is used by the Ackawoi. A Makuxi, an Arecuna, and an Ackawoi speak quite intelligibly the one to the other."

Yekuana (Maquiritare), on the other hand, is not intelligible to a Pemon-speaker. There are, however, Pemon in the middle Caroni and Paragua who have extensive trading contacts with the Yekuana and who are consequently bilingual in Pemon and Yekuana.

As might be expected after more than 200 years of contact with European civilization, the Pemon language now contains a fair number of terms from other languages, largely borrowing from Spanish. These borrowings are mostly related to tools and other items of material culture or to domestic animals acquired in postconquest times.

History — The Eighteenth and Nineteenth Centuries

The first real penetration of Pemon territory by outsiders came in the middle of the eighteenth century, with the Spanish-Portuguese boundary commission around 1750. Centurion, the Spanish colonial governor of Guayana in the 1770s, still searching for the fabled Lake of Manoa, or Parime, and the El Dorado supposedly alongside it, sent expeditions up the Paragua in the 1770s: "These expeditions began in 1772. The first, led by Lieutenant Nicholas Martinez, having left Angostura in January, tried to open passage to the Parime through the Alto Caura, but almost all of the party having fallen ill, they stopped at the Cuata River. There they were told that the Paragua River offered the best route to the Parime" (Ojer, 1966: clxxii). They crossed to the Paragua via C. Sabaru and ascended to the headwaters, but returned without reaching "Parime." This expedition, however, brought home the lesson that it was necessary to found settlements as way stations for future expeditions.

At about the same time (February 18, 1772; see Armellada, 1960: 118ff.) the Capuchin missionaries set out on an expedition up the Caroni and Icabaru. The difficulties of navigating the Caroni are well described by Fray Tomas de Mataro (ibid.:119):

> Leaving on the planned date from the harbor of the Mission of San Buenaventura of Auguri, we embarked on the aforementioned Caroni River. This river is almost unnavigable because of the torrents and rapids that almost touch one another. So that in the month and a half that we traveled on it, we can swear that we were not on board more than six days at a time without having to leave the canoes, casting ourselves on the rocks to raise the canoes; many of these times we even had to remove the baggage and help raise the canoes with ropes. It is unexplainable, even unthinkable, how bad and dangerous this navigation is.

Fray Mataro continues with observations about the Indians of the region (ibid.: 120):

> Having come this distance on the Caroni, we arrived at the Icabaru River, where we camped, in order to leave the Caroni and take this other river, the Icabaru, to continue our course. It should be known that since we began to navigate the Caroni, up until this place, we spent a month and a day, and if we had continued, we would have spent seven days to arrive at the headwaters, which are called Pamguau. All along this Caroni River, from the mouth of the Paragua to this place, there are many Indians of the Camaragota nation, which are impossible to remove by means of this river in order to subdue them. . . . [on the Icabaru] there are many Indians of the Hipurugota nation. We found many fields, and at the ports very wide paths.

In the same year Fray Benito de la Garriga observed (Armellada, 1960: 139): "In the already mentioned journey I saw Barinagotos, Cucuicotos, Ipurugotos, Mapisanas, and these without leaving the banks of the Caroni and Icabaro Rivers. They kill each other frequently, and we found empty houses, in which hammocks hung with bones of dead people and heads broken by wooden clubs."

In 1774, Fray F. de Vich recorded the burning by Indians of a settlement of Spanish soldiers (San Jose de Caroni Chiquito) at the mouth of the Carun River. There is no doubt that in the latter part of the eighteenth century the Capuchins, in "reducing and civilizing" the indigenous population in the missionary Prefectura del Caroni, brought Pemon downriver from the middle reaches of the Caroni to mission sites at San Pedro and Guri. In 1789 Fray Mariano de Cervera, recounting a voyage to the mid-Caroni in the area just below Uriman, stated (Armellada, 1960: 156): "We arrived at a tributary called *Capaure*, from which we took 80 souls last year. . . . " These captures must have had some effect, since he says further on in the same letter (ibid.: 156): "And now in almost a month of navigation we have not found any Indians from the woodlands, until one day . . . we found two Indians, who were coming down the river fishing." In the accounts dating from the year 1772, the Indians of the Icabaru area are reported by the Capuchins to have had firearms, probably of Dutch origin.

Some insight into the process of extracting Indians from their territory for use as a labor force on the mission cattle ranches can be gained from the words of Fray R. Bueno, who worked in the Orinoco missions from 1785 to 1804 (quoted in Simpson, 1940: 217):

> The Camaracotos, Guayanos, and Guaicas are mixed nations; the first and last flee continually to the mountains and the Guayanos, being mostly creoles, return to the mountains to bring them out. The RR PP Capuchinos Catalanes of the lower Orinoco have several settlements of these nations, and aside from the subjugation in which they hold them, give them plenty to think about: they make them wear clothing, the men in trousers and

shirt, the women in a piece of coarse cloth worn crosswise; each settlement
having a herd in common, whose products are used to pay this and the expense of trips into the mountains, one taking place every year.

The boundary commission had explored the economic resources of
the Guiana Highlands area. From the time of the commission onward
there were projects for the exploitation of cinnamon and of forest cacao
of the upper Orinoco and Paraguamuxi. Also, the old interests in
timber, gold, and silver reawakened, as well as interest in forests of qui-
nine. Both missionaries and civil authorities looked at the establishment
of settlements as the single way to consolidate control over the Spanish
possessions of Guayana.

In the 1750s and 1760s the Capuchins began to push eastward toward
the upper Cuyuni, which was one of the main avenues for slave-raiding
coastal Caribs. By the 1780s, with the establishment of a mission at
Tumeremo (1788), this consolidation of the upper Cuyuni area was
almost complete.

On the western flank of Pemon territory, San Pedro de las Bocas and
Vila de la Barceloneta, both at the confluence of the Paragua and
Caroni, came into being around 1770. The basis of the Capuchin mission economy was cattle, and by the late eighteenth century the Capuchins had almost 95,000 head of cattle and 2,800 horses on their mission
ranches. By 1779 the Capuchins had 20 "pueblos de indios" or mission
stations with attached indigenous populations. At the time of its foun-
dation in 1770, San Pedro de las Bocas had a population of 332, part of
which was almost certainly Pemon (see Ojer, 1966: clxxviii).

Since many of the settlements founded by the Spanish civil authorities
were along the main course of the Orinoco, the Capuchins were by far
the most important influence on the Pemon in the later eighteenth century and the first few years of the nineteenth.

Of course, the Spanish colonial effort was contested by the Dutch and
Portuguese. The Dutch were active in the upper Cuyuni area before
1700 and up until about the middle of the eighteenth century. The
Spanish expansion in the latter half of the eighteenth century coincided
with the waning of Dutch influence in the upper Cuyuni. By 1814 the
Dutch colonies of Essequibo and Demerara were transferred to the British, and from that time on the influences on the eastern side of Pemon
territory were British.

In 1817, with the outbreak of the civil war in Venezuela, the
Capuchin missions in the Prefectura del Caroni were abandoned and
the mission villages disappeared. Thus the direct pressure on the north
and west sides of Pemon territory subsided.

In 1838-39 R. H. Schomburgk reached Mt. Roraima in the course of
his exploration from Pirara in British Guiana to Esmeralda on the upper
Orinoco. He was the first of many expeditionaries to come into Pemon

territory, particularly the Roraima area, throughout the nineteenth century.

Pemon during the early and middle nineteenth century were making long trips outside the territory, for trading and visits to missions. It is probable that northeastern Pemon along the headwaters of the Kamarang and Venamo rivers used the routes of the Mazaruni and Cuyuni rivers to make trading voyages to Georgetown in the nineteenth century. Present-day Pemon recount trading trips to Georgetown in the early part of this century via the Kamarang-Mazaruni route. Brett (1868: 267) notes that in 1863 there came to the Waramuri mission at the headwaters of the Moruca River (which flows directly into the Atlantic northwest of Georgetown) "a large party, about seventy in number, of mixed Acawoios and (to our surprise) Arecunas. The latter, whom we had not seen before, had journeyed from the high lands between the head of the Cuyuni and the Caroni. . . . " In a subsequent book Brett (n.d.: 208–9) recalls what appears to have been the same visit:

> In the year 1865 we were surprised (and our timid Waraus alarmed) by the arrival of about seventy Arecunas, from the highest, wildest, and most interesting region of Guiana, the vicinity of Mt. Roraima.
>
> Some of the people we already had were sufficiently wild in their appearance, but these Arecunas were wilder still. The men were tall, and well limbed. They seemed at first to have large, bushy whiskers, but when you got a nearer view, those facial ornaments proved to be only bunches of black feathers, attached to reeds fixed in the lobes of their ears. In the dividing cartilage of the nostrils they had also the reed ornament usually worn by the Acawoios.
>
> The men of this race wore little clothing, certainly, but their women had less. Females of mature age had only small aprons of beads. Yet they were modest, and perfectly unconscious of any offense or impropriety.
>
> Being tatooed around the mouth, they seemed to have lips of enormous size. And in addition to this artificial beauty many of those poor females had lines in imitation of moustachios, commencing on the upper lip, and going in flowing curves over the cheeks, and towards the ears.
>
> Several of these Arecunas stayed with us permanently, clothing themselves after a time like the Christian Indians around them. Their indelibly tatooed faces were soon noted as regularly appearing at Divine service, and (when they had become Church members) at Holy Communion.

Brett's observations indicate that the easternmost Pemon, though still in traditional garb, were looking outward to the British colony. By this time, undoubtedly, British Guiana was an established source of trade goods for the Pemon.

In the interim between Schomburgk's expeditions and the missionary efforts within Pemon territory in the early part of this century, the Hallelujah religion came into being. A syncretistic combination of Carib (Makuxi, Akawaio, Pemon) elements and the teachings of the

Anglican missionaries of the mid-1800s in British Guiana, the Hallelujah religion swept through the Makuxi, Akawaio, Patamona, and the eastern and southern Pemon. Butt (1960: 85) states: "My guess is that the eighteen-seventies and eighteen-eighties saw the birth and establishment of Hallelujah in the Carib-speaking tribes of the western borderlands of British Guiana. My Akawaio informants seemed to think that, in the first instance, the Arekuna and Patamona tribefolk got most of their Hallelujah knowledge direct from the Makuxi. . . . "

Up to the present century the most important external influences on the Pemon were missionary ones. By the time the relative isolation of the Pemon was definitely broken in the first decades of the twentieth century, vast changes must already have taken place in the tool and crop inventories, in the necessity for outside sources of metal goods, and in the population structure, as a function of disease. There are stories of widespread epidemics, apparently mostly measles, in the 1890s, according to my older informants in 1970. Of the actual disease history of the Pemon population, virtually nothing is known.

The relative isolation of the upper Caroni drainage basin, hemmed in by mountains on three sides and by the rapids and waterfalls of the Caroni on the fourth, kept the Pemon from being decimated as were the peoples in the flatlands from the Carrao and Cuyuni to the Orinoco. Cattle flourished on the lands of the Caroni Prefectura in the eighteenth century, but the Indians did not. How many Pemon were taken from their native lands to become laborers at San Pedro or San Buenaventura de Auguri (Guri) or even farther afield we shall never know. How many escaped and returned to the bush with metal implements and new knowledge to be incorporated into the tribal tradition is likewise unknown.

From the accounts of the Capuchins, the Pemon (including the Hipurugoto of the Icabaru River, as the Capuchins called the Pemon of that area) were fighting among themselves in the 1770s-80s, sometimes with weapons provided by the Dutch. From a variety of sources (Schomburgk, Im Thurn, Brett) it is clear that warfare had virtually ceased among the peoples of the Guiana Highlands by the third or fourth decade of the nineteenth century. Whether or not the warfare recorded by the Capuchins was instigated by Spanish, Portuguese, and Dutch penetration and the alliances set up by the conflicting colonial powers with different groups of natives, or to what extent it was an autochtonous development, will probably never be known in full. Pemon oral tradition on the subject of warfare is quite hazy (see Armellada, 1964: 24).

It is my feeling that the present-day Pemon ethic of repressing overt demonstration of hostility and of censuring persons given to violent behavior (even at the level of fisticuffs) is of long standing. This ethic and its persistence in Pemon society argue strongly for an external cause or causes for past warfare. Certain inferences from the Capuchins' letters coincide with this interpretation. There are repeated references to going over long stretches of the Caroni without finding any Indians; this indicates that the Pemon kept their settlements off the main river and well hidden. The dispersion which appears to have characterized the Pemon settlement pattern in the past (and at present) is consonant with a policy of flight and hiding from an external enemy. Possibly both external and internal causes were at work, the Capuchin penetrations forcing the move off the main rivers, and traditional norms of dispersion and ecological factors preventing large agglomeration for defensive purposes. (Dispersion may in fact be a better defense then agglomeration in the face of a technologically superior opponent.)

History — The Twentieth Century

Following the dispute, through much of the nineteenth century, between Venezuela and Britain over the boundary between Venezuela and British Guiana, the Venezuelan government began to make efforts to establish its presence in the southeastern corner of the country. A major part of that effort was the signing, in 1922, of an agreement between the Capuchin order and the Venezuelan government, re-establishing a missionary jurisdiction in southeast Venezuela for the first time since the wars of independence.

> The Venezuelan government appeared to be moving towards acceptance of responsibility in regard to the problem of the Indians when it promulgated the *Ley de Misiones* in 1915. In virtue of this law the Venezuelan nation delegated to the missionaries the task of "converting and drawing into civil life the native tribes and groups which still exist in different regions of the Republic. . . ." The rules for the implementation of this statute appeared in 1921. Successive additions to them gradually endowed the missions with even greater concessions regarding the control of native tribes and their territories and also regarding the course to be mapped out for them in order eventually to incorporate them in the national life. The missions were organized in vicariates to suit the regions of the country with Indian inhabitants, and the vicariates assumed direct responsibility to the national government. In 1922 the first contract under this law was concluded with the Caroni Mission. (Arvelo-Jimenez, 1972: 31)

But missionary penetration in Pemon territory in this century antedates the Capuchin missions by some 20 years. Armellada (1949: 448) mentions the excursions of Cary-Elwes, a Jesuit from Brazil, into the Gran Sabana in 1912, 1916, and 1920, and the Adventist missionary O.E. Davis penetrated the Roraima area in 1911, if only temporarily. Koch-Grunberg (1916–28), I: 102) states: "The influence of the English Akawaio mission, which in Roraima never had a lasting place, can here hardly be felt." He was speaking of a Pemon community on the upper Kukenan, south of Roraima. Armellada (1949: 448) also mentions the efforts of the Benedictines from the Surumu River in Brazil, who built chapels in Santa Elena, Apoipo, and Uonken from 1923 to 1931. Major missionary efforts on the part of the Adventists began with the efforts of the Reverend and Mrs. A. W. Cott in the mid-1920s. They established centers on the Arabopo River and in Acurima (now Santa Elena) and evangelized in the valleys of the Apanguao and Karuai rivers until their expulsion by the Venezuelan government in 1929-30.

The Capuchins were most eager to assert their part in this expulsion:

> By the same road Father Ignacio used, behind him penetrated Protestant Seventh Day Adventist Missionaries in 1922, who managed to establish themselves with a house, chapel, and English elementary school in Akurima, Kamuaran, and Luepa.
> This penetration represented a true danger to territorial integrity, because in addition to teaching the English language, they stamped their documents with the address "British Guiana," as we could see on various papers, left behind when they were expelled from the region at the founding of our Capuchin Missions. (Armellada, 1949: 448)

The Capuchin vision of their alliance with the Venezuelan government is further exemplified in the same issue of *Venezuela Misionera* from which the above quotes were taken:

> The Capuchin missionaries, basing themselves on official documents, have repeatedly given assurances, both orally and in writing, that it was they who in 1930 suggested to the government the desirability of expelling the foreign Adventist Protestants from the Gran Sabana, in which Venezuelan region they had established themselves illegally; likewise that it was they who advised the establishment there of the Catholic missions and the creation of a Frontier Inspector to safeguard the interests of Venezuela. (Armellada, 1949: 467)

The Adventists were readmitted to Venezuela after 1945, when a new constitution ensuring freedom of religion was passed, and their early efforts in the 1920s were followed up in the postwar period. In addition, many Pemon journeyed in the 1930s and 1950s to Adventist missions on the Kamarang and Mazaruni in British Guiana. Some converts returned to proselytize their fellow Pemon in the southern part of the territory, and by 1970 there were five Adventist Pemon communities: La Colonia and Maurak, both near Santa Elena; Apoipo, Betania (Pemon Wariwantei), and Yuruani (Pemon Kumarakapai).

Meanwhile the Capuchin missionization program went on apace. Capuchin missions were founded at Santa Elena (1931), Luepa (1933, vacated 1942), Kavanayen (1942), Kamarata (1954), and Uonken (1959). The history of direct outside influence on the savanna Pemon is largely the story of religious teachings and economic and social life at these centers. In assessing the impact of the Capuchin missionary effort on the Pemon, one must remember that the government had vested civil as well as ecclesiastical power in the Catholic missions. The Capuchins, in describing their objectives, still (1949) used the terms of the Spanish conquest: "The conversion and civilization of the natives that populate the territory of the specified mission of the Caroni — all of the Amacuro Delta and part of the state of Bolivar — was entrusted by the National Government to the Franciscan-Capuchin Order in conformity with norms established in the CONVENIO signed by both parties the 21st of February of 1922" (Armellada, 1949: 537).

The discussion of the budget assigned to the missions by the government continues:

> By Article 9 of the cited CONVENIO, the Government committed itself to contribute to the support of the personnel of the Mission with the sum of 30 thousand bolivars (Bs. 30,000.00) a year; but nothing was assigned for the construction of buildings or offices, purchase of agricultural tools and implements, support of schools and native boarding students, etc., etc., which does not fail to be an enormous defect in the aforementioned Convenio. (Ibid.)

In 1939 the amount given to the Caroni missions was raised to Bs. 50,000.00 per year, and in 1949–50 the Venezuelan government gave the Caroni mission Bs. 50,000.00 under the rules of the contract of 1922, and an additional Bs. 120,000.00 for clothing, medicines, agricultural equipment, building construction, and other like expenditures.

The 1922 contract was superseded by a new one in 1956, which separated the mission of the Caroni into two parts, one for the Gran Sabana and one for the Delta Amacuro (which became known as the Mision de Tucupita). In 1966 a third contract was signed, in which the Caroni mission (Gran Sabana and neighboring areas) was given an annual governmental subsidy of Bs. 287,784.00 to cover " . . . ordinary expenses of travel, maintenance, objects for the personal use of the missionaries and other activities of the Mission, as well as for food, clothing and other equipment for the natives . . ." (B.I.V., 1966: 37).

It has long been the policy of the Capuchins to run boarding schools for Pemon children. Accounts by Pemon from the Uonken area of years spent at the Santa Elena mission school in the 1930s are rather grim. The small children were made to work in the mission fields and attended class only about two hours a day. Speaking their native tongue was forbidden them. Food was inadequate, and several of the informants stated that the privations of the mission school forced them to escape to the bush for a long four-or-five day trek back to their home region. Conditions have improved over the years, but as late as the early 1960s a local boy in Uonken became something of a hero by fleeing from the boarding school at Kavanayen and hiding out in the bush for several weeks to avoid the chance of being sent back.

In some cases the mission schools now employ bilingual Pemon as teachers, but much of the teaching is still done in Spanish by Franciscan nuns who speak not a word of Pemon. Most mission personnel were born in Spain, including skilled craftsmen brought in by the priests to supervise mission construction work. It is my experience that few of the present-day (1970) Capuchins speak Pemon to any degree. At the Uonken mission in 1970–71 communication between priests and nuns and Pemon was entirely in Spanish, with the exception of some short passages during religious services.

One of the most important relationships between the Pemon and the Catholic missions is the employment of Pemon as wage laborers in mission construction work. In many areas (Kavanayen, Kamarata, and Uonken especially), working for the mission is the only way to obtain cash to buy salt, fishhooks, soap, clothing, powder and shot, and other outside items which have become necessities in Pemon life. It should not be forgotten that the mission buildings, fields, and workshops are a product of Pemon labor, often at very low wage rates.

The total scope of the effects of Capuchin and Adventist missionary efforts among the Pemon would require a special study. Adventist efforts have seemingly produced more far-reaching changes in basic Pemon lifeways: Adventist communities are large, laid out in rectangular grid patterns with cleared streets; the native Pemon manioc beer *(cachiri)* is prohibited, as are certain kinds of fish and certain game animals; and adult males usually possess a Western-style suit, for use at Saturday religious services. The most important fact is, of course, that the friction and competition between Capuchins and Adventists have produced a deep rift in the society of their converts. The Adventist communities, as a group, now have a tendency toward endogamy, and these communities appear to be moving away from traditional Pemon life at a more rapid rate than other segments of the population.

Other outside influences have been at work in this century, including scientific and exploratory expeditions. Most notable among these was the 1939 expedition to the Gran Sabana, sponsored by the Venezuelan government (Aguerrevere et al., 1939). This expedition was the most thorough scientific effort concerning the characteristics of southeastern Venezuela yet undertaken. Other expeditions include those of Tate (1930a, 1930b), Rice (1937), and Holdridge (1931). Slightly earlier, the Capuchins Armellada and Matallana had explored the Paragua (see Armellada and Matallana, 1942). The expedition of Felix Cardona and Juan Mundo in 1927–28, up the Caroni and its tributary the Tirika River to the Gran Sabana, was followed by a 1929 expedition of Capuchin missionaries up the Caroni as far as Uriman, then north into the valley of Kamarata, and back across the Serrania de Lema to El Dorado on the Cuyuni.

An important influence on the Pemon in the valleys of the Caroni and Paragua, and sporadically at places in the Gran Sabana, is alluvial diamond mining (see Thomas, 1979b). Mostly confined to pick-and-shovel type work, it brings as a consequence a series of "bullas" or booms. These booms establish large (sometimes upward of 5,000 individuals) temporary communities of miners of all nationalities and cultural backgrounds (principally Brazilian, Guyanese, and Venezuelan, but including Italians, Syrians, Lebanese, and others as well). The diamond diggings provide the Pemon with the opportunity to obtain small amounts of cash income which are almost immediately converted into goods produced in the external Venezuelan economy. A principal feature of this alluvial diamond mining is its sporadic nature; stream deposits are found, opened up, a community or small group of miners is founded and disappears, all within a matter of months, perhaps years in some cases. Alluvial diamond mining may range from a small encampment of two or four miners working a small section of stream to a boom community containing merchants, miners, diamond buyers, prostitutes, vendors of every description, and Pemon Indians.

In 1948 the "bulla" of Abekri created the airstrip and commercial center at Uriman, which survives to this day with a few Venezuelan merchants selling goods and buying diamonds from the Pemon and a few other miners who still work the middle reaches of the Caroni. Uriman is a few short dirt streets of mud-walled, concrete-floored, tin-roofed dwellings, some doubling as general stores, with a neighboring group of Pemon dwellings, fluctuating in numbers over the years. It is a stop on the route of the Linea Aeropostal Venezolana, which has, under various names, been shuttling DC3s and earlier vintage aircraft to the upper Caroni area since around 1936.

The anthropology of the diamond diggings and the "bulla" or boom has yet to be written, since the "bulla" is an ephemeral phenomenon, difficult to catch and describe because it happens so fast. Yet the effects of the diamond diggings over the years on the Pemon are profound. The free-for-all nature of alluvial diamond mining means that partnerships are formed, streambeds are dug, the take is whatever it turns out to be, and the partnership dissolves when the deposit is played out. The Spanish word "socio" or partner in the diamond diggings denotes a concept which has been adopted by those Pemon who go to the diggings. Rather than any long-term reciprocal relationship, the word denotes a limited-term contract, good for as long as the job holds out.

The ephemeral nature of the diamond boom is expressed in the thrown-together appearance of the camp which grows up near the diggings. Open-walled four-corner shelters, roofed with canvas tarpaulins or with plastic, are set up by the merchants, selling mostly food and hardware, clothes, mining sieves, shovels, and the like. Near the port, a stretch of cleared mud along the riverbank, the merchants' shacks are clustered helter-skelter, with narrow paths leading between them, paths that twist and jump around the rough posts and occasional tin walls of structures set down in no apparent order. Here and there under an awning a diamond buyer plies his trade, using his eyeglass and small, hand-held scale in a never-ceasing effort to classify diamonds into as low a class as possible, thus squeezing his profit out of the miner's need for ready cash. The camp hums from before dawn until well after dark, since the miners often spend twelve hours of daylight at the diggings and come in early and late to buy and sell, or whenever they can get free. Every conceivable type of clothing item suitable for wear in the tropics — and some not so suitable — is for sale at one shack or another; transistor radios are everywhere, and are an attractive item for men in the bush — the radio message hour "Correo de Guayana" is a main channel of communication for miners at different locations. Private messenger services — "representaciones" — serve the mines, miners, merchants, and diamond buyers alike. They come and go by canoe and by air, daily during the height of the boom.

The boom camp at Guacharaka on the Caroni downstream from Uriman was active during September, October, and November of 1970. The river port and merchants' shacks made up the center of the camp, strung out for some distance along the left bank of the Caroni. Shacks and lean-tos were built among the trees — there was no time to do anything but clear the underbrush. Many miners had their lean-tos, for sleeping at night, on the periphery of the merchants' section or just off the trails leading back into the forest to the streambed that was being worked. Pemon — some 70-80 men in a peak population of about 3,000 at Guacharaka — spread themselves out upstream from the camp, building small thatch lean-tos. A group clustered around a local leader (capitan) from Uriman who attempted for a short time to organize a short section of streambed "for Pemon only." Many Pemon, however, were in partnership with criollo miners, and the organizing didn't last long. Even so, small groups of Pemon organized themselves in knots of two, three, or four to exploit particular stretches of streambed, always of course as "socios" or partners, just like their criollo counterparts. Insofar as I could tell, there were no special preferences for kin as "socios," though a few father-son and brother-brother pairs turned up.

Prices of food, especially staples such as rice, usually keep Pemon from staying very long at booms such as Guacharaka. Unless they can start to bring in money from diamonds or casual labor fairly quickly, most Pemon do not have the money resources to last long at mining camp prices. Even if they do start bringing in money, the tendency for Pemon who still have fields and family back home is to stay long enough to buy needed items of clothing and equipment and then to head out.

Some Pemon have opted completely for the mining life, and these may be found all over Estado Bolivar wherever the mines happen to be. This includes sites as far away as the Guaniamo mines on the upper Cuchivero.

The business of buying and selling diamonds is regulated by the Venezuelan government in the form of taxes administered by the Ministry of Mines and Hydrocarbons. Within Pemon territory there are offices in Santa Elena, and inspectors from the MMH visit the mining town of San Salvador de Paul, near the headwaters of the Chiguao and just inland from the bank of the Caroni, some distance north of Uriman. Government may also be present in the mining centers in the form of the Guardia Nacional, government troops sent in small detachments for purposes of ensuring order. (In connection with Venezuelan frontier policy, some armed forces personnel are stationed in Santa Elena.)

Venezuelan government presence in Pemon territory is not limited to military detachments and various outposts of the MMH and MAC (Ministry of Agriculture and Stockbreeding) in Santa Elena. The Ministry of Health and Social Assistance (MSAS) maintains a Division of Malaria and Environmental Sanitation with regional headquarters in Cd. Bolivar. During the 1950s and 1960s the Malariologia employed several bilingual Pemon as part of its successful antimalarial campaign in the valleys of the Caroni and Paragua, as well as at selected locations in the Gran Sabana.

The OCAI of the Ministry of Justice (Oficina Central de Asuntos Indigenas, Ministerio de Justicia) has, since about 1951, been an instrument of governmental policy toward the aboriginal population, acting under the National Indigenist Commission, set up in 1948. While the OCAI regulates expeditions into areas inhabited by Indians, and operates a series of "Indigenous Centers" at various places in Bolivar, Apure, and Amazonas, its influence on the Pemon has been slight. A small dispensary set up on Isla Casabe to serve the Pemon and Yekuana populations of the lower Paragua was virtually inoperative in mid-1970, and no other centers exist in Pemon territory except for one in El Dorado (in the town of El Dorado). In general, OCAI has delegated work among the Pemon to the Capuchins, at both policy levels and the level of practical affairs.

While influences from Venezuelan national society have been most important over the last 50 years, influences from Brazil have likewise affected the Pemon, L. F. Peña, a Spaniard who came into Pemon territory from Brazil, established a ranch and founded Santa Elena in 1924, bringing Brazilian cattle to start his herds. Across the border from Brazil has come a steady stream of *garimpeiros* (pick-and-shovel miners) who come from as far away as the states of Ceara and Pernambuco in Brazil's impoverished northeast. There were, in 1970, mining camps on the Caroni where as much Portuguese as Spanish was spoken, and some Brazilian miners reported having lived and worked in Venezuela for over 25 years. One of the most important items in the Pemon trade network, the single-shot shotgun, also comes from Brazil, via traders who operate on the Brazilian side and sell to Pemon who come across from Venezuela. The availability of these shotguns at prices the Pemon can afford has been a major stimulus to the Pemon trade network and particularly to the shotgun/manioc-grater trade with their western neighbors the Yekuana.

Cattle have been imported from Brazil, by the Capuchins and by some Pemon. Though the grasses of the Gran Sabana are very poor pasturage, being remarkably low in calcium and potassium, the Capuchins have rather extensive herds at Kamarata, Chinadai near Kavanayen, and Divina Pastora near Santa Elena.

The poor quality of Pemon agricultural land, the poor grasses of the Gran Sabana, and the sporadic and intermittent quality of diamond mining operations have meant that the Pemon have largely — at least up until 1970 — been spared permanent influx of settlers and workers in extractive industries. The pick-and-shovel techniques of the diamond diggings have affected the Pemon technological repertoire relatively little, outside of the introduction of outboard motors financed from mining work. Cattle-keeping by Pemon has not become widespread, and so far (1970) there have been no major land invasions in the Gran Sabana. In some areas, such as the lower Paragua and the valley of the upper Cuyuni, Pemon are side-by-side with the rural version of Venezuelan national culture, in its frontier form — *conuqueros* or subsistence peasant farmers in the forest areas, *hatos* or cattle ranches in the savannas.

So far the Pemon have not had enough of anything valuable to Venezuelan national society to make wholesale colonization of Pemon territory worthwhile. The diamonds are there, but booms come and go and miners are always moving on to the next "bulla," usually somewhere outside the Pemon tribal territory. The power of the missions and the relative absence of penetration by other forces of Venezuelan national society have meant that the Pemon have been subjected to external influences more Spanish than Venezuelan, more rooted in the tradition of the colonizing Capuchins of yesteryear than in the traditions of the modern nation-state (all the trappings of supply by air and radio contact notwithstanding). On the one hand, the Capuchins have been a kind of total institution, whose province is not only religion but also wage labor and outside goods; on the other, they have provided a modicum of education and a buffer against the loss of land to other interests. The amount of land appropriated by the Capuchins for their mission buildings, fields, and herds is considerable, but it is certainly much less than that which would be taken up by land-hungry settlers.

The Capuchins themselves see their purpose as "civilizing and evangelizing" the Pemon as a means of "integrating" them into the national life. The Pemon, of course, are already part of the national life—they work for wages at the missions, work in the mines, buy Venezuelan goods, depend on axes, machetes, and the like for their very subsistence.

Traditional economic and social life goes on even in the shadow of the missions. Pemon in 1970 still danced Hallelujah, itself a combination of Anglican missionary and Pemon elements, now a traditional form. For those Pemon growing up in 1970, Hallelujah was as much of a tradition as the *tukui* and *parichara* dances had been to their grandparents' generation. In spite of the overlay of Catholicism, most Pemon still believe in Kanaima (the spirit of evil) and are sure that evil shamans or sorcerers can do harm; many continue to observe the cross-cousin marriage rule though the church is against it. All are now baptized, but most are married and buried on their own, in traditional ways, and even baptism serves well the Pemon purpose of hiding one's Pemon name by overlaying it with a Spanish-language one.

The Pemon have undoubtedly been much changed by the missionary forces of the twentieth century, but beneath the surface the forces of tradition are strong. The Capuchins and Adventists have wrought changes, but the Pemon still pursue many of their old purposes in many of the old ways. Those ways are the focus of this book.

Land, Subsistence, and Material Life

The huge massifs and choppily rolling savannas of southeast Venezuela present the observer's eye with varying shades of green on the slopes and flats, and blazes of white, cream, or rose-colored rock higher up. In many places in the valleys of the Karuai, Apanguao, and Kukenan rivers huge masses of rock rise right out of the ground, straight up for hundreds of feet. The picture strikes one as a green version of some parts of southern Utah.

The Caroni drainage starts at Roraima, a huge mass strung together with others in a line along the eastern edge of Pemon territory. It winds its way first south, toward Brazil, then west, and finally north toward its end in the Orinoco. The culture heroes of the Pemon cut down a tree of life (from which all cultigens are ultimately derived) at Roraima, loosing a flood upon the land and leaving the stump of the tree in the form of the giant mesa.

Though Pemon seem to take the grandeur of their Gran Sabana environment pretty much for granted, place names of rock formations, waterfalls and rapids, lakes and streams all have their origins specified in myth. Some features of the landscape date from the time of the culture heroes, some from other mythological sequences. Whatever their origin, the giant mesas, flat-topped and steep-sided, are still the homes of the *mawari*, spirits in the form of men who may steal the souls of the living, and the white blazes on the cliff faces are the windows of *mawari* houses, watchful of what goes on below.

An ever-present contrast pervades the areas of the Caroni and Paragua drainages inhabited by the Pemon, that between the savanna and neighboring forest. This is expressed in several terms, which codify the division of the tribal territory into an eastern or savanna portion and a western portion which is almost exclusively riverine tropical forest. Pemon speak of *itei*, the savanna, open, green or yellow-brown, but unfit for cultivation, and the forest, *tureta*, the place of cultivated plots, game animals, and, sometimes, demons. The inhabitants of the middle Caroni and Paragua drainages, a mixed Arekuna-Kamarakoto population, speak of those Pemon east and south of Kamarata and Uriman as *iteikoi* or savanna people. Almost all Pemon, even those who live surrounded by forest, express a preference for building their houses out in the open, in the savanna, *iteibo*. One Christmas, in a settlement known as Kamadak in the western part of the valley of the Karuai, a man arrived for a holiday visit after a long trip from his home in the forest to the west at Kunken, Tirika. His first comments were how good it was to be in the open again, back on the savanna.

Pemon build their houses along or near watercourses, and settlements most often take their names from the name of the adjacent watercourse. Since many settlements are found at or near spots where smaller tributaries join larger streams, the suffix — *ken* or "mouth of" (used only with reference to a watercourse) is frequently found in settlement names (e.g. Urimanken, Karuaiken). Other prominent, proximate features of the landscape, such as rock formations, rapids, or waterfalls, also appear as settlement names. I have never come upon a watercourse, however small, for which local informants could not provide a name. Settlements are, in a sense, indexed to the toponomy of the tribal territory. Social space is inextricably bound up with geographical space, and persons are classified by place through the convenient suffixes *-pon* or *-kon*, or *-kok* meaning "people of," or *-koto*, *-goto*, meaning "inhabitant of." Place (of birth and of residence) is an important part of personhood in Pemon culture, and people are often lumped with their neighbors or regional confederates, and then stereotyped in accordance with the experience of the speaker with "those people." Sometimes disparaging characterizations are made by reference to place of origin or of residence, thus avoiding a reference in terms of kinship or other relationship.

Cultivating in the forest and living on the savanna often make for a considerable distance between home and the fields, and Pemon sometimes make daily trips totaling as much as two and a half hours on foot to get to the fields and back. Most often there is some type of roofed structure on the plot where one can sling a hammock and stay the night if need be, but rather lengthy commuting to and from their fields does not seem to bother the Pemon. Women and elder children, and often whole families, will be found on the trails into the forest shortly after the sun is fully up and about midafternoon, on the way back after the day's work.

The dispersion of settlements, the frequent journeys to the plots or farther on to hunting and fishing areas, and endless rounds of stopping by neighbors' places for short visits, a drink of cachiri, or to return another's visit, all combine to make a situation where people are away from home quite often. One of the most frequently heard Pemon expressions is *atimboro autɨ*, "where are you going?" An accurate image of Pemon society would be a large scatter of dots, all connected by innumerable cross-cutting and overlapping lines, representing settlements and visits between them. This dispersion and the countervailing frequency of visits make for particular characteristics of the gossip network, since one person may not have many others in sight at a given moment, for the greater part of the time. I will later go into more detail on the implications of dispersion and frequent visits for Pemon life.

The land, however beautiful, is not bountiful, and Pemon often complain of the scarcity of fish and game nowadays. Large fish, such as the much-sought-after *aimara*, are not found above Otovanta Falls. Only small fish (usually 10-12 inches or under) are found in the valleys of the Kukenan, Karuai, and Apanguao, all above Otovanta. The savanna itself, except along the watercourses, is virtually devoid of the game animals and birds which make the forest so important. The numerous tiny savanna birds would make no one a meal. The extremely sandy, leached soils of the savanna provide no basis for cultivation, and with the exception of a few fruit trees or a moriche palm standing beside a stream, the savanna itself contributes nothing to Pemon subsistence. Though life is lived in part on the savanna, the forest and the waters, not the savanna, sustain it. The Pemon are keenly cognizant of all parts of their environment, even those parts which prove of little direct benefit to them. Numerous species of savanna grasses and shrubs are known and named, and birds and insects which abound on the savanna are known to all.

The basis of Pemon subsistence is slash-and-burn horticulture in which the principal cultigen is bitter manioc. The subsistence round includes horticulture, fishing, and hunting, and a very minor segment of gathering wild fruits and insects in season. Simpson (1940: 387–88) lists the following crops cultivated by the Kamarakoto in 1939: bitter manioc, yams, arum, sweet potatoes, banana, plantain, squash, sugar cane, watermelon, corn, peppers, peanuts, black beans, papaya, cotton, and tobacco. At the present time bitter manioc, peppers, and a green, leafy, spinach-like plant known as *aurosa* form the bulk of the Pemon diet. Corn does poorly in the soils of southeast Venezuela, and though I have seen large plantings of corn in the Antabari River area of the Paragua drainage, corn is not widely grown by Pemon today. Peanuts likewise are not often found. Banana, plantain, squash, bottle gourds, sugar cane, and pineapple are found somewhat more frequently. The growing of cotton and tobacco has recently declined given the availability of commercial cotton and commercial cigarettes at mission and mining centers.

In terms of frequency of use or consumption, we can classify Pemon crops as follows: (1) daily: bitter manioc (up to ten varieties), peppers, *aurosa*; (2) moderate frequency (once a week to once a month): sweet manioc, banana, plantain, pineapple, ocumo, arum, sugar cane; (3) infrequently (less than once a month): corn, yams, peanuts, beans.

The soils of the forested portions of the Gran Sabana and of the middle reaches of the Caroni (San Pedro to the mouth of the Icabaru River) have spottily distributed fertile patches; large areas of extremely sandy soil are found upstream from Uriman along both banks of the Caroni. Informants from the Uriman area say that in many locations there a plot is good for only one planting of bitter manioc (and virtually no other crops), after which it must be allowed to return to forest fallow. They attribute this to the extreme sandiness of the soils in the Uriman area.

Rainfall in the tribal territory varies between 1,000 and 2,000 millimeters per year, and varies somewhat in distribution over time as well. In the south, along the Brazilian border and in the area of Santa Elena de Uairen, the distribution is bimodal, with a short dry period from mid-August to early October and a longer one from January through March. As one goes north, the shorter dry period is somewhat attenuated. Also, as one moves from east to west across the tribal territory, rainfall tends to be more evenly distributed throughout the year.

Pemon speak of two divisions within their year, wet (*konokdatai*—rain time) and dry (*weipechi*—sun being out), and mark the passage of the year with the longer dry period from January to March. Koch-Grunberg (1916–28, III: 283) states that Tamekan, a constellation which represents a one-legged man and is nearly congruent with the Pleiades, marks the height of the rainy season when it goes down in the east. When Tamekan comes up again in the east, this marks the cessation of heavy rains. When it comes up about 4 or 5 o'clock in the morning, then the dry season begins. Koch-Grunberg was describing the situation in the Roraima area, and the western portions of the tribal territory differ somewhat in the onset and duration of the dry season.

There is no word for "year" in the Pemon language, and the wet/dry contrast marks the extent of Pemon concern with seasonality. In fact, concern with time in any sense is minimal in Pemon aboriginal concepts. The day is divided into dawning *(yayukapupe)*, morning *(penanimarɨ)*, noontime *(weitachipe)*, and afternoon *(koamunbe)*, and contrasted with *walpɨ*, dark or nighttime. Finer distinctions as to time of day are rarely drawn. The lack of concern for time and seasonality is related to the fact that Pemon crops ripen continuously, for the most part, and agricultural work knows no single harvest time. Most temporal references do not go beyond yesterday *(koamunyak)*, today *(serɨ-datai)*, or tomorrow *(penane)*, unless they are to *pena*, time past, date and duration unspecified.

Pemon take advantage of either of the two dry periods to cut fields, since around two or three weeks of continuous dry weather are needed to dry the plot sufficiently for burning. Clearing about a one-acre plot can take two weeks of continuous work for two men, equipped with axe and machete. First the undergrowth is cleared, using a machete and forked stick. This may take two men a week or more. Then trees are felled, larger trees being cut so as to take whole stands of smaller ones with them, domino-fashion, when they fall. Trees are cut so as to fall more or less toward the center of the plot, thus providing no avenue for flames to escape into the surrounding forest when the plot is burned. The smaller trees are merely notched enough so that they will break and tumble when the larger trees hit them on their way down. Larger trees are left lying as they fall, while smaller ones may be cut into pieces after being felled, in order to facilitate rearranging and clearing after the first burning takes place.

Following the two- or three-week period, the plot is burned. The man who has been in charge — the owner of the field — lights small fires in the brush collected at numerous points about the plot, taking care not to be caught with no exit as the fire comes toward him. Normally the first burn is not enough to clear the plot sufficiently to allow planting. All of the underbrush has burned away, but many smaller trees and branches have not burned completely. Two days after the first burn, or as soon as the trunks and soil have cooled, collecting branches, stacking, and reburning take place. This usually takes two days at most. Finally, after the second cooling, the whole family is ready to begin planting.

Cut stalks of manioc plants are brought from the old, exhausted plot in lengths of about 18-24 inches. They must be fresh enough so that sap is still flowing in them when they are planted. Small mounds of charred earth are built up with a hoe, and three or four stalks are placed in each mound. The mounds are built up randomly throughout the plot, whereever stumps and the criss-crossed larger trunks leave space. With the whole family, down to young children, participating, planting of previously gathered cuttings seldom takes more than a couple of days.

With planting, the intensive six-to-eight week work period of the men on the new plot comes to an end. While weeding and harvesting are women's work, in the main, men often help their wives and daughters when the weeding gets especially rough, at different times throughout the life of the field.

Bitter manioc must be grown from cuttings. It does not set seed. (*Aurosa*, however, grows wild in the plots and flourishes with the elimination of other weeds.) Bitter manioc begins to produce usable roots some six to eight months after planting and continues to do so until 20-24 months after planting. After this time the roots begin to rot. Digging out the usable roots with a machete or digging stick is a time-consuming task, and the women spend about one day out of four harvesting and transporting manioc. Their loads are heavy, especially if they take them home in their fiber backpacks rather than doing the processing in the workshop usually found in the fields. Often the manioc will be used for preparing *cachiri*, and this is done at home to avoid the difficulties of transporting large quantities of the rich red beer.

Processing bitter manioc, whether for conversion into flour for manioc bread cakes (Pemon *ikei*) or into paste for the preparation of *cachiri* or other fermented beverage, is a process which constrains the women to a rather monotonous round of digging, carrying, peeling, grating, squeezing and drying the roots and their resultant product. Nevertheless, the work is lightened by the aid and companionship of other women, mothers, daughters, sisters, or sisters-in-law, and no picture of the process could omit the banter and gossip that accompany it. With the baby laid in a small hammock strung up in the work shed, and a daughter at work on the grater, a woman talks to her mother, sister, or sister-in-law as they sit peeling the rough brown husks with bits of metal that are the remains of past machetes.

Peeling and grating done, the white paste left in the wooden trough is lifted in clumps into the fiber squeezer, an ingenious tube-like device which expands its diameter when compressed and reduces it when stretched. Strung between an upper and a lower pole and stretched, the squeezer forces out the poisonous prussic acid and renders the paste fit for use as flour. If *cachiri* rather than manioc cakes is being prepared, the squeezer is not necessary as the poison is boiled off in the beer-making process.

The flour is then set aside and dried or else used immediately in baking manioc cakes. These thin, round (usually about 24 inches in diameter, if not larger) white cakes are baked on a flat, round, stone griddle, set on three supporting stones which elevate it from the fire placed underneath. Baking takes around 15 minutes a side; the baked round cakes are set on a rack to dry in the sun for several hours.

Much of the women's effort goes into preparing fermented drinks. While there are at least three kinds of these, the red *cachiri* is the everyday drink and is by far the most frequently prepared. *Parakari*, a white drink made by a somewhat different process than *cachiri*, is made for festive occasions. *Paiwa*, a murky drink made from fermented, burnt pieces of manioc cakes, is seldom prepared nowadays. *Cachiri* preparation in its simplest form involves taking the grated manioc paste and mixing it with water and a red root, also grated, in a large clay or metal pot and boiling it over a fire for about a day. The resulting mixture is then strained into a long, open drum made for the purpose out of a hollowed log, by means of an open-weave fiber strainer (Pemon *panka*). The large drum is then covered with fiber mats and the liquid is allowed to ferment for a day or so, after which it is consumed. The fermentation process may get an initial boost from chewed (by the women) balls of manioc paste placed in the mixture of paste and water and red root before boiling. *Parakari* is prepared by allowing the manioc paste to remain in a trough together with masticated leaves which are placed in the paste to speed fermentation. The paste is covered with banana leaves for three days, then boiled for a day. It is not strained before it is consumed, and the fermented bits of leaves must be removed as one drinks.

Other daily women's tasks include gathering peppers and *aurosa* for the pepper pot which forms part of every meal. Peppers (Pemon *pumui*) are grown in the slash-and-burn plots, and variety is greatly sought after. The different varieties of peppers, which come in various shades of red, yellow, and green, often have names linking them with animals and fishes, as for example *kurwapupai* ("head of the kurwa fish") or *maʔwai yenu* ("eye of the crab"). Women make special trips to the fields of friends or relatives to get new varieties of pepper plants. Meat and fish are boiled right in the pepper pot, and whenever possible the pot is enriched with products of the waters or the results of the hunt.

Sometime in the course of their day in the fields, or in the late afternoon, women gather firewood to be loaded home for tonight's and tomorrow morning's fire. If a special trip to a nearby field is required, their husbands accompany them and transport a load themselves. The wee hours of the morning are cold on the Gran Sabana, and people like to have a small fire burning near their hammocks through the night if possible.

In addition to manioc and *cachiri* preparation, cooking and looking after their children, women may most often be found spinning cotton, weaving, or tying hammocks. Sitting on small stools in front of horizontal strands of cotton wrapped in a continuous warp around two upright

sticks sunk in the ground, the women tie knots every two strands, verti-
cally all the way up the width of the hammock.. Numerous vertical lines
or ribbing thus bind the horizontal strands into a tight net. Since women
work so intermittently at tying hammocks, it is virtually impossible to
tell how many hours of labor go into making one. A small X-frame hand
loom, steadied between the toes while sitting with legs stretched out on
the ground, is used to weave the *weinek* or baby sling which the mother
uses to hold the infant on her hip while walking or working.

Women, since they harvest and process bitter manioc and prepare the
foodstuffs which are made from it, in effect can run a household well
enough by themselves, if there are older children around to do some
fishing and if they have some male around to cut and clear a field for
them. While the complementary arrangement of men's clearing fields,
hunting, and fishing with women's harvesting and processing the crops
is the most common situation, women often make do for long periods in
the absence of their husbands on trading trips, working at missions, or
working in the diamond diggings.

A basic constrast between the women's work regime and that of the
men stands out: the women's work regime is more or less regular, with a
relatively constant level of effort required, while that of the men is intermittent, with highly variable intensities of effort required. The
women are more tied to the fields, the men to the rivers and the forest.
Women do the day-to-day production of foodstuffs, men manufacture
or obtain from outside sources the tools and equipment to carry on the
work. Most Pemon males, even today in an era when imported articles
are fast replacing Pemon-made goods, manufacture all basketry and
fiber articles, including the eating mats (Pemon *orori*), strainers
(*panka*), baskets (*waikarapɨ*), and squeezers (*tungkui*) used in everyday
household production.

Women provide carbohydrates and beer, and men provide, with fishing and game animals, the protein necessary for a society whose basic
staple is almost pure starch. The contrast in work regimes is part of a basic complementarity which is re-enacted daily and continuously in all
Pemon households. For, while it is true that the women can manage the
household in the absence of their husbands, things don't go as well as
normally, and they are essentially "making do." If the husbands are
gone for too long, another male may appear and a new conjugal production unit replace the old one, destroyed by the husband's prolonged
absence.

Men's work — house building, basketry, hunting and fishing, clearing
and burning the fields — has also been more extensively transformed by
new technology than has women's work. The introduction of machetes
and steel axes in ever-increasing numbers since the Spanish conquest has
undoubtedly greatly reduced the necessary labor of cutting and clearing

fields. Men now can clear larger plots than before, and many do not cut a new field every year but only every other year, or every 18 months. The shotgun, mostly the single-shot, breech-loading Brazilian type which has penetrated the tribal territory since the 1940s, has transformed hunting and increased its efficiency to the point where game is now very scarce in many areas and long trips are necessary for the hunter to find any prey. The short-run efficiency of the shotgun is evident, but insofar as it permits hunting out parts of the territory, it may bring about more effort in the long run. Of course, it is only with the increased availability of shells, powder, and shot from the mission centers of the Gran Sabana since the 1930s that continuous use of the shotgun has become feasible.

Hunting was formerly a marginal activity in terms of quantity of food brought in. Koch-Grunberg (at Roraima in 1911) classified the inhabitants of the Roraima area as "almost vegetarians." Simpson (1940: 392) stated that the return from hunting on the part of Kamarakoto males was minimal. Though the Kamarakoto at the time of Simpson's visit (1939) possessed firearms, they had virtually no powder and shot and their firearms were rendered useless.

Pemon today hunt paca, agouti, deer (three types), tapir, white-lipped peccary, collared peccary, and numerous birds. Birds form an important part of the hunter's quest, and Pemon eat the following: curassow, guan, great tinamou, and, with some prohibitions, cinereous tinamou and crested bobwhite. Vultures and the numerous types of hawks present on the savanna, as well as the numerous types of small savanna birds, are not eaten.

Fishing is generally a more productive and constant source of protein than hunting, and men generally invest more time in fishing than in hunting. A person adept with hook and line often can bring home enough for the evening meal, unless there have been heavy rains, causing the fish to rush upstream to the headwaters. Fishing is at its best in the dry season, and it is during periods of relatively lower water levels that people undertake fish poisoning, using barbasco (Pemon *inek;* Venezuelan Spanish *barbasco*, a general name for both wild and cultivated plants of several different genera used to poison fish). One type of barbasco is gathered from the forest, where the vine is cut from the tree upon which it is hanging and partitioned into lengths of about two feet. Bundles of these cut-up vines are then taken to a section of stream which has been selected and possibly blocked off by a weir with fish traps set in it. At some convenient point upstream, one man pounds the bundles into fibers and repeatedly soaks the fibers in the water to release the poisonous fluid. The poison acts only to stun the fish and bring them to the surface, where they can easily be netted by family and friends waiting downstream. The fish will flee the poison, and the barbasco may be released at a rock or rapids which blocks their movement in the upstream direction. My observation of several barbasco fishing parties in 1970–71 leads me to believe that they are rather inefficient, as the small streams where the poison has most chance of being effective usually contain only small fish, and not too many of these.

Fish were formerly shot with a small bow and unfeathered arrows, and though such bows and arrows are still around, they are no longer used. Likewise, the blowgun, formerly used to hunt birds, with its curare poison darts, is no longer in use, except by small boys who enjoy the sport. Curare and blowguns are still occasionally obtained in trade from the Yekuana.

Gathered foods form a very small part of the Pemon diet, and are eaten for variety or as snacks. Two types of palm fruits, *kuai* or *moriche* palm fruit, and *kun*, fruit of the *kunwada* palm, are eaten boiled. Both are exceptionally dry to the taste and have only a small amount of meat between the skin and a proportionally large seed. Certain larvae found in the *moriche* palm are eaten, sometimes raw, sometimes cooked over the fire in a packet of leaves. In the month of April, at the start of the rainy season, large numbers of flying ants (Pemon *kaivayun*) settle on the savanna and are gathered up and eaten.

Domestic animals kept by the Pemon today include dogs, chickens, pigs, horses, and cattle. Horses and cattle are found mostly in the southern portion of the tribal territory and there only in the more prosperous settlements. Relatively few Pemon own horses or cattle. Chickens and pigs, though kept, provide almost no input into the diet, and chicken eggs are not eaten to my knowledge. By far the most important domestic animal is the dog. These scrawny, undernourished, but never-tiring animals are indispensable in hunting, and good hunting dogs are occasionally valuable items in trade.

House building is an important male task. Like the women's work on hammocks, it is done gradually and intermittently, sometimes even over a span of years. Pemon house styles are various and three types are in use today: a circular form with a conical roof, an oblong form with a pitched roof, and a rectangular form with a pitched roof. All three are made of the same materials, though tin roofs have replaced thatch on some houses, particularly in mission areas. The walls are wattle-and-daub construction. A latticework of small saplings is tied between the wall posts, forming a series of vertical compartments into which mud, mixed with dried grasses, is stuffed. In the riverine forest areas bark slats often take the place of the mixed mud and grasses. Three types of thatch are in use: the leaves of the *moriche* palm (Pemon *kuaiyare*), of the *kunwada* palm, or of a forest plant called *waramiya* (Brazilian Portuguese "Sao Paulo"). *Waramiya* is by far the most durable roofing material, though it requires more time spent in gathering materials, as the plant grows in small stands on the forest floor.

Wall posts and roof support posts are first set into the ground, and then the roof poles are laid on and tied with thin, cordlike vines. Thatching the roof is the lengthiest part of the work, and in the case of *waramiya* each set of leaves must be bound over a transverse lath one set at a time. Often a man will obtain help from his brothers in gathering and placing roofing materials. It is too big a job for one man alone, as scores of bundles of *waramiya* must be cut and carried from the forest to the house site. Houses are often in partial use for long periods after the roof is completed, with the walls left open. The *waramiya* roofs may last six or seven years without needing repair.

Round houses (Pemon *waipa*), especially the large communal round house used for dancing and for housing visitors, are seldom built nowadays, and the rectangular forms are now most common. A recent practice deriving from white and mission influence is the division of the house into rooms. In the past Pemon houses were not internally subdivided, and most are open inside even today. House sizes vary with family sizes, of course, but an average Pemon dwelling has about 40 square meters of floor space.

While the Pemon economy is not self-contained, almost all their necessities other than clothing and some tools are provided by the land and water around them. Houses and household items are constructed from the products of forest and savanna, and the daily manioc bread is a constant reminder of dependence on the land. Work is not some portion of life cut out and separated from the rest of it, as it is with us. In fact, the Pemon verb which comes closest to our word for working, *senneka*, does not connote the idea of laboring. When Pemon began to work on the construction of mission buildings, or in the diamond diggings, they adopted the Spanish word "trabajo" (work) into their language and produced the form "trabasoman" to characterize work done after the white man's fashion. In his own idiom a Pemon will simply say, if asked, that he or she is "going to the fields" (*mɨ dao tɨ dai*) or going hunting (*awomɨ*) or fishing (*morokmai*). The verb *senneka* has more the meaning of "being active" than it does the meaning of "laboring." Work is part of life, not separate and estranged from it, and the pace may be steady but seldom forced.

The rhythm of work in Pemon subsistence activities is varied, even for the women, by the need to switch over from one activity to another and perform a variety of tasks in the course of a series of work days. The women may be making manioc bread on one day in the shed in the fields, be home making *cachiri* the next, be back weeding the fields the third day, and visiting relatives or neighbors the fourth. Pemon do not work to build up a surplus, as manioc stores best underground in the plots, and tomorrow's tasks are best taken care of when the time comes and not before. Pemon are capable of prolonged and intensive effort when the need arises, as in clearing fields, making up enough manioc to last for a trip, or going on a long hunting trip where the men may work from dawn to dusk for three or four days running. Pemon value proficiency in subsistence tasks very highly, but they certainly do not subscribe to anything like a "Protestant ethic" of work.

The irregularity and variety of the normal, subsistence work regime have made the grind of mission labor onerous for those Pemon who have to take it up to provide things that come from the outside and are now necessities. A regular work day in one's own fields goes from about 7:30 A.M. to 2 P.M. continuously. Then people may break and go home or move to some other activity, such as fishing, in the late afternoon and early evening. They may go visit a neighbor or head home and occupy themselves around the house. One works as much as is necessary to obtain what one needs, and no more.

By contrast, 8 to 5 in the hot sun wielding a machete, with an hour off for lunch, brought $1.75 per day (Bs. 8) with a mandatory six-day work week in 1970–71 at the Uonken mission.

John Gillin (1936: 132), who studied the Barama River Carib of British Guiana, summed up their attitude toward work and acquisition, an attitude which is also quite characteristic of the Pemon, as follows:

> One of the reasons for the surprisingly considerate treatment which Indians receive from outsiders in this region is the fact that the latter have been forced to recognize that beyond a certain point, the mere possession of property means nothing to the Caribs. Every gold digger, lumber operator, and balata bleeder who has traveled on the Barama will tell you of the difficulty he has in keeping his Indian boatmen and laborers at work. "An Indian will work only until he gets what he wants and then he will quit cold," is a common observation. Consequently, anyone who relies on a native crew must depend upon the personal relations which he establishes with his workmen to a larger extent than the trade goods which he can give them.

The intermittent quality of the Pemon work regime (true of the women to a lesser extent than of the men) must have been more pronounced in the past, when the reciprocal visiting of the *cachiri* parties was in full swing. People would work intensely building up a huge quantity of *cachiri*, then throw a party which would last for days, until all the supply was drunk up. The social round still includes large amounts of *cachiri* drinking, but the three- or four-day fests seem now to be a thing of the past.

As Gillin's quote indicates, the fact of possession beyond a certain point is not an obsession with the Barama River Carib; the same holds for the Pemon. What is important is the fact of use, and of having definite rights to the fruits of one's labor. Simpson (1940: 544) described this well for the Kamarakoto:

> By the general rule, what an individual makes or uses is his. When he finishes using it, it is ownerless.

> So, then, you could say that in theory the land belongs to the tribe in general, or that it belongs to nobody. But when a man clears a field or builds a house on a piece of land, the land is his. No one has the right to use it, or even enter it without his permission, while he occupies it; its products are exclusively his without any obligation to share or divide them. Nevertheless, when he leaves it, he cannot transfer title of ownership to anyone else; ownership returns to the community and the first comer can occupy it and enjoy its fruits. The same happens with houses as with worked land.

> You could say that this ownership belongs to the group of houses or to the *to-esa* as director and representative of the group. A special and very important case of ownership is that of fishing rights. According to custom, which naturally is equivalent to an unwritten law, a dwelling situated on the banks of or in proximity to a river holds the fishing rights to it in the stretch between it and the next house. These rights are maintained with utmost strictness, to the point that a fish that is pulled downriver by the current does not belong to the fisherman if he does not collect it in his own waters. Of course several or many households use barbasco poisoning in association, along stretches of varying lengths of the river, dividing the fish among themselves, but this is done only at the invitation of the owner of rights to his water. Violation of this right is counted among the most serious offenses the Indians know, as is indicated by the fact that the last bloody war, of which a vivid although confused memory is recalled, was motivated, it is said, by a violation of this type. With hunting, it seems that there are no rights of ownership.

As Simpson notes, land among the Pemon belongs to the community until it is cultivated, at which time the right to dispose of its products is held by those who cultivate it. Theoretically, a field belongs to the man who cuts and clears it, but in fact it belongs to the man-woman pair who jointly are responsible for its clearing and maintenance.

It is true that land, once fallow, reverts to the community, and that theoretically anyone may cultivate it when it regenerates sufficiently to sustain cultivation. But the situation is more complex than that, and the tendency of relatives and settlement mates to maintain fields proximate to their settlement and to each other means that, in practice, people often return to recultivate old lands during their lifetime. Settlements are frequently rebuilt close to an older settlement site. One sees new houses going up or nearly completed beside the ruins of an old, broken-down structure. Many Pemon settlements stay on virtually the same site for 20 years or more. During this time the occupants of that settlement will have utilized the nearby forest for one round of shifting cultivation and will begin to re-use forest fallowed land cut many years before. Thus the stability of settlements tends to create patterns of continued land use by groups of relatives, and the dispersion of settlements is a response which serves, among other things, to ensure long-term adequacy of land in reasonable proximity to the settlement.

It would be wrong to give the impression that blocks of land are "held" by groups of relatives. There are no corporate kin groups, land-holding or otherwise, in Pemon society. The only actual land-holding unit, with use rights only, is the man-woman pair which forms the core of the Pemon household. What these groups of relatives actually "have" is simply some permanence in an area over time, and the continuity of use rights which goes with it. The dispersion of settlements in the savanna portion of the tribal territory is almost surely a function of needed dispersion of fishing sites as well as agricultural needs. In the western, or riverine forest portion, of the tribal territory the ecological explanation for the extreme dispersion of settlements becomes less appropriate. Also, there are large concentrations in some settlements, in mission areas, in Adventist settlements, and some others — e.g. Peraitepui de Roraima — in the southern portion of the territory. Agglomeration into settlements of 90–100 people or more, though not the rule, is possible and does occur.

Simpson is not the only source which indicates that fishing rights may in the past have caused conflict. A Pemon tale recorded by Armellada (1964: 24) goes as follows, in part:

> Our grandfathers tell us that in their time the Pichaukok fought with the Kukuyikok.
>
> The Pichaukok lived in Kukenan, toward Roraima, in Uairen, near Uonken. But the Kukuyikok lived in Kamarakata, Uriman, Kavanayen and Iken.
>
> They came to be many, and then fought for their women, for hunting and fishing places and for places to use barbasco.

Whatever the historical veracity of this tale — it is hard to envision a large-scale conflict of northern versus southern Pemon in the light of local fishing rights, where one would be most in conflict with an immediate neighbor — it is significant that fishing and hunting rights are mentioned as sources of conflict. Whether the tale served more as an admonition for right conduct or as a description of historical fact, the *possibility* of conflict in these areas was important. On the other hand, it is my experience that there are a sufficient number of areas where fish poisoning or other fishing may be carried out at a reasonable distance from most settlements, and no historically known case of conflict of this type ever came to my attention. It is always easy enough to ask permission from a neighbor where necessary, or to go a little farther than one's neighbor's rights extend if need be.

Ultimately, rights in cultivable land and in fishing sites cannot be held without exercising them. There is no inheritance of either land or fishing rights, except by staying on the same land as one's forebears. The myth cited above refers to "hunting . . . places," but, as Simpson remarked, there are no proprietary rights in hunting territories, and hunters are free to roam at will. Since game animals are seldom found near settlements and not often near the fields, hunting is carried on in the vast spaces open to all.

Rights in cultivable land and in fishing locations pertain to three different contextual levels: (1) the level of individual use rights, (2) the level of household use rights, and (3) the level of the community at large. Where the individual acts for himself, he must still act as a member of some household; thus level 1 taken singly applies primarily in those instances where an individual may fish for his own immediate consumption. In considerations involving cultivable land, a man-woman partnership of some sort is always involved, and by implication one or more households. Thus the individual character is acting not only in accord with his individual use rights, but more importantly in accord with the right of a household to retain control over the means of production and the product of its labor. The third, or community level, is a level of custodial right which comes into play when the rights of individuals and households lapse or come into conflict.

It is difficult to separate exactly the rights in productive resources which are vested in the individual as individual from those vested in the individual as household member. It can be said that the head of household (the eldest active male member) "owns" the fields which his household cultivates, yet it could equally well be said that the woman who weeds and harvests the plot in fact "owns" it. Both men and women will refer to u-mɨrɨ, "my field," when talking about their family plot.

Ownership of tools and household items is by individuals, even in the case of things — for example, manioc graters — which are used in producing subsistence for the whole household. An individual owns his own hammock, clothing, grater, fishhooks and line, shotgun, bow and arrow, flashlight, cardboard suitcase, and so on. Eating bowls and basketry are individually held, usually by the women. Women own the knives, wooden troughs, and other paraphernalia used in manioc processing. Manoic graters, though often obtained by men in the shotgun/grater trade, are owned by either men or women. Canoes, an important item for many households, are owned by male heads of household.

Pemon society exists at a machete-axe-fishhook-shotgun level of technology geared to obtaining sustenance directly from the land. While many of the important tools used in subsistence tasks are obtained from sources ultimately outside of Pemon society itself, these tools are found in every household and all households have some means of acquiring these items, whether through labor or trade.

The use, manufacture, and possession of household items can be understood readily by seeing the association of items with daily activities. The axe, hoe, and machete are part of daily work in the fields, cutting firewood, weeding, digging up manioc roots, and so on. Only men use and own the axe; both women and men use and own machete and hoe. Items used by the women in processing manioc are knives, stone or metal griddles, the squeezer (Spanish *sebucan*, Pemon *tungkui*), strainers for flour, manioc graters, wooden troughs to hold the grated paste, and *orori* or fiber mats for handling the hot manioc cakes while baking. *Cachiri* processing involves the same equipment plus the hollowed-out log drum for holding the *cachiri*, gourds for water, and large metal or clay pots (Pemon *murai:* large clay pot) for boiling the *cachiri* mix over the fire. These items are most often owned by the women, although griddles, graters, and pots may be owned by men and used by women of their household.

Morning and evening, and sometimes in between, the clay bowls used for the pepper pot are taken from the corner and heated up over an open fire. These bowls are known as *oini* and are made only in the Kamarata and Uriman areas, by women who know the techniques and have an available supply of good clay. In spite of the widespread presence of metal pots, Pemon still prefer to be served the pepper pot in the traditional clay bowl. The Kamarakoto *oini* bowls are widely traded, and another type, of somewhat heavier construction, known as *wairang* is made by the Inagriko to the east of Roraima and extensively traded by them to the southern Pemon. No evening meal is unaccompanied by *cachiri* (unless the supply is temporarily exhausted), served in hemispherical drinking gourds known as *pishao* (or *kamok*). Small metal bowls have replaced the gourds in some households.

If you come into a house during the day, you will find a series of hammocks rolled up and bound to the rafters, clothes strung over twine loops attached to the walls, glass bottles full of green, yellow, and red peppers standing in the corners, fishing poles and shotguns (if not in use that day) hanging from the rafters or placed horizontally on slats between the rafters, and possibly a canoe paddle and fiber backpack or two leaning against a wall. Perhaps some of the small wooden stools known as *murei* will be lying about on the ground. No firewood will be in evidence, and the fire stones placed in threes around one or two hearths will be cold.

Come back in the early morning or the late afternoon hours and the house, full of family, will present a different picture. Firewood is piled against one wall. A pepper pot sits on the fire stones with kindling blazing underneath. Hammocks are strung between rafters and house posts, in the corners from wall to wall, and in the center of the house from rafter to rafter. Conversation is animated as the family gathers around the pepper pot, dipping in bits of manioc cake torn off in small chunks from the half-cakes placed on mats on the floor. If guests are present, the men will eat first, the women and children following. Otherwise the family eats together. If it is evening, the hammocks have been strung; if morning, they will be rolled up and stowed after the meal. Blankets, if they are available, are rolled up inside the hammocks, and mosquito coverings — valuable items not owned by everyone — will be rolled up with the hammock still inside.

Any visitor from our own culture is immediately struck by the contrasts found in the inventory of goods in a Pemon household. The mixture of indigenous and outside items is curious at first, since the outside items have penetrated piecemeal, and have by no means taken over the scene. Glass bottles are used to store peppers, cardboard suitcases contain not just clothes but trade beads *(kasuru)* as well, the blankets rolled up in the Pemon-made hammocks were brought at the mission store. Powdered milk for the children is stirred and mixed with a *kurukuru-matok*, a wooden beater used for *cachiri*. Occasionally even a pair of *pɨrai*, Pemon sandals made from parts of the moriche palm leaf stalk, are found beside Venezuelan *alpargatas* or Western-style shoes.

Our subject here is the Pemon way of life as it was lived in 1970, and there is no escaping the fact that Pemon life now contains many elements of exogenous, Western origin, not only as tools and equipment but also as parts of the realm of ideas. Shotguns, for example, were long ago incorporated into Pemon myths (see Armellada, 1964, for myths recorded since the 1930s), even before they became widely incorporated into the actual hunting pattern. Fishhooks likewise are part of the Makunaima creation myths (Armellada, 1964: 46). For a meticulous and detailed treatment of the material culture of the Guiana Indians, the Pemon (Arekuna) included, the reader may consult Roth (1924).

Both men and women sometimes possess skills as individuals which are not uniformly distributed among all Pemon. As we have mentioned, only certain women in the Kamarata and Uriman areas command the skills necessary to manufacture the *oinɨ* clay bowls. Certain men are skilled at making complexly patterned baskets, while others can fabricate only the rudimentary types. On the other hand, certain skills which are fundamental, such as tying cord fish nets *(pentɨ)* or tying cotton hammocks *(kami)* or sewing for women, and the making of mats, baskets, and sifters for men, are pretty much universally found.

Every Pemon man is hunter, fisherman, woodsman, and clearer of fields, maker of fiber basketwork, and house builder. Every Pemon woman is manioc processer, weaver and tier of cotton, seamstress, and tier of fish nets. Some are better at the basic skills than others, but all know them well enough to get by. It is customary to characterize this situation as one of "absence of specialization" or "simple division of labor." A positive characterization of Pemon working life seems more appropriate. In Pemon society each adult is master of the requisite skills necessary to provide food, shelter, and other basic necessities when he or she forms part of an ongoing household unit. Rather than the division of labor being master of the individual, the individual is master of the multiplicity of tasks necessary to sustain life. An adult in Pemon society is simultaneously master of a whole range of tasks, no single one to the exclusion of all the others. In the case of many individuals there is special emphasis on some, but not to the neglect of the remaining ones.

The mastery of a minimally complete inventory of subsistence-related skills by each person in the process of becoming an adult is the precondition and concomitant of the relative autonomy of the household unit. It does not preclude specialization but, rather, provides a "floor" for Pemon society, an assurance that the component household units, though not completely autonomous, are able by and large to sustain themselves. We will later consider the limit on this household autonomy imposed by local variations in raw materials and the cultural constraints and possibilities of exchange. We shall also see how these relatively autonomous households are, through numerous ties, linked together and welded into a societal whole.

CHAPTER III

Relatives, Residents, and Neighborhoods

Kinship and marriage among the Pemon can only be understood against the background of the dispersed settlement pattern. In many ways kinship and friendship relations are reflected in physical space. Gillin (1936: 127) remarked of the various clusters of houses in a Barama River Carib settlement: "In each of these groupings there is a high correlation between the personal influence of the dominant character, his blood relationships with the members of the group centering about him, and the spatial grouping of the households concerned." If we substitute the word "kinship" for "blood relationships," the statement would apply to the arrangement of households within Pemon settlements. The nature of the correspondences between social relationships and physical space is treated at some length below, simply because space is itself an inherent part of the quality of Pemon life. When first among the Pemon, I was struck by the distances between settlements, and often as well by the spread-out pattern of the settlements themselves. When I asked Pemon about this, the reply was, "When we get too close together, there are fights." Now, as we shall see, there are some fights even with spatial separation. Nevertheless, it can be said that the Pemon settlement pattern makes a concentration of individuals in any one place something that must be accomplished by individuals acting separately. The normal state is one of apartness, with individuals and small groups carrying out the basic tasks of Pemon life. It requires an effort to get together, though it should be noted that Pemon are indefatigable walkers and boatmen and do not consider vast distances much of a deterrent to undertaking visits, provided one wants or needs to.

The constant round of visits within and between neighborhoods, combined with the small size of most settlements, means that interaction can be spaced out in time. Gossip can become particularly effective and important in a situation like this, since parties depicted in some bit of hearsay need not face each other directly but, by arranging visits and schedules properly, can keep out of each other's way.

The Pemon system of kinship and marriage can be thought of as forming the principal lines which link households and settlements together.
The distribution of kinsmen over the land, seen from a number of individual vantage points, forms a crucial part of the understanding of
Pemon society. The word "network" has been much used in recent anthropology, perhaps overused. Yet, if we think of a series of overlapping
networks, spread out in time as well as space, connecting the various
households and settlements over the Pemon landscape, we have an accurate metaphor for much of Pemon social life.

Household Relationships

There is no word in the Pemon language for "family" in either the
broad or narrow sense, despite the importance of the nuclear family and
the extended family in Pemon society. Pemon speak of *utapui*, "my
house," or alternatively *uyewɨk*, "my dwelling." Both of these terms
refer to the physical structure itself, and not do have the connotation of
the English "home." When Pemon refer to "home," it is inevitably with
the term *upata*, literally "my place." One's *-pata* is the place from which
one comes, the place where one resides most of the time.

The most common household form found among Pemon is the nuclear family. Extended family households are usually of short duration,
at least until the time when the members of the elder generation become
less active economically and need the support of a son, daughter, and/or
son-in-law. Even in the cases in which a young bridegroom takes up
residence with his parent-in-law, he may reside in their dwelling only
long enough to complete the construction of his own nuclear family's
dwelling a short distance away.

The virtual autonomy of the household may be broken in several
situations, and in fact an individual household is continuously dependent on other households or on extratribal (usually Yekuana) sources for
some trade items, such as clay bowls and manioc graters. Those situations in which a household comes to depend on kinsmen and neighbors
outside it for assistance are inevitably due to absence or illness of one or
more of its members. For example, during my fieldwork a young man
and his wife were both taken ill and confined themselves to their hammocks. The females of the man's FB's household took charge of processing manioc from the man's plots, and the efforts of the FB and his household sustained the man's family (the young man had four quite young
daughters at the time) for the duration of their illness. This required
considerable effort on the part of the FB's household, since they lived in
another settlement some distance away and had to walk long distances
to work the FBS's fields. The household, then, is autonomous but never
isolated.

One must be a member of a household to subsist. In one rather extraordinary case an older widow was left with a small child after her second husband died. Though she had a half-brother to the south of Uonken, she attached herself to the household of an unrelated couple in the Uonken area. The couple's household was already large, and the woman and her child barely got by most of the time. This was the only case I know of where an unattached person did not have available or did not exercise the option of attachment to the household of a kinsman during hard times. I was unable to ascertain why she did not seek aid from her half-brother; she eventually left for the settlement of her deceased husband's brother, eastward and outside the Uonken region.

The boundaries of food sharing on a daily basis are fairly strictly limited to the household, except that meat and fish, in that order, are often distributed to other households in the settlement (if such there be) or to relatives in other settlements. Also, Pemon etiquette regarding hospitality requires that even a casual visitor be offered the traditional pepper pot and calabash of *cachiri*. If the head of household or his son or son-in-law has killed a game animal, the meat will be rapidly distributed, usually boiled and eaten in short order. However, many households also smoke a portion of the meat and put it by for members of the household only. Food items never enter into formal or informal exchange between different households — the only return for food and hospitality is food and hospitality provided in one's turn. While food transfers do occur across household boundaries in times of need, these transfers cannot be paid for except by incurring a future obligation to provide food to the former donor should the need arise. Pemon do not count debits and credits in the sphere of hospitality (in the manner of dinner invitations in middle-class American culture, say) but simply recognize the imperative of providing hospitality when they are able to do so. If the *cachiri* has run out, the visitor will be so informed and offered water if he requests it, along with the hint that "so-and-so has *cachiri* available." If one household in a settlement receives visitors and has no manioc cakes *(ikei)* available, someone will quickly hustle next door to tap another stock and provide the visitor with something to dip in the pepper pot.

Patterns of ownership reinforce the autonomy of the household. Items used in production — *sebucan*, the trough for holding manioc paste, manioc graters, fishing poles, fiber baskets and backpacks, fishhooks and line, shotguns and shells, knives and machetes, stone or metal platters for baking manioc — are individually owned but freely used, except for shotguns, by any member of the household involved in daily tasks. For example, manioc graters may be held by males or females, and the right to trade or in rare cases sell them outside the household rests with the owner. They are used exclusively by females, regardless of who owns them. Likewise, males make the fiber products used so often in daily tasks, yet they are in effect often given to the females of the household who own and use them. As a general rule, whatever a person makes or produces with his or her own labor belongs to that person to dispose of as he or she deems fit, with the exception of food. Food belongs to the household as a whole, and no member would contemplate withholding it or barring other household members' access.

The house structure itself is technically owned by the man who sponsors its construction, though in almost all cases he will be aided in building it by his own male siblings, his offspring, or in some cases his brother-in-law. The house structure, though owned and occupied by members of a household, nearly always involves labor by members of other households during construction. Rights to the household structure on the part of its principal builder and the members of his household endure until the structure either disintegrates or is abandoned for some other reason. Once abandoned, the house structure belongs to no one, and anyone may come and build on that site if he chooses to do so.

Rights involving factors of production — land, labor, and tools — are thus vested in the household. There are no supravening claims on the product or the productive activity of individuals beyond the claims of the household itself. There are obligations to be met — hospitality, trade, and so on — but no one outside the household has any overright on what the household produces. Pemon society exemplifies in almost pure form what Sahlins (1972) has called "the domestic mode of production."

Household composition among the Pemon is highly variable, but certain characteristics stand out when looking at the overall pattern. About 40 percent of Pemon households are of the nuclear family form. Almost all Pemon households are male-headed households, though 4 percent female-headed households can be found in my data from Uonken in 1971. Many households contain the wife's mother (10 percent) or the head of household's own mother (12 percent), though in no case were the mothers of both spouses present simultaneously in the household. Forty-two percent of the households contained members of three separate generations. Overwhelmingly, even in those households which are not nuclear family households, those present are primary relatives or immediate affines of the husband and wife making up the focus of the household. It is rather common for a household which is not a nuclear family household to contain siblings of either of the focal husband-wife pair. The importance of primary kin relationships in the make-up of the Pemon household (H, W, M, F, S, D, B, Z) is evident from a brief look at household composition patterns (see Thomas, 1973: 114–18).

Attachment of primary relatives other than the offspring of the focal couple usually comes about through death or divorce. The cases in which mothers or mothers-in-law of the head of household are present simply represent the effects of death or divorce and the inability of an elder female to maintain an independent household. Consequently she takes up residence with a son or daughter. Elder females in Pemon society participate actively in manioc production (and often in the fabrication of potential trade items, such as bowls, hammocks, or fish nets) and thus are welcome in the households of their offspring. Brothers or sisters of one or the other of the focal couple may also attach themselves to the household if they have not yet married or if they are divorced. The usual recourse for a divorced female is to take up residence with one of her siblings if her parents are deceased or divorced.

It is easiest to portray the cycle of development of Pemon households starting at the time of marriage. In the normal sequence of events, a young man upon marriage goes to live in the house of his parents-in-law and does brideservice for several years. Usually, however, he will attempt soon after the birth of the first child to construct a house near that of his parents-in-law, for his own nuclear family. This is the first stage in establishing the autonomy of the young bridegroom and his family, as opposed to his initial subordination to his parents-in-law. As the parents-in-law grow older, and as visits to the groom's own parents become frequent, the young man may eventually relocate his family in an area where his own parents or siblings live, there to take on sons-in-law in his turn and begin the cycle anew. As we have seen, elder parents or parents-in-law will take up residence in the household of their offspring. Each household, then, goes from its formation in the shadow of the groom's parents-in-law, to independence during the period of children growing up, to having its own satellites as daughters marry, and finally toward dissolution in old age as a surviving member takes up residence with a younger couple. There are circumstances which alter this idealized sequence; these will be dealt with later.

The informality which pervades so much of Pemon life is found within the household as well, but cross-sex and age divisions are clear in most interaction. One important element in the life of the individual is that elder siblings of both sexes play an important part in one's upbringing. For the first-born, the eldest of a sibling set, this doesn't hold, as parental influence is correspondingly more direct. A nearby father's younger brother or mother's younger brother or sister may play an important part in the upbringing of these first-to-come-along children.

The domestic unit is hierarchically organized, but the hierarchy is not recognizable in any patterns of orders, commands, or injunctions; it is rather subtly manifested in certain patterns of deference and restraint. Also, the hierarchy is consonant with the patterns of complementarity which must reign if the household is to work well as a production unit and as an interaction sphere. The primacy of the male head of household is evident but not emphasized. In the presence of outsiders, the males, including the head of household, his elder male offspring (over about ten years of age), and any male guests will eat prior to the women and children. The pepper pot and *cachiri* will be served by the wife or an elder daughter. There is no order of necessary precedence in the male eating circle, nor among the women and children after the males have finished. At times when outsiders are not present, the household members usually eat at the same time, with little or no deference to the males.

Sleeping arrangements — where one's hammock is slung — manifest the separation of the sexes and age gradations. A man and wife will sling their hammocks at one end of the house, on opposite sides of the fire, and the smaller children's hammocks will be slung quite close to their mother. Moving away from the fire toward the center of the house, the daughters sling their hammocks relatively proximate to their parents. Next farthest away come the sons (from about six years old on up). If a married daughter and a son-in-law are in the house, their hammocks will be slung at the opposite end of the house from her parents, possibly around a second fire.

Eating and sleeping arrangements are the most overt manifestations of the separation of the household into behaviorally marked segments, hierarchically arranged. While father and mother both maintain dominance over their own offspring of both sexes until the parents are quite advanced in years, the patterns of relationship among siblings depend directly on cross- versus same-sex divisions combined with relative age. An elder sister (Pemon *naʔnai*) usually has a "caretaker" role with respect to younger brothers and sisters. She often takes on a "mothering" role toward these younger siblings, and they accord her a corresponding respect and affection. The relative separation of boys and girls does not begin until about five years, when the females begin helping their mothers and elder sisters in daily domestic chores, such as fetching and carrying water from the nearby stream, putting manioc flour or *cachiri* paste through a sieve, clearing away the hard earth floor with a makeshift broom, and so on. After the age of five or six the daughters begin rapidly to participate in tasks around the house or in the manioc preparation process in the field lean-tos or at home. I have often seen young girls of eight years of age grating manioc on small manioc graters set aside for them. They work alongside their mother or elder sister. Young boys usually start going fishing — their first crack at subsistence tasks — around the age of eight years, but they do this only sporadically until they are in their teens.

Sibling relationships, whether own-sex or cross-sex, are always mediated by relative age. While a male is separated from both an elder and a younger sister by cross-sex social distance, he is subordinate to his elder sister (and will have no chance of any say in her marriage arrangements or participation in activities, visits, etc., outside the household) and in a superordinate, guardianship relationship to his younger sister. While the most clear-cut lines of daily interaction in work and play point to a separation of siblings along sex lines, in fact brother/sister ties often remain quite strong throughout life. As we shall see later, there is a tendency for adult male siblings to try to localize themselves and their nuclear families in the same area. Many times, however, a localization of both the males and females of a sibling set occurs. In some cases of divorce or marital dispute, a woman's best refuge is with her own elder brother or, failing that, an elder sister. While the elder brother cannot be said to control or influence the remarriage possibilities of a divorced sister, he can and does provide a refuge in line with the "guardianship" relationship with his younger sister.

The husband-wife relationship, basically one of complementarity, does show some subordination of the wife to the husband, though this is often difficult to detect. Though husbands may help in weeding fields and gathering firewood (both culturally defined as women's tasks), they will seldom, if ever, get up at night to replenish the fire from the stock of wood by the door—this falls to the wife to do. Though the husband may, on a trip, shoulder the burden of his own hammock and a few personal items in his backpack (if he carries one), the burden of carrying manioc cakes in sufficient quantity to last the journey falls to the wife. These slight—sometimes not so slight—differences in who shoulders what burden point up the dominance aspect of the complementary relationship.

Though the hierarchy of father, mother, offspring is present in the nuclear family household, it is not a hierarchy which is very manifest in day-to-day life. Pemon etiquette seems to go counter to any kind of direct giving of orders. A simple remark like *Tuna bra man*—"There is no water"—from her mother during the course of *cachiri* preparation will send a young daughter, gourds in hand, off to the stream to fetch the necessary water. Likewise, early morning will often find her brother, aged eight or so, outside chopping wood for the cooking fire, without a direct word having been said to him.

Many households, of course, are not limited to the nuclear family in membership, and nonnuclear family relationships within the household change the overall tenor of interaction, rendering it somewhat more formal, depending on the length of time that the "other" members have been present. Pemon behavior toward the spouse's parents is always deferential, though the formality eases off considerably after children have been born and the marriage is consolidated. Of Pemon households in the Uonken region, 22 percent contained the mother or wife's mother of the head of household. These elder females participate actively in the tasks of the household, and are somehow always engaged in a bit of work whenever one encounters them. They weave fish nets, make cotton baby slings for their grandchildren, work in the fields, and care for their grandchildren in conjunction with their daughter or daughter-in-law. Most are quite active traders, some even entering into the normally male shotgun-grater exchanges.

Brothers of either spouse in the household are almost invariably younger siblings and are usually unmarried. A man's younger brother-in-law (wife's brother) or his own younger brother will become a helper in major subsistence tasks such as the clearing, cutting, and burning of the plots, fish poisoning efforts which require the gathering of barbasco (Pemon *inek*) vines in the forest, or extended hunting forays away from the home settlement.

In some cases an unmarried or divorced wife's sister of the head of household may be present, but these arrangements are often temporary until a marriage or remarriage takes place. Some rather large "conglomerate" households contain members of the natal families of both spouses. In such cases, except where a man is supporting his parents-in-law and wife's unmarried siblings (as well as some of his own siblings), the arrangements are usually due to economic circumstances, in which some persons with newly established marriages have not cut their own fields and have to attach themselves to a sibling's or in-law's household in order to make do. Only a few households in which married brothers-in-law are found together under the same roof exist over a long period of time. Households containing two married brothers and their wives also exist but are not very common. The only nonpolygynous household where two married sisters were found was a somewhat anomalous case in which a man and his son (by a previous wife) were married to two sisters.

All members of Pemon society are thus part of a production and consumption unit which maintains all of the equipment necessary to fish, hunt, gather, and cultivate. While the process of production is almost totally a household affair, consumption patterns compose a wider field, one embracing household, settlement, and neighborhood. Though the household is relatively autonomous in the production sphere (with the exception of the items brought into it through trade), the household is not the society in microcosm and no Pemon would ever conceive of the household as an isolated unit. Each household is embedded in the wider ties of its members, which both individually and as group ties extend beyond the household. From the household domain we go to the domain of "relatives." Even so, we shall continually refer back to the household context, since Pemon continually move within and between households.

While the injunction to share inevitably extends beyond the individual household, it is mainly within the household that holding back or being stingy (*amunek*) is unthinkable.

The Kindred and Terms for Kinsmen

Any account which attempts a translation and interpretation of another way of life must be clear about two sets of terms, ours and theirs, and about where these two sets of terms do and do not overlap. Nowhere is this more important than in the realm of kinship and marriage, where our everyday familiarity with domestic and familial events leads us to think that we have ready-to-hand concepts for thinking about these facts. In addition, there is little standardization of concepts in the social studies, so one must ask of each writer in turn just what he means by certain "key" words.

One anthropologist (Schneider, 1972: 51) has gone so far as to claim that kinship is a "nonsubject," an idiosyncratic category set up by anthropologists which doesn't correspond "to any cultural category known to man" (ibid.: 50). At another pole are those who claim that kinship universally has to do with the basic facts of sexual access, procreation, birth, and death. Most anthropologists, while granting the grounding of kinship and marriage in the universal facts of human biology, insist (and rightly so) on the *social* nature of kinship and marriage and its character as a system of rights and duties, moral and affective ties, and so on. The extent to which the social is viewed as rooted in the biological varies quite a bit in different treatments.

We are faced with an anthropological tradition which views kinship as a domain which can be defined in terms of genealogically specified relationships (see Goodenough, 1970), though many state that the genealogical connections are indicators based on indigenous notions of parenthood, descent, and the parent-child relationship. The treatment of Pemon social life requires attention to the problem of genealogically defined relationships, but no adequate definition of the domain of kinship and marriage in Pemon society could be limited to the properties of genealogical space. Kinship in Pemon society has a genealogical component, but this component is only a part of what comprises kinship. Nor are all other aspects of kinship able to be directly derived from notions inhering in the genealogies.

Fortes (1969) has characterized kinship as an "irreducible" domain of social life which is characterized by the "axiom of amity" or "prescriptive altruism." Kinship involves sharing without the expectation of return. This sharing is in a sense obligatory. As Robert Frost put it, "Home is the place where, when you have to go there, they have to take you in." And home (*upata*) for the Pemon, as for us, is always associated

with kinship. Kinship in Pemon society is a domain of binding obligations, sometimes diffuse, sometimes specific, which sets the tenor of
social relations in the society at large.

While Fortes's "axiom of amity" is a useful starting point in bounding
the domain of kinship in Pemon society, several of the attendant propo-
sitions he puts forth do not adequately fit the Pemon case. He (1969:
242) states, "What I wish to stress is the basic premise: kinship is binding; it creates inescapable moral claims and obligations. Diffuse as these
claims and obligations appear to be, they are, nevertheless, correlated
to morphological and institutional distinctions which put kinship
proper on one side, and the complementary or coordinate spheres, no-
tably those of affinity, locality, and polity on the other." He separates
kinship and affinity, and kinship and locality. While these separations
are analytically all right for the societies which Fortes analyzes, they do
not fit the Pemon.

The relationship of the "axiom of amity" to biological considerations,
to the folk biology of a society as well as to the "real" biological facts, is
problematic. It is usually handled by a description of the indigenous
theory of conception and procreation, and with notions of parenthood
derived from that theory, and we will in part follow this course here.
This done, the anthropologist goes back to his description of kin terms
and social relationships in terms of genealogical designations and proceeds to omit the question of just how closely the genealogical designations fit the folk theory of human reproduction or the social theories of
fatherhood, motherhood, and childhood based on it or superimposed on
it. It is clear that in discussing kinship we are in the realm of rights and
duties, moral and affective considerations, which are somehow given,
ascribed (see Fortes, 1969: 235). Yet, for all that, kinship relations are
not fixed and immutable, and people become kinsmen through processes other than the round of birth, marriage, and death or "discov-
ered" genealogical connection. An adequate understanding of Pemon
life would mean understanding the processes by which people become
kinsmen, processes by which the contingent is made over into the given,
the ex post facto into a pre-existing condition.

The Pemon concept of kinship begins with a single term, *uyomba* —
"my relative." The term has several levels of meaning. At the broadest
level all Pemon are kinsmen — *tukari̇ri̇ uyombaton*. This usage is meta-
phoric and is not found in everyday reference but in the explanations of
informants upon direct questioning. The second level refers to the personal kindred of an individual, a circle of relatives defined on the basis
of terminological references built on the usages of Ego's parents, on the
basis of spatial proximity, and on the basis of frequency and quality of
social interaction. The third level, the core kindred, consists of a genealogically definable set of relatives. It consists of parents and parents' sib-

lings in the first ascending generation and their spouses, and all descendants of parents and parents' siblings, and includes the spouses of descendants. In addition, parents of spouses of relatives are often known and included in the genealogical core kindred. The core kindred is thus a kindred of first-cousin range which includes affines. Grandparents are often remembered and considered part of the core kindred. Grandparents' siblings are virtually never known. In no case did genealogical reckoning extend above the second ascending generation.

The concept of the kindred has come in for considerable discussion in recent years (Yalman, 1962, 1967; Goodenough, 1962, 1970; Mitchell, 1963, 1965) and one anthropologist (Gulliver, 1971) has concluded that the concept is of so little utility that it should be discarded. Following Goodenough (1962: 5), we limit the use of the term kindred to mean an ego-centered circle of relatives. For the Pemon, the connections between relatives need not be traced genealogically, and relatives include affines as well as consanguines. The concepts of "affine" and "consanguine" are foreign to the Pemon, though they are perfectly well aware of the existence of relatives by marriage. There is, however, only one specifically affinal term other than the husband and wife terms. This is the term -*payɨnu* or son-in-law, a term which has special significance in Pemon marital and residential arrangements and to which we shall return. Throughout our discussion, it should be remembered that the concepts "affine" — relative by marriage — and "consanguine" — relative connected to Ego by a genealogical chain containing only parent-child links — are concepts of the anthropologist, not of the Pemon. The glosses for Pemon kinship terms can be given in two ways. The first, which I have previously put into print (Thomas, 1971), consists of defining the terms on the basis of the genealogical grid consisting of consanguineal and affinal relatives of a given Ego in five generations: Ego's own, the two above, and the two below. The second consists of the translations of Pemon descriptions of relatives, including the rules for assigning someone a place in the terminological scheme of relatives. The structure of the Pemon language permits the tracing of relationships to relatives in two ways, which we shall call genealogical and terminological. The ability of the Pemon to operate with both of these schemes shows that both genealogical (resulting in the core kindred) and terminological (resulting in the personal kindred) means of tracing relationships to relatives have meaning for them.

The genealogical manner of tracing relationships relies on the iterative possibilities of the Pemon language, on the possibility of a descriptive calculus of relationships. Thus there are two ways in which to refer to a grandfather: as (1) the father of a parent: *papaiyun* (father's father) or *amaiyun* (mother's father), or as (2) male relative of the second ascending generation (*utaamo*). In fact, there is also a third way to refer to a grandfather, using a self-reciprocal term which operates between grandparent and grandchild. It is possible to construct, in the Pemon language, a descriptive calculus for genealogical reckoning using the terms which subsume the meanings of father, mother, elder sibling (male or female), younger sibling (male or female), children, son, daughter, husband, and wife. I say "which subsume the meanings of" rather than "which mean" in order to point out that the terms themselves, if defined in terms of our own descriptive genealogical calculus, have broader meanings *which define their use* in the terminological calculus of relationships. The use of the Pemon terms in a genealogical calculus proceeds as follows.

First, four grandparents, if known, are ascertained by use of the terms which can be constructed for FF, FM, MF, and MM. These are *papaiyun, papaiyan, amaiyun,* and *amaiyan,* respectively. Now the astute reader who refers to the list of terms will note that the gloss for *papai* and for *uyun* is F, FB, MZH, and that for *amai* and for *usan* is M, MZ, FBW. But by referring to the second ascending generation, we are in effect asking for the common parent of F, FB or M, MZ, that is FF or FM, MF or MM as the case may be. From this point on, the genealogical calculus proceeds with names and an appended reference to "the children of" (Pemon *imukuton*). Thus if we wish to ask about father's sibling set, we simply use the phrase *ɨ kin papaiyun imukuton* — "who are your father's father's children?"

This is quite clearly a roundabout way of doing things, and *does not* correspond to everyday Pemon calculation of relationships. It nevertheless represents a possibility inherent in the Pemon language (all genealogies, covering a population of about 600 living people, were taken in the Pemon language), one wl.ich they themselves do not exploit except on occasion. The core kindred which is defined by genealogical reckoning is a reality which can only be found by direct inquiry, and as such is open to the criticism that it is an artifact of anthropological questioning rather than a set of concepts in minds of the Pemon. Since we are after the totality of the Pemon way of looking at and doing things, or at least aspects of that totality, we must show that the genealogical calculus is part of Pemon conceptualization, however covert it may be in everyday usage.

The place to start is with the Pemon concept of parent-child relationship, with what anthropologists have called "filiation," the fact of being the child of a particular parent. The Pemon have various words for children, depending on whether the father or the mother is the point of reference. In the singular, a man refers to his son by the word -*mu*, which also means, quite significantly, semen. His daughter he refers to as -*yensi*. When referring to all his children, he uses the term -*mukuton* (-*muku* also means both son and semen). A woman does not distinguish the sex of her children, referring to a child of either sex with the terms *-me*, *-rume*. The plural of the latter term is *mureton*, the everyday word for children, used by both sexes to refer to children of both sexes, in the general sense. When own children are meant specifically, the term *-mu-kuton* is used. Armellada (1943–44, II: 137) notes of the term *-rume*: "This word is most certainly a simple metastasis of *mure*, and hence can be used for both sexes." The word *mure* in the singular means child of either sex.

The significant characteristic of all these terms (except for *-yensi*) is that they center on the stem *-mu*. Armellada (1943–44, II: 95) gives the following definitions for this stem: "semen, son; starch, fertile substance, flour." *I-mu* is also used to refer to the white, starchy root of the bitter manioc plant, which forms the basis of Pemon subsistence. The stem *-mu* thus connects the parent-child relationship with the fecundating power of semen as well as with the growth of manioc roots from the transplanted stalks. Through the multiple meanings of the stem *-mu*, the child is seen as connected not only to its parents but more generally to the principle of growth manifested in the plant world surrounding the Pemon.

According to the Pemon theory of conception, the male, by repeated copulation, engenders the growth of the fetus by adding semen progressively over time. The female provides the blood, the male the white substance which will form the flesh and bone of the child. In all senses the roles of the male and of the female in producing the child are co-equal, since it is only the progressive melding of semen and blood which can produce the child and assure its development before birth. Parenthood is based upon this notion of common substance with the child, and the basis for genealogical reckoning, for the core kindred, is the parent-child tie and the principle of growth or fecundity with which it is associated. The explicitness of these associations is encapsulated in the term *-mu*.

The parent-child tie is directional, from parent to child, in the sense that it is necessarily the one which brings about the other. But genealogical reckoning on the part of the Pemon always starts in the present and moves backward into the past by child-parent links, links of filiation. Descent, in the sense of genealogical relationship to a specific apical ancestor (ancestor focus) is not a principle of Pemon social organization. What are present are successive links of filiation traced backward two generations. The filiative links move outward and backward in time from Ego, not downward from the ancestor as in the case of descent. When asked as to why their genealogies are so shallow, why they did not know of their great-grandparents (or in some cases, grandparents), the answer was inevitably, "Well, I never knew them (saw them)." The this-worldly orientation of the Pemon is not quite as complete as this statement suggests, as there is a generalized word for ancestor (*piato*). Nevertheless, links of filiation are only important insofar as Ego can actually know the persons involved. They are not the basis for links with the long-dead, except in the vaguest and most generalized sense — we all have ancestors back there somewhere.

The most frequently used Pemon kinship terms can be represented on the basis of a genealogical paradigm (see Figures 4 and 5 and Table 1). The terms have the possessive *u*, except in cases where the term is not normally conjugated (as, for example, the term *waʔnɨ*). This representation does not include some of the affines which are included under some terms, and it is not possible, as we have noted, to represent the totality of the definition of the terms with a genealogical paradigm (the descriptive definition is a minimum one).

The descriptive genealogical calculus which can be constructed in the Pemon language is based on the parent-child relationship, summed up in the words -*mu* and -*mure*. The terminological calculus which Pemon utilize and which forms the basis of the personal kindred is likewise based on the notion of parent-child relationship, but in a more generalized sense. In the terminological calculus the point of reference is the usage of one's parents in designating others of their generation. The terminological calculus makes extensive use of the concepts of "sibling/ parallel cousin" and "cross-cousin/in-law" used to refer to persons in one's own generation. These within-generation concepts are effectively prior to the between-generation parent-child concept which is linked to them to constitute the terminological calculus. The category "cross-cousin/in-law" is troublesome because a single Pemon term subsumes two divergent meanings in English. Anthropologists have been wont to give priority to the affinal meaning of this category. To do so here would result in error. The two meanings are bound together as one in the Pemon terms -*yese* (male Ego term for "male cross-cousin/brother-in-law") and -*yeruk* (female Ego term for "female cross-cousin/sister-in-law").

The rules for classifying kinsmen are based on the usage of Ego's parents (see Tables 2 and 3). Their importance lies in the fact that the rules can be manipulated to include persons who might not be included on the basis of strict genealogical reckoning. Pemon will use both the genealogical mode and the terminological mode of reckoning depending on their needs in a given situation. Social interaction in Ego's parents' time may take precedence over genealogical reckoning. An example will illustrate this. Evaristo (male) designates Santos *urui* (eB, elder parallel cousin). The genealogical connection between the two from Evaristo's point of view is ZDH. Santos would be *upoitorɨ*, not *urui*, from this genealogical perspective. When questioned as to why he designated Santos as *urui*, Evaristo gave the following answer: "Since my father

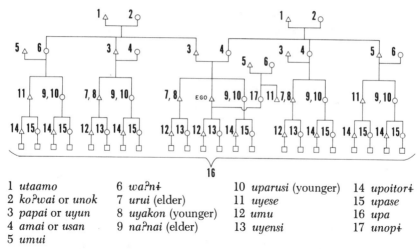

1 *utaamo*	6 *waʔnɨ*	10 *uparusi* (younger)	14 *upoitorɨ*
2 *koʔwai* or *unok*	7 *urui* (elder)	11 *uyese*	15 *upase*
3 *papai* or *uyun*	8 *uyakon* (younger)	12 *umu*	16 *upa*
4 *amai* or *usan*	9 *naʔnai* (elder)	13 *uyensi*	17 *unopɨ*
5 *umui*			

Numbers refer to chart only, not to text. All terms given in first person.

For a complete description of all Pemon kin terms, see Thomas, 1971.

Figure 4. Most frequently used Pemon kin terms (male Ego).

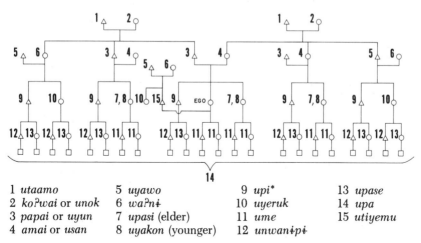

1 *utaamo*	5 *uyawo*	9 *upi**	13 *upase*
2 *koʔwai* or *unok*	6 *waʔnɨ*	10 *uyeruk*	14 *upa*
3 *papai* or *uyun*	7 *upasi* (elder)	11 *ume*	15 *utiyemu*
4 *amai* or *usan*	8 *uyakon* (younger)	12 *unwanɨpɨ*	

Numbers refer to chart only, not to text. All terms given in first person.

The *upi* term is broken up in address into /*pipi*/ (elder) and /*sioko*/ (younger).

Figure 5. Most frequently used Pemon kin terms (female Ego).

Symbols used in kinship diagrams: □ *person of either sex;* △ *male;* ○ *female;*
|___| *marriage link;* |‾‾| *sibling link;* | *parent-child link;* BLACKENED CHARACTER *deceased;*
|_X_| *divorced;* ╱ *married outside the settlement;* ·═══·═ *co-resident relationship;*
═══ *putative genealogical link;* ··═══·· *"capitan-segundo" relationship.*

Table 1. Pemon Kinship Terms.

Reference Terms	Vocative Terms	Descriptive Definition
utamo		man of second ascending generation
unok	koʔwai	woman of second ascending generation
uyun	papai	F, FB, MZH
usan	amai	M, MZ, FBW
umui (male Ego)		MB, FZH, WF
uyawo (female Ego)		MB, FZH, HF
waʔnɨ		FZ, MBW, spouse's mother
urui (male Ego)		eB, elder male parallel cousin
upasi (female Ego)		eZ, elder female parallel cousin
uyakon		same sex younger sibling; same sex younger parallel cousin
naʔnai (male Ego)		eZ, elder female cross- or parallel cousin, WeZ
uparusi (male Ego)		yZ, younger female cross- or parallel cousin, WyZ
upi (female Ego)	pipi	B, male cross- or parallel cousin, HB
uyese (male Ego)		male cross-cousin, WB, ZH
uyeruk (female Ego)	miʔmi	female cross-cousin, BW, HZ
upoitolɨ (male Ego)		ZS, MZDS, MBSS, MBDS, FBDS, FZSS, FZDS, DH
unwanɨpɨ (female Ego)		BS, FBSS, FZSS, FZDS, MZSS, MBSS, MBDS, DH
upase (male Ego)		ZD, MZDD, MBSD, MBDD, FBDD, FZSD, FZDD, SW
upase (female Ego)		BD, MZSD, MBSD, MBDD, FBSD, FZSD, FZDD, SW
umu (male Ego)		S, BS, FBSS, MZSS, WZS
uyensi (male Ego)		D, BD, FBSD, MZSD, WZD
ume (female Ego)		S, D, ZS, ZD, FBDS, FBDD, MZDS, MZDD, HBS, HBD
upa		male or female of second ascending or descending generation (self-reciprocal term)
unopɨ		W
utiyemu		H

Table 1 (Cont)

Reference Terms	Vocative Terms	Descriptive Definition
upayɨnu		DH
	maʔnon	younger female kinsman of Ego's generation or of first descending generation
	moyi	younger male kinsman of Ego's generation or of first descending generation
uyomba		any relative

called his father brother, I call him (elder) brother." Upon further questioning Evaristo stated that Paulo Plaza (Santos's father, now dead) had migrated into the Uonken area from Roraima, five or six days' walk to the east, and had no antecedents in Uonken. Evaristo described how the group from Paulo's settlement would come to dance at his father's settlement. Evaristo's father, head of a large settlement, and Paulo, leader of the other large settlement in the area at the time (1940s), set up visiting relations and denominated each other "brother." Evaristo's version of the story *excludes* possible genealogical connection of his father with Paulo (and the genealogies bear him out). The visiting relations among proximate settlements were transformed into kinship relations, and these transformed social relationships of his father's generation took precedence in his kin classifications over the ZDH connection, based on a current marriage tie.

Other classifications made by Evaristo reveal much the same attention paid to the actual classifications in use by his parents' generation, as opposed to concern with genealogical connections. Lisandro Bernal called Evaristo's father *umu* (son). Evaristo's father then called Lisandro's son Horacio *uyakon* (yB, younger parallel cousin). Horacio thus became *papai* (F, FB) to Evaristo. The genealogical connection between Evaristo and Horacio is (from Evaristo's point of view) WMFS = WMB. Now, if FZD marriage had occurred, Evaristo's WMB would be his "F" (WMB = F). Since FZD marriage is part of the Pemon ideal of marriage with a person in a category including FZD and MBD, his marriage is consistent with his classification of Horacio as *papai*. The social relations of the parental generation form not only a basis for his kin classification but are consonant with his marriage choice in terms of Pemon ideals.

The above two examples center on the overriding of genealogical criteria for kin classification by "situational" criteria inherited from the parent's generation. "Situational" criteria also may apply to Ego's classification of persons in his own generation or descending generations

Table 2. Terminological Calculus Based on Male Ego's Parents' Usage.

If	X calls	Y,	Y is Ego's Z.	Y's male offspring are	V.
1.	papai	urui (e) uyakon (y)	papai	urui (e) uyakon (y)
2.	papai	uyese	umui	uyese
3.	papai	naʔnai (e) uparusi (y)	waʔnɨ	uyese
4.	amai	upasi (e) uyakon (y)	amai	urui (e) uyakon (y)
5.	amai	uyeruk	waʔnɨ	uyese
6.	amai	upi	umui	uyese

7. All female offspring of parents' own-generation relatives are *naʔnai* (e) or *uparusi* (y).

8. Own offspring and offspring of own *urui* (e), *uyakon* (y) are *umu* if male and *uyensi* if female.

9. Offspring of own *uyese* or of *naʔnai* (e), *uparusi* (y) are *upoitorɨ* if male and *upase* if female, except WZC = own child.

Table 3. Terminological Calculus Based on Female Ego's Parents' Usage.

If	X calls	Y,	Y is Ego's Z.	Y's female offspring are	V.
1.	papai	urui (e) uyakon (y)	papai	upasi (e) uyakon (y)
2.	papai	uyese	uyawo	uyeruk
3.	papai	naʔnai (e) uparusi (y)	waʔnɨ	uyeruk
4.	amai	upasi (e) uyakon (y)	amai	upasi (e) uyakon (y)
5.	amai	uyeruk	waʔnɨ	uyeruk
6.	amai	upi	uyawo	uyeruk

7. All male offspring of parents' own-generation relatives are *upi* (in address broken up into *pipi* (e) and *sioko* (y)).

8. Own offspring and offspring of *upasi* (e), *uyakon* (y) are *ume*.

9. Offspring of *uyeruk* or of *upi* are *unwanɨpɨ* if male and *upase* if female, except HBC = own child.

based on current social practice. Thus Evaristo classifies a man in a relatively distant (four hours' walk overland) settlement, as eB (*urui*), since Evaristo and his family visit the man's settlement on festive occasions to celebrate observances of the Chochiman cult (the man is a leader of the Chochiman cult). Evaristo justifies his classification with a simple statement to the effect that he visits the man and considers him a "brother."

In some cases genealogical criteria can be used to transform a social situation by in effect excluding someone from a category into which they would normally fall on the basis of a specific social situation (in this case, a marital relationship). Uslar had a dispute with Anton, the step-father of his wife, a man who was nominally his *umui* (the MB, FZH, WF term) on several counts:

1) Anton was Uslar's WFB, and was married to Uslar's WM in accordance with leviratic norms. Hence, as a stepfather to Uslar's wife, Anton was in the position of *umui* = WF.

2) The WFB relationship is sufficient in itself for the application of the *umui* term. Uslar argued, however, that Anton was not his "true" *umui* — that he was not related to Anton by ties in his parents' generation and that hence Anton had no right to criticize Uslar's behavior. Uslar thus used the absence of a genealogical tie in the first ascending generation as an excuse to break off relations with Anton.

The above examples illustrate the importance of situational factors — e.g. visiting relationships, future marriage plans, or past marriage choices — in a person's classification of kinsmen. The categories into which persons fall reflect notions which underlie the system of categories as a whole. These underlying notions can be summed up by three terms which interlock: siblingship, filiation, and affinity. Since these three terms have been used by Fortes (1969) in the analysis of societies quite different from the Pemon, and since my account differs markedly from the analysis employed by Fortes, care must be taken in their definition.

By siblingship I mean the quality that inheres in the cooperative relationship of offspring of the same parents. In Pemon life siblingship must be thought of as a horizontal tie which is not necessarily always mediated by a vertical tie (that of connection to a common set of parents). To be sure, siblingship implies common substance (the result of the combination of *mu* = semen and *min* = blood), but as a principle for organizing social life it is best understood as a tie which links members of a single generation in a single trajectory through time. The ties of common substance may be secondary, in any given case, to the ties of unreserved cooperation. The ties of cooperation in one generation may engender the statement (as in the case of Evaristo and the Chochiman cult leader discussed above) that "we are brothers," and offspring of these "brothers" in the next generation will consider themselves "brothers and sisters." In Pemon life the principle of siblingship is coequal with, not subordinate to, the principles of filiation (the parent-child tie) and affinity (any tie which contains a marriage link). Siblings are allied not just by birth but by the circumstance of moving through life in solidary formation. As adults, Pemon turn first to their siblings for cooperation and backing and, if possible, will create sibling ties if cooperation is forthcoming from a valued other person.

Siblingship, then, is a principle which is simultaneously vertical (being offspring of a common set of parents) and horizontal (unreserved solidarity within a single generation); in Pemon society the horizontal aspect most often predominates, but the dual nature of siblingship can be seen as the bridge between the genealogical and the terminological calculi for kinsmen.

We recognize several levels of meaning and implication for Pemon terms for kinsmen. These are (see Geertz and Geertz, 1975: 154-55): (1) the cognitive level, defined primarily by genealogical specifications which in turn derive from the arrangement of parent-child ties and actual marriage connections; (2) the level of rights and duties, the so-called "normative" level; (3) the "affective" level, including sentiments and attitudes associated with specific terms; and (4) the "symbolic" level, mainly concerning the representation of types of kinsmen in myths and stories.

All of these levels interact in the use of any given term, and any one of them may, alone or in combination with the other levels, assume primacy in the application of a specific term to a fellow Pemon. The level of rights and duties and the "affective" level involve certain expectations of behavior on the part of the incumbent of a category (the "symbolic" level will be treated below, in the course of a discussion of Pemon tales).

To see the sequence of links between the genealogical and terminological calculi as mediated by the principles of siblingship, filiation, and affinity, consider the diagram in Figure 6. The generative power of semen and blood give rise to common substance, the basis of the genealogical calculus. This genealogical calculus is the basis for a cognitive map which is one component of Ego's parents' usage, which (as described above) is the basis for Ego's terminological calculus. Ego's terminological calculus is then, in whole or in part, mapped back onto the level of common substance and the genealogical calculus. Siblingship is the focal principle in the combinatorial process which brings together affective connotations, notions of rights and duties, and the thinking about genealogy, resulting in actual usage, since it is siblings who embody common substance in the fullest sense. Pemon society can be thought of not only as individuals and families perpetuating themselves but, more widely and more importantly, as sibling sets trying to recreate themselves down through the generations. In the Pemon case we must learn to take the horizontal lines — the lines linking siblings — in

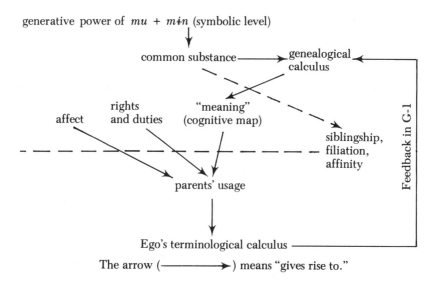

generative power of *mu* + *min* (symbolic level)

Figure 6. Relationship of the genealogical and terminological calculi.

the genealogies quite seriously, and not subordinate them automatically to the parental links which connect them to a common source.

In order to define the domain of the principles of siblingship, filiation, and affinity in Pemon society, we will briefly set forth their components in tabular form (see Table 4).

With this rather abbreviated summary of the principles underlying Pemon designation of kinsmen, we are now able to embark on the account of how Pemon use, elaborate on, and contradict these principles in the course of social life.

Distribution of Kinsmen in the Settlement Pattern

At any given moment an individual's core kindred contains some relatives who are long distances away and some who are close by. Those who are close by will almost invariably be members of Ego's own sibling set, though seldom are all siblings collected in one area. There is a tendency for male siblings to attempt to live together in the same area after they have established families of their own and completed (or avoided) their obligations to their parents-in-law. Failing this, some males may choose either to stay on in the area where their wife's relatives live or to go to the vicinity of a female sibling's family of procreation. Since there is no lineal principle of descent in Pemon society, and since each succeeding generation of male siblings must "marry out" in

Table 4. Siblingship, Filiation, and Affinity in Pemon Society.

Principle	Rights and Duties	Sentiments and Attitudes
Siblingship (fully common substance)	1) balanced obligation only in very long run	1) same sex: solidarity + respect + affection
	2) unquestioned back-up in disputes	2) cross-sex: separation + respect + affection + sexual restraint
	3) economic cooperation in house building and setting up residence	3) elder/younger: respect from y to e; protective attitude from e to y
	4) unquestioned support in misfortune (e.g. illness, divorce, bereavement)	
Filiation (common substance in part)	1) unidirectional nurturance: parent → child (reversed only in very old age)	1) Mo-child affection strongest single bond
	2) transmission of skills: parent → child (same sex)	2) familiarity, love, pride, permissiveness (parent → child), respect (c → p)
	3) unquestioning allegiance	
Affinity (assertion of common substance via previous generation; no common substance in own generation)	1) exchange; quid pro quo; strict reckoning	1) veiled hostility, mistrust (except H-W tie)
	2) short-term balancing of obligations	a) same-sex: veiled hostility, mistrust
	3) reciprocal economic services	b) opposite sex: distance, separation, sexual access
	4) cross-generation (younger to elder): provision of services (unidirectional); exchange permanently out of balance	2) elder to younger (cross-generation only): expectation of deference, subordinate attitude
		3) younger to elder (cross-generation only): resentment, chafing at demands

its turn, the sibling sets spread out and reconstitute themselves repeatedly over the generations.

The push and pull of affinal ties versus sibling ties could, of course, be resolved if Pemon ideals were carried out over enough generations, and if demographic contingency and personal likes and dislikes could be left out. If the Pemon verbal ideal of bilateral cross-cousin marriage were carried out and suitable spouses could be found — of proper age, sex, and disposition — within the category of "near" relatives, there would be no opposition, no dialectic, to bother about. All affines would also be consanguines, and the ultimate — a world with no outsiders — would be achieved.

Of course this does not happen, and the push and pull referred to is a constant feature of Pemon life. We shall argue that, far from being just a departure from expressed ideals, the interaction of sibling and affinal ties over the course of three generations — children, young adults, and the senior generation — represents a series of fundamental mechanisms which prevent the concentration of power and allegiance in Pemon society. In a very real sense, for the Pemon, it is the contradictions in the norms of obligation to siblings and to affines which disperse power, which keep Pemon society egalitarian.

Reference points for grouping Pemon in physical space are not "given" or obvious. One of the levels of grouping, the neighborhood, is not explicitly recognized by the Pemon and must be partitioned out of the continuous scatter of settlements by a combination of spatial and behavioral criteria. The household is easily recognized by the daily pooling of resources and effort by its members, and most often by a single dwelling (there are some cases where a single household extends to two dwellings, but these are quite rare). The settlement, a named cluster of houses anywhere from immediately adjacent to five minutes' walk apart, is also a "given" unit. To the Pemon, there is no ambiguity about the notion of settlement (*upata*). All settlements, with the exception of those in immediate proximity to missions or criollo centers, are named for a watercourse nearby, or possibly for a prominent landmark in the immediate vicinity. Almost all Pemon settlements are close to a small watercourse which serves as the water supply for the settlement. The settlement pattern in the savanna portion of the tribal territory tends to be somewhat more uniform than that in the riverine forest portion. While both patterns can only be described as riverine, the settlements in the western, or riverine forest, area fall more easily into "clumps" along a stretch of the main river or tributaries. "Clumping" or clustering is rather less evident in the Gran Sabana area around Uonken, where detailed residence and census data were obtained.

Pemon in general do not recognize any levels of spatial organization between the settlement and the region, a very loose concept with ill-defined boundaries. They do classify persons in terms of space, however (see above, p. 34), and in that context sometimes refer to the large river nearest the settlement of the person referred to, a level between the settlement and the region. The neighborhood is a group of spatially proximate settlements (usually no more than an hour's travel across on foot or by canoe) which manifest frequent intersettlement visiting and some concentration of genealogical ties, reckoned cognatically. Neighborhood boundaries are drawn using this combination of spatial and behavioral criteria. The Uonken region can be divided into seven neighborhoods in this way. The region can only be defined loosely, and for our purposes will consist of 36 named settlements in the valley of the Karuai River and the Caroni itself upstream from Otovanta Falls as far as the mouth of the Surukun (see Thomas, 1973: 100).

Analysis of the distribution of kinsmen (including affines) in the settlement pattern shows that, for heads of settlement, members of their core kindreds are dispersed throughout the levels of the settlement pattern; many heads of settlement have primary relatives *outside the Uonken region altogether* (see Thomas, 1973: 114–18). Many heads of settlement also have primary relatives (other than their wives and children) within the same settlement. There is no discernible tendency for concentration of particular genealogical kin types at any level of the settlement pattern, at least for heads of settlement (adult males usually 30 years of age or older). As we move down the age scale, the concentration of relatives within the neighborhood and settlement would of course tend to increase, reaching its maximum for persons aged below ten years. These results show that, even though the neighborhood is more or less composed of cognatically related persons, the core kindreds of adults span the whole of the tribal territory — the regional population cannot be considered closed in any real sense, since some of its members move out, usually to marry and set up residence in another region of the tribal territory. We shall see that the existence of near relatives in other regions has crucial significance for the options available in disputes within settlements and neighborhoods.

The neighborhood level of organization stands out if we compare concentrations of certain types of relationships at the settlement level and at the neighborhood level. Taking only heads of settlements as foci, we find the configurations of selected affinal relationships at the two levels shown in Tables 5 and 6. Likewise, concentration of sibling relationships (of heads of settlement) becomes more apparent at the neighborhood level, as comparison of Tables 7 and 8 shows.

If we look at residential patterns for all adults (not just heads of settlement), we find, with reference to own parents and spouse's parents, own full and half-siblings, and same-generation same-sex affines, the following results (see Thomas, 1973: 130–40):

Table 5. Affinal Relationships within Settlements.

	Total	DH Present	SW	WB	ZH
Single household	16	2	1	1	0
Multiple household	17	6	6	3	1
No household data	3	2	1	0	0
	36	10	8	4	1

Table 6. Affinal Relationships within Neighborhoods.
(heads of settlements used as foci)

Neighborhood No.	Number of settlements	DH	SW	WB	ZH
1	5	2	2	2	1
2	3	2	1	1	1
3	11	4	4	1	2
4	7	1	1	3	2
5	4	1	2	1	0
6	4	1	1	0	0
7	2	1	4	0	0
	36	12	11	8	6

Table 7. Siblings within Settlements.
(heads of settlements as foci)

	Total	B (or MS, FS)	Z (or MD, FD)
Single household	16	2	1
Multiple household	17	0	2
No household data	3	1	1
	36	3	4

Table 8. Siblings within Neighborhoods.
(heads of settlements as foci)

Neighborhood No.	Number of Settlements	B (or MS, FS)	Z (or MD, FD)
1	5	1	1
2	3	3	2
3	11	3	3
4	7	2	4
5	4	0	0
6	4	1	0
7	2	0	1
	36	10	11

1) For about two-thirds of all adult males and of all adult females, one or the other surviving parent lives in the same neighborhood, and the spouse's parents live in the same neighborhood.

2) Three types of sibling ties (bro/bro, bro/sis, sis/sis) are considered. At the level of settlements, adult siblings are predominantly in different settlements. Sibling pairs of all three types, however, are found mostly together in the same neighborhood, with the exception of the bro/bro relationship, where the united and separated categories break up about evenly. (In assessing sibling relationships, siblings found outside the region are not considered. Remember, however, that many adults have siblings outside the region.)

3) At the settlement level, 37 percent of adult males and of adult females have same-sex in-laws of the same generation residing with them in the same settlement (some of these affines are also consanguines). At the settlement level, there is a slightly greater tendency to live with same-sex same-generation affines rather than with siblings (all types of sibling pairs). At the neighborhood level, the two tendencies (living in the same neighborhood as one's sibling, living in the same neighborhood as a same-sex same-generation affine) are almost the same strength in percentage terms, except for the slightly lower percentage of bro/bro sibling pairs living together.

In order to see how choices with regard to these types of near relatives (both consanguines and affines) are involved in the constitution of actual settlements, we can compare personal genealogies and the actual composition of settlements. Several settlements, which can be regarded as "mature" at the time of study, provide the basis for a retrospective look at how they came to be as they are.

The Maikanden settlement

The current head of the Maikanden settlement, Jaime Portales, was born just upstream from the mouth of the Karuai, on the main course of the Caroni, around 1923. (See Figure 7 for a chart of the genealogical relationships in 1970.) As a young man he left the Uonken area and married Cilia, a Makusi woman, in Santa Elena around 1941. Upon his return to the Uonken area in the mid-1940s, he resided with his family at Aruameru, a site overlooking the Makarupai River, some ten minutes' walk from the present site of Maikanden. Then, around 1953, Jaime Portales took a second wife and spent part of his time at his new wife's father's settlement, across the Karuai River and some distance away by canoe and on foot. In the late 1950s the settlement at Aruameru was abandoned, and its members, who included Jaime Portales's first wife and her offspring, as well as his mother, moved to the present site at Maikanden. Jaime's sister's children, Anibal and Videlia, had been raised by his mother, Riabi, after the death of his sister. Anibal

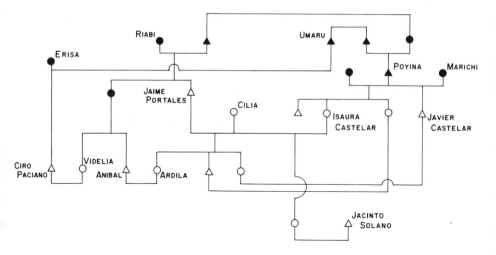

Figure 7. Genealogical relationships at Maikanden (1970).

married Ardila Portales, Jaime's daughter, about 1956 and then moved with his wife and mother-in-law to Maikanden in the late fifties. Anibal's sister, Videlia, had married Ciro Paciano in 1951, and Ciro and Videlia were also part of the Aruameru settlement in the fifties and moved to Maikanden in the late fifties.

Jaime, having married out as a young man, brought his first wife (an orphan) and offspring back to his natal area and contracted a second, rather irregular (FZSD, a "sister's daughter" union, about which more later) marriage which aligned him with his new father-in-law, Poyina. Poyina was an important man in the Makarupai River area who had assumed a leadership role taken over from his own father's brother, Umaru. Umaru was a powerful shaman who died in 1942 at a site very close to the present site of Maikanden. Umaru had fathered numerous children by many wives, and had used the threat of his spiritual powers to obtain women. Umaru had taken as one wife a woman named Erisa. Poyina later took Erisa's half-brother's daughter Marichi as one of his wives (a "MBD," or regular, marriage). Poyina established himself and his wives and children at Uakautei, a site across the Karuai River, inland from the banks of the Karuai and almost due west of Maikanden, in the early 1950s, after having lived mostly in the area of Wadaraden, Umaru's principal home site, south of the Makarupai. Jaime Portales's new relationship with Poyina, beginning in 1953 with his marriage to Poyina's daughter Isaura Castelar, was not only the taking of a second wife but an attempt to reintegrate himself into the community of the neighborhood after his out-marriage in Santa Elena, and thereby to be in line to move into the leadership position which Poyina had taken over from Umaru. However, he was involved in commuting between two wives in two different settlements for some time during the 1960s, since his wife Isaura and their children spent much time at Uakautei. Poyina died at Uakautei in 1956, but some of Poyina's children remained there.

Jaime's attempt to assume the position left open on Poyina's death was based on the following ties: his own marriage tie to Poyina's daughter, and the marriages of two of his offspring by Cilia to offspring of Poyina, and the MB/ZS, father-in-law/son-in-law tie to Anibal. Anibal in turn had a close tie to his sister's husband, Ciro Paciano. Jaime's position was strengthened in the mid-1960s by the construction of a large, communal-type round house (a relatively rare event among present-day Pemon) at Maikanden, a house which was used to accommodate numerous visitors and to carry on the Hallelujah dancing ceremonies, which brought people from as far away as Uonken proper, some two and a half hours' walk. In 1969, upon the visit of a capitan from the Uriman area (the Uriman capitan was a man whose mother had come from the Uonken area; his mother had been a true sister of Erisa, one of the wives of Umaru), Jaime Portales became a capitan of the Uonken region. This was the outcome of a large assembly at Maikanden called by the capitan from Uriman. The Uriman capitan had come to express his concern over the fact that the Uonken region people had no capitan, since Baco Bandino, a previous capitan who had lived in the Old Mission settlement two hours to the north of Maikanden, had died in 1965 and no one had replaced him.

By 1970 some difficulties with Jaime's following within the Maikanden settlement had begun to appear. Ciro Paciano, linked to Jaime mainly by his own tie to Anibal (Ciro's WB and Jaime's son-in-law), maintained an alternate residence downstream on the Caroni (almost a day's canoe trip away, paddling) where he spent considerable time with his family, maintained manioc fields, and eventually (April, 1971) married his eldest son to a girl resident in that neighborhood. There were many complaints (quite guarded, of course) from members of Ciro Paciano's household about the fact that there was never any *cachiri* for visitors at Jaime's house (which was true, as far as I could tell) and that visitors always ended up at Ciro's house, where there was plenty of *cachiri*. In addition, relations between Anibal and Jaime Portales were not all that close, and Anibal was mainly concerned with helping his aging mother-in-law Cilia. Also, Javier Castelar, Jaime's daughter's husband and simultaneously his second wife's half-brother was in the same household as Cilia, and was also concerned with supporting Cilia. Cilia and Jaime were at this time in separate households, side by side. Both Anibal and Javier maintained their own subsistence plots, worked by them and their wives, and though both contributed to the support of Cilia, there was not much support given Jaime's household in *cachiri* production or contributions of fish by either Javier or Anibal. Most particularly, the segment of the settlement focused around Ciro Paciano's and Anibal's families was, by 1970, increasingly distancing itself from Jaime Portales.

Meanwhile Jaime had been unable to retain a third son-in-law, Jacinto Solano, at Maikanden after the completion of his brideservice. Jacinto was married to Jaime's daughter (by his second wife) in late 1967, and had not yet built a separate dwelling in the Maikanden settlement by 1970. Early in 1971 Jacinto took his wife and their offspring to live at Pampetameru with his brother Abelio Solano, citing among other things the need to help his brother in cutting new manioc plots for the following year (January through March is a dry period, a principal time for the cutting of fields). Jaime's second wife's brother, Jorge Castelar, was completing a house close by at a site ten minutes' walk from and in plain sight of Maikanden, and Jorge frequently visited Jaime and vice versa. Jorge had resided for some time in the large round house owned by Jaime, at Maikanden, before beginning his house a short distance away. Jorge Castelar was married to Jacinto Solano's sister Belisa, but relations between Jorge and Jacinto, and between Javier Castelar and Jacinto, were marred by the fact that a sister of Javier (a half-sister of Jorge) had left Jacinto's brother Abelio for another man. Jacinto's brother Abelio was much hurt in this abandonment, and Jacinto's desire to remove himself from the Maikanden settlement was undoubtedly conditioned by the presence there of Javier and, nearby, of Jorge.

Several factors, then, militated against the further buildup of the Maikanden settlement after 1970. Foremost among these was Jaime Portales's inability to persuade his sons-in-law Anibal and Javier to take a more active part in providing the wherewithal for traditional Pemon hospitality. Further, Jaime's relative neglect of his first wife Cilia must have been keenly felt by her two daughters (the wives of Anibal and Javier), who were strongly identified with Cilia and who influenced their husbands accordingly. Jaime Portales's only surviving full sibling Rigoberto Portales had married out downstream on the Caroni (still in the Uonken region but a good day's canoe trip away, paddling), and while he and Jaime maintained visiting ties, Rigoberto was never in a position to support Jaime's efforts at consolidating the Maikanden settlement. Jaime had had the misfortune to have two elder siblings die young and thus to have relatively little possibility of backing by his own siblings. By his own rather irregular second marriage he had drawn on the support not only of Poyina while he lived but also of Poyina's offspring, to whom he married a son and a daughter, in an attempt to consolidate support of the upcoming generation. However, conflicts between two sibling sets (the Castelars and the Solanos) in the first descending generation effectively prevented him from building a solid set of sons and sons-in-law at the Maikanden settlement.

Several things stand out in this account:

1) The interaction of members of sibling sets in the generation 20-35 years of age can have marked effects on the outcome of leadership attempts by members of the generation 35-50.

2) Mother-daughter and mother-son ties can be very important in determining lines of possible cleavage within a settlement.

3) A member of the generation 20-35 will often be confronted with deciding between obligation and affection toward his or her own family of orientation and obligation to the family of orientation or the adult siblings of the spouse. This holds for both men and women.

4) Virtually all individuals have siblings outside their own neighborhood and within the region (Thomas, 1973: 114–18, 133), and this, while it can decrease their base of support if they have no true siblings left in their own neighborhood (the case of Jaime Portales), also provides each individual with the option of someone to count on if things are not going well in the immediate surroundings. Thus, while the ideal is the concentration of adult members of a sibling set in a given neighborhood, the dispersion of male members which occurs as a result of the norm of matrilocal residence at marriage provides a basis for options on the part of the individual. In real terms, for a given individual's siblings to be either all concentrated in one neighborhood or to be all elsewhere would both be bad alternatives, even though the former is an "ideal" state.

The Old Mission Settlement

Some further lessons can be drawn from examination of a large settlement at and near the former mission site, just above the stream known as Tereyen, which flows into the Karuai. This site is about one and one-half to two hours' walk north of Maikanden. Though much larger than the average Pemon settlement, and having no real single leader (a nominal "senior" male was around, but not active in a leadership role, and a second, "capitan segundo" of the Uonken region, moved out during the year to a site not far from Maikanden), the settlement and its close satellites demonstrate a concentration of consanguineal and affinal ties among the residents. This settlement and the nearby areas show how the descendants of a brother and sister, respectively, often form the main portion of the population of a neighborhood.

The story of the Old Mission settlement goes something as follows. Candido Rulfo (born around 1900, died 1965) had raised his family in the 1920s and '30s at Uakauyen, south of the Makarupai River, an hour and a half walk southeast of Maikanden. Lisandro Bernal (born around

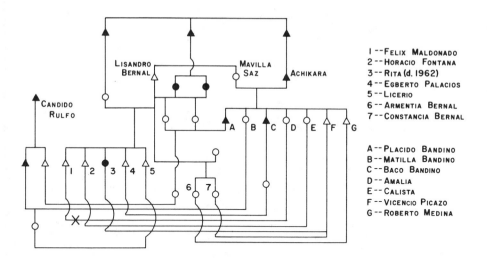

Figure 8. Genealogical relationships in the Old Mission neighborhood (1970).

1900, died 1974) had lived most of his life just to the south of the present Old Mission settlement. He had been engaged in several sister (actually parallel cousin; see Figure 8) exchanges with his sister's husband, Achikara, and both Lisandro and Achikara had lived at the site named Kuaiparu, just south of the Old Mission settlement close to the bank of the Karuai River, through the 1920s and '30s while raising their families.

Candido moved upon arranging several marriages between some of his offspring and persons in the settlement at Kuaiparu, and lived in the area of Iramata, a large stream east of the present Old Mission site. The bulk of the persons living in the Old Mission settlement in 1970-71 were either (1) offspring of Candido by his first or second wife, or his grandchildren or (2) offspring or grandchildren of either Lisandro Bernal or his sister Mavilla Saz. Candido had been a supporter of the missionaries coming in the late 1950s, and had sent one of his younger sons, Evaristo, to the mission at Santa Elena in the early 1940s. He was the acknowledged capitan of the Uonken region during the 1950s and up until his death in 1965, having during that time considerable competition from Paulo Plaza, the leader of a rather large settlement at Uonken proper, just to the north of the Old Mission site. Lisandro and his sister Mavilla were, in 1970, venerable and respected in the neighborhood of the Old Mission, though they were both too old to be economically active or to get around much.

Candido had moved into the Iramata area sometime in the late 1930s or early '40s, and Lisandro and his sister, after the death of her husband Achikara around 1940, continued to live near the present Old Mission area at several sites. Candido's offspring had mostly married into the Iramata–Old Mission area during the late 1930s and early '40s, and Candido attracted several sons-in-law to his settlement in the Iramata area during the '40s. There were at the time three main settlements in the areas now known as the Old Mission and Uonken (here referred to as Uonken proper): one, headed by Paulo Plaza at Uonken; a second, headed by Candido Rulfo at a site on the Iramata stream; and a third, rather dispersed settlement along the Tereyen stream, occupied by Lisandro Bernal, his wives and offspring, and his widowed sister and her offspring. The Tereyen stream is immediately to the south of the present Old Mission settlement, and several houses of the Old Mission settlement are two minutes' walk from the stream. According to informants, there was extensive visiting and *cachiri*-party giving among these settlements during this period, and informants recount that the old-style dances, *parichara* and *tukui*, were still performed in those days.

With the coming of the Capuchins to the Uonken region in the mid-1950s (the earliest recorded baptisms in the mission books date from October, 1956), Candido moved his settlement (several of his sons had already married offspring of Mavilla, Lisandro's sister) to the Old Mission area near Tereyen. Meanwhile, during the 1940s and '50s, there were numerous marriages between the offspring of the Lisandro-Mavilla sibling pair. These included the following unions:

Mavilla offspring	to	*Lisandro Bernal offspring*
Placido Bandino		-Lida Bernal and Maya Bernal (simultaneous)
Amalia		-Felix Maldonado (ended in divorce)
Anton		-Maya Bernal (second marriage for both)
Calista		-Horacio Fontana
Vicencio Picazo		-Rita (died 1962) -Cilia Bernal (sororate: married wife's half-sister upon first wife's death)
Roberto Medina		-Armentia Bernal

There were also some rather irregular (in the genealogical sense) marriages which connected descendants of this brother-sister pair. For example, the marriage of Egberto Palacios, a son of Lisandro Bernal, to the daughter of one of Mavilla Saz's elder sons was a FZSD marriage (the *upase* or "sister's daughter" category), and the marriage of Licerio, Egberto's younger brother, to a granddaughter of Mavilla was a FZDD marriage (also *upase* category). While there were offspring of other members of Lisandro Bernal's generation in the neighborhood which surrounded the Old Mission settlement in 1970, both the Old Mission settlement and in fact the whole of the neighborhood were dominated by his and his sister's descendants.

The large number of surviving offspring produced by this brother-sister pair (Lisandro Bernal had a total of four wives, two of whom died young and two of whom he maintained in a polygynous union until his death) provided ample opportunity for the fulfillment of the Pemon ideal marriage rule (marriage with a cross-cousin) in its most direct form. Though there were others at the Old Mission settlement in 1970 (particularly Candido's surviving offspring), they were almost all attached in some way to one or the other of the two intermarrying sibling sets which comprised the bulk of the neighborhood. The degree to which these sibling sets (even including half-siblings) remained localized over the period 1940–70 is indeed extraordinary. For example, of the seven surviving offspring of the Lisandro Bernal–Artemisa union, four were living in the neighborhood (one in the Old Mission settlement; one at Tereyenken, three minutes away; one at the Old Mission airstrip, also three minutes away; and one at Paruyapa, 20-25 minutes away). Of eight surviving offspring of the Lisandro Bernal–Arsenia union, five were living in the neighborhood, two in the Old Mission settlement. Of six surviving offspring of the Mavilla Saz–Achikara union, three were living in the Old Mission settlement, two at Tereyeken three minutes away, and one at Uoctapa, about a half-hour away, all of course in the neighborhood.

This concentration of marriages must be seen in the light of the large numbers of surviving offspring produced by both Lisandro and Mavilla. Candido Rulfo married two daughters to two brothers who initially lived with him at his settlement in the Iramata area, but both the daughters died and the offspring remained with their fathers, who subsequently remarried and moved out of Candido's influence, settling at Warmo, about 40 minutes to the west of the Old Mission settlement. Likewise, Candido's grandchildren contracted marriages which pulled many of them outside of the neighbborhood.

The neighborhood surrounding the Old Mission represents that rare situation in which ideals are nearly realized in practice and a cohesive group of near kin comes into being through intermarriage between two sibling sets which are related by consanguineal ties in their parents' generation. Many neighborhoods are rather more heterogeneous, and have more of a tendency to generate long-distance marriages. Also, many of the individual settlements in this neighborhood have close visiting and consanguineal ties to distant settlements within the region, as, for example, the ties which several of Lisandro Bernal's offspring and their children have to his deceased sister's offspring and their children at Kamadak, four hours' walk to the northwest.

Even in as highly "concentrated" a neighborhood as that which centers on the Old Mission settlements, persons have extensive kin and visiting ties outside their own neighborhood. This points up a significant result of our discussion thus far — there is *no endogamous unit* in Pemon society, at the household, settlement, neighborhood, regional, or even tribal (along certain borders, e.g. with the Akawaio, Patamona, and Makusi) levels. Endogamy is a word that is not applicable to Pemon society — there is a clear preference for marrying "close" both spatially and genealogically (we have mentioned one marriage occurring between members of the same settlement, that of Anibal and Ardila Portales at Aruameru in the mid-1950s); there are not units within which one *must* marry. Likewise, the only exogamous unit in Pemon society is, strictly speaking, the individual household. In fact, to speak of endogamy and exogamy in a society like the Pemon is simply superfluous and to a large extent misleading, since neither one of the two terms can be attached to any definable unit (above the household) with any accuracy. Ultimately, all units above the settlement level in fact overlap, and there are always links which connect different neighborhoods and different regions. Quite a few marriages in the Uonken region are with persons from other regions, and by no means are all of these found at the peripheries of the region (one of these marriages, in which the in-married male's natal settlement is several days away on the Kukenan, is found at the Old Mission settlement, in the center of the region).

What does this mean for individual Pemon? Each adult individual, no matter how concentrated his relatives are in one area, will almost always have a sibling or parallel cousin outside his or her own neighborhood and often outside the region as well. This is not merely a phenomenon of demographic time and chance, but is a structural tendency inherent in the pushes and pulls between different sibling sets over the course of several generations. Cross-generational ties (parent-child and parents–children-in-law) are never strong enough for a long enough time to produce very large settlements (we will discuss below the conditions which do produce such settlements, and discuss their characteristics). Even given the Pemon suspicion of strangers, every individual is glad to have an "out." In short, the personal kindred acts toward the end of dispersion, even in the face of an ideal of concentration of near relatives.

Siblings through Time

The strength of sibling ties varies through the life cycle, as in all cultures, but in Pemon society this strength is extremely enduring even over much space and time. An elder sibling is always, in some sense, in the role of guardian and protector of a younger sibling of either sex. Thus, for example, in the relationship of an elder sister to a younger brother, the brother will be in a subordinate role and have virtually no influence in the marriage arrangements of the sister. If the sister is younger, however, the brother assumes a guardianship role and can have some influence in the sister's marriage arrangements. The males of the sibling set are dispersed gradually as they marry out. This dispersion is mitigated, however, by the fact that young couples often spend a fair amount of time visiting the parents of the groom, even when residing matrilocally. Theoretically, since males usually marry in the order of their birth, there is no necessary competition among brothers for eligible females at any given moment in time. In practice this is not always the case. Since marriage in its early stages is subject to vicissitudes and may end up having been only a "trial" that failed, elder brothers may at times be attempting to arrange unions at the same time as younger ones.

In many cases, after the death of one or both parents, younger siblings will be found attached to the households of elder ones, who have taken on responsibility for them. Likewise, small children of deceased siblings will be cared for by a brother or sister of the deceased (in the event of remarriage of the children's surviving parent), usually a mother's brother or mother's sister. Finally, while movable property capable of being inherited upon death is scarce among the Pemon, what items a man owns will almost inevitably go to his brother if he dies before his children are fully adult (I refer here to such items as shotguns and manioc graters, important trade goods which are not buried with the dead or destroyed).

The extent to which siblings act in concert can be illustrated by several cases taken from everyday life. The first, a divorce case, shows the degree to which a younger sister is able to count on her elder brothers for support (see Figure 9). Maria Solano was a half-sibling of Abelio Solano and his brother Jacinto, both of whom lived at Pampetameru, a site in the southern portion of the Uonken region. Their common father had died when Maria was a small girl, and Maria's mother had subsequently remarried. Maria had married a man from Kamarata and had gone to live with him at a site on the Caroni known as Cachimbo (Pemon Avikara), which by 1970 was a thriving center of the Cochiman cult and a fairly large settlement (well over 50 people). During a dancing party at Cachimbo in mid-1970, Maria behaved very provocatively toward a

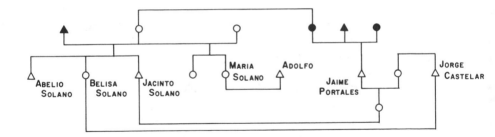

Figure 9. Genealogical relationships in Maria Solano's divorce case.

visitor and, according to reports, had intercourse with him while her
husband was away from the settlement. This incident was apparently a
manifestation of the rocky state of the marriage and of Maria's desire to
be out of it. Her husband later claimed that this was only one of several
instances in which she had "gone with another."

Finally, early in 1971 Maria had left Cachimbo, gone downriver to
Uriman, and come from there to Uonken. Upon arriving in Uonken she
found that her half-brother Jacinto had finished his brideservice in Maikanden and gone to Pampetameru. She immediately set out for Pampetameru and took up residence there in the household of her elder half-
brother, Abelio. Her husband soon followed her from Uriman and had
long and lamenting conversations with the head of the Maikanden settlement, the capitan of the Uonken region and father-in-law of Jacinto,
Maria's half-brother. These conversations took place in the house of the
capitan's brother-in-law, Jorge Castelar, who was married to Maria's
half-sister. Maria's husband claimed that he was willing to forget the
past, to make a new start and overlook his wife's transgressions. The
capitan, acting as a counselor in the matter, listened at some length over
many gourds of *cachiri* provided by his brother-in-law Jorge to the lam-
entations of Maria's husband.

Maria's half-brother Jacinto, despite the intercessions of his father-in-
law the capitan, defended his sister (at a later time, since he was a half-
day's journey away during the talks between Maria's husband and the
capitan). Jacinto claimed that she had been beaten by her husband, and
that her husband was a "Kamarakoto," not one of our people anyway
(i.e. not from the Uonken region), and a bad provider to boot. Jacinto,
in conversations with me after the husband had departed from Maikanden, talked disparagingly of those "Kamarakoto" and said his sister did
not want to go back to the man in any case. Jacinto repeatedly referred
to *inaparusi* — "our younger sister," emphasizing the unity of the sibling

group. Thus despite the intercessions of his father-in-law, Jacinto, along with his elder brother Abelio, made a solid front with their half-sister's cause, and the husband's efforts at reconciliation failed. Jacinto's vigorous defense of his half-sister's rights may have been in part selfishly motivated, since he had on several occasions expressed to me his desire for "many women" and may have planned adding a second wife using his newly divorced younger sister as part of an exchange. It should be noted that Jacinto's accusation of wife-beating on the part of the husband was a serious one, since this practice is quite frowned upon by Pemon (rumors of wife-beating are very serious matters in everyday gossip discussions and can result in the isolation of a man from even his near kin, as will be shown below).

The extent to which siblings are localized, of course, places limits on the amount of cooperation between them, but people may travel extensively to undertake cooperative effort. For example, two brothers in the Uonken region had a virtual monopoly on the manufacture of dugout canoes in the region, a skill which both had learned far to the west, in the Paragua drainage. One of them lived in the southern portion of the region and the other far to the northwest, almost a day's journey by canoe and on foot. Periodically, however, as need to manufacture a canoe would arise, the two brothers and their sons would gather at the mouth of the Karuai River and go downstream on the main course of the Caroni on a canoe-making expedition.

In another instance of a similar nature, Javier Castelar was in the process of putting a roof on his house in Maikanden. This was a job which he wished to do in a reasonably short time, as his current quarters were becoming too small. In addition to his younger brother, who was resident in Maikanden (in Javier's household, for the most part) at the time, he called in his elder brother, who was across the Karuai at their father's old home site. The two brothers aided Javier for several weeks in the rather involved process of gathering the needed plants, vines, and saplings for the roof thatch, ties, and stringers, and putting them all in place, a job which requires considerable persistence and skill. Although Javier had several resident wife's brothers at Maikanden at the time, they were not called upon to aid in the roofing project.

In some cases the males of a sibling set may localize themselves in one settlement, even a short time after their marriages. One settlement north of the Old Mission was composed of a group of half-brothers (common father, who had married four sisters, their mothers), their wives, and their own mothers, as well as their mother's brother and his wife. In almost all cases these co-resident half-brothers had married wives whose parents were deceased or divorced. Since they thus had virtually no affinal obligations, they continued on in the settlement of their father. Their ability to coalesce in this fashion was directly dependent

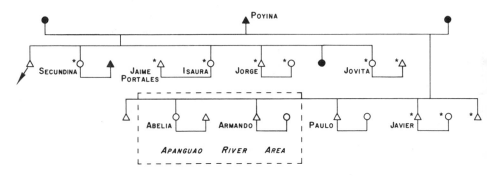

"*" indicates residence within ten minutes' walk of Maikanden.

Figure 10. Chart of Poyina's offspring (1970).

on the break-up of the natal families of their spouses and on the relative disunity of their wives' sibling sets. We shall return to this theme of "absent affines" later on.

In order to see the dynamics of sibling relationships as the sibling set matures, we can follow the changing situation of two groups of half-siblings who were virtually all adults in 1970; one, the youngest male, remained unmarried at that time. Both sets were the offspring of Poyina (see Figure 10), mentioned above in the account of the Maikanden settlement. The offspring of one of Poyina's wives were all in Maikanden or nearby in 1970, except for the eldest male, who had married again after the death of his first wife and was living downstream on the Caroni, just above the Otovanta Falls, in the southwest corner of the Uonken region. Secundina, the eldest female of this set, was widowed and living in Maikanden with her children and two married sisters, Isaura and Jovita. Their full brother Jorge Castelar was residing a short distance from Maikanden, and in fact Jorge's family had lived off the manioc from his sister's plots while he was setting up his new house site. The offspring of their deceased sister, Maria Castelar, were living in the household of Isaura and Jovita (the household of Jaime Portales, head of the Maikanden settlement). Secundina was recently widowed (1968) and her daughters were all married in 1970; her sons-in-law, however, with one exception were not living at Maikanden and in 1971 she moved out to the same area as her eldest brother (in the southwest part of the region), where her eldest and youngest daughters were living. Isaura and Jovita were married to the head of the Maikanden settlement and to his son, respectively, and had moved to Maikanden from their natal settlement (now defunct) at Uakautei.

Poyina's offspring by his second wife were not so concentrated in space. One surviving elder male of this sibling set had disappeared in Caracas while the next two siblings, Abelia and Armando, were both, with their spouses, living to the east of the Uonken region at a site on the Apanguao River. Javier Castelar, son-in-law of the head of the Maikanden settlement, resided in the house next door to the head of the settlement, and his younger unmarried brother formed part of his household. Javier's elder brother Paulo Castelar spent most of his time downriver on the Caroni, just above Otovanta Falls, where his father-in-law's settlement was located. Javier made frequent visits to his other brother's settlement on the Apanguao, but was still residing at Maikanden in 1975 even after his father-in-law had left to found a new settlement. His permanence at Maikanden may have been due to the frequency with which he undertook day labor at the nearby mission.

Secundina's experience indicates an important tendency for a woman whose husband dies before her offspring have married and set up viable households, the tendency to attempt to remain near the families of her adult siblings, preferably a sister who already has a functioning household and manioc plot. The widow or divorcee will generally be welcomed in the household of her sister, since she provides an addition to the labor force available for the time-consuming processing of manioc. A sister's household is preferred over that of a brother in most instances, since relationships between a woman and her brother's wife are liable to be more distant and they would be compelled to work together on a daily basis if they lived in the same household.

Within a given household, no equivalence among siblings can obtain, and the kinship terminology recognizes and stresses this hierarchical ordering. However, any sibling set may be looked at from the outside, and in the field of relationships beyond and outside the household siblings of the same sex at any rate are regarded as socially equivalent. Thus each individual grows up into a realm of equal standing with same-sex siblings, even though he or she continues formally to recognize the elder/younger distinctions throughout life, and with respect to both sexes. Above we have emphasized three aspects of the relations among siblings: (1) the sibling, particularly an elder sibling, as a person with whom refuge can be sought in situations of domestic (or other, to be detailed below) conflict; (2) the sibling, particularly a same-sex sibling, as economic support in certain tasks too difficult or unwieldy for the individual; and (3) the sibling group as a more or less localized group of close kin which dominates a particular area.

Sibling sets move through a cycle as their members do, and certain

patterns emerge in the degree of co-residence or proximate residence
over time. While the families of the sibling set are more likely to be localized during their late teens and 20s, particularly if they have a strong
father who can keep his sons-in-law about him, brother/sister pairs
become more important as children of the members of the sibling
set begin to reach adulthood. If prospective cross-cousin marriages
among these offspring are contemplated, the brother/sister bond
becomes important. At the same time, when the males of the sibling set
reach the ages from their early 30s to their 50s, there is a strong desire on
the part of males, who may be heads of settlements at this point in their
lives, to have a nearby male sibling as an ally in the neighborhood *as
well* as a nearby sister. There is no firm continuity across generations in
either the male or the female lines — by the time the males attempt to
regroup the sibling set after having married out, a new generation is beginning to marry and they must be concerned with cross-generational
ties to their own offspring and the spouses of their offspring.

For the females, who under ideal circumstances remain together the
longest, as they reach their middle 30s and their husbands attempt to
regroup with their (the husband's) siblings, sisters and the daughters of
sisters will be split up. There is no male line continuity because of marrying out, and ultimately there is no female line continuity because of
the regrouping after marriages have been consolidated. Even though
the strongest degree of co-residence was found for sister/sister sibling
pairs, this reflects the concentration of persons in the younger age
brackets in the Pemon population (see Thomas, 1973: 57), and the only
possibility for "perpetuation" of the sibling set is the marriage of offspring of a brother/sister pair (an outcome which we have shown above
in the Old Mission settlement and surrounding neighborhood). Of
course, siblingship in one generation gives way to marriage in the next,
and Pemon society must thus literally recreate itself in each generation
through the marriages which are contracted by members of that generation.

In a sense, then, the relative strength of a group of siblings in a given
neighborhood is always contingent on the relative strengths of the sibling sets to which the set is tied through the marriages of its members.
Every spouse who resides with is or her affines is in a sense a loss for one
set and a gain for another. There is, of course, the limit to concentration
provided by the need for refuge and by the concern for the marriages of
the upcoming generation.

The idiom of siblingship goes even beyond one's own generation in
certain cases. We have noted above that all cross-sex own-generation relationships other than that of husband and wife are subsumed under
sibling terms. The implications of this usage are far-reaching, since it
eliminates a category which would be maximally distant in one's own

generation (we will treat the effects of this usage further in the discussion of marriage and relations with relatives by marriage). Females, in referring to the category "women," most often use the phrase *pemon pasiton* to refer to their fellow females in general. *Upasi* (*u* is a prefix meaning "my") is the female speaker term for elder sister/elder parallel cousin, and the phrase could be reasonably translated as "Pemon sister." Their usage is in contrast to that of the males, who refer to *wurisan*, literally, "women." Where solidarity or the characteristics of the Pemon as a whole are concerned, the women would invoke the sibling term.

It might seem from the discussion above that the sibling set is in a sense broken down the middle, with same-sex siblings forming each of the two halves of it. However, this is not the case, since links of similarity or identity are seen not only as strict likeness but also as complementarity. This is not so much because of the interests of those involved in so-called "sister-exchange" marriages, where one must relinquish a sister to get a wife, but because the basic idiom of male-female relationships in Pemon society is one of complementarity, and brothers and sisters within the household differ from husbands and wives in the matter of sexual access but not in the matter of economic complementarity. The little boy who goes fishing after the manner of his father and the little girl who grates manioc alongside her mother (or sister) are putting in their share to the household, as brother and sister, long before they must assume the roles of maintaining their own household, the one as a husband and the other as a wife. They are in complementary economic roles long before the question of sex and marriage comes up. The husband/wife relationship in Pemon society differs from the elder brother/younger sister relationship, not in terms of economic complementarity, relative dominance (often slight in observed behavior) by the male, or the slightly asymmetrical dimension of a "protective" relationship, but in the dimension of sexual access.

The complementary nature of the male-female relation was rather vividly brought home to me in observing a joking discussion between a sister and her brother's wife on the one hand and her brothers on the other, during some festivities where the men had brought in a deer and a tapir after being out on a three-day hunt. The discussion started out with the brother avowing that meat was really important food, and that it was, after all, the men who brought in the meat. But who, his sister shot back at him, prepares the manioc cakes and *cachiri* that give the men the strength to go out and hunt? And who, the brother replied in turn, cuts the forest so that the manioc can be planted? And who, the sister and her sister-in-law asked, tends the plots so that the manioc will not be swamped by weeds, and who brings it home and grates, squeezes, and bakes it? Who, said the brother, makes the manioc squeezer so that the manioc will be rendered edible? Round and round it went, for the space of half an hour or so, till finally the discussion left off in a few joking barbs and the grudging admission on both sides that one thing supported another, ad infinitum. (Everyone was quite agreed that no meal was really complete without meat (or fish) and manioc cakes.) What intrigued me about the repartee was not only the theme but its joking nature and its outcome — no one could be topped, there was always a comeback for every one-upping line which preceded it. The result was not just a draw but simply that there was no end to the trade-offs.

One must not confuse separation and opposition (our own situation) with separation and complementarity. Linguistic usages are important in interpreting the wide currency of a "brother/sister" idiom of cross-sex social interaction. Men, if they interact with a female older than themselves, will almost always use the "elder sister" term *naʔnai*, even if the woman is in fact of their own parental generation. This broad use of the *naʔnai* term by the males means that implications of sexual access are avoided (whether or not they are intended in practice), an element of deference is expressed, and the sibling idiom is extended to the widest range of persons.

The Pemon relationship terminology makes no distinctions between half and full siblings, but the offspring of one female may, with their mother as a focus, differentiate themselves from their paternal half-siblings. It is remarkable that in Pemon myths a recurrent theme surrounding the out-married male (who often, in the myths, marries the daughter of a spirit being and travels to his father-in-law's abode in the spirit land) is his desire to return home "to see his mother" (not father, brother, or sister). Though half-siblings linked by a common mother may have little contact and may not act cooperatively, offspring normally stay with the mother in the event of divorce or death of her husband, and usually half-siblings of a common mother will form a solidary unit. The only cases in which a woman's offspring by different males will not be solidary are found when the woman migrates a long distance upon remarriage. In cases that I know of, widowed females remarried long distances from their natal areas and left the children by their first husbands to be cared for by either their deceased husbands' sisters or their own mothers, the children's maternal grandmothers. The normal procedure upon divorce is for the children to remain with their mother, and the mother will, if not in the settlement of her parents, undertake to move to a settlement where she has a brother or sister.

Lines of cleavage between offspring of co-wives can produce strains which tend to split settlements and prevent the build-up of a cohesive following on the part of a polygynous head of settlement. This was the case in the account of the Maikanden settlement presented above.

Siblings will not defend one another in all situations, and isolation of a member of a sibling set can occur and be maintained even in a populous settlement. For example, one man in the Old Mission settlement was known to get angry (Pemon *sakorope*, a word we shall have more to say about later) and beat his wife. It was noised about, even by one of his brothers, that his first wife (a half-sister of his present wife) had died as a result of the long-term effects of his beating her. This man seldom participated in the rounds of *cachiri* drinking which moved from house to house around the settlement, or in any hunting trips with either his brothers or brothers-in-law who resided nearby. Both his brothers and his wife's sisters were quite upset at his behavior, but the only results of their distress were the increasing isolation of this man and occasional times when his wife would leave to spend some time at her sister's house, some 40 minutes away from the Old Mission settlement. The man's children by his first wife (deceased) spent most of their time in the household of their mother's sister, a strong and energetic woman who practically single-handedly maintained them as well as her own children. The man's wife's father was old and infirm, and his wife's full brothers were young and still residing in the household of their brother-in-law, who in this case was also the full brother of the wife-beater. The only response which the man's siblings and near affines could produce was increasing isolation and the offering of refuge to the wife. Since his behavior was inside the context of his own household, the reputation of his siblings resident in the neighborhood was diminished, but they did not become involved in intersettlement or interhousehold disputes as a result of it, and therefore their efforts at restraining him were not too pronounced.

Cycles of Households and Settlements

The ranges of settlement size found in Pemon territory are large. In the Uonken region the largest settlement in 1970–71 was the Old Mission site with ten households and 76 people, the minimum a single household settlement with five people. The Old Mission settlement does not represent an upper limit for contemporary Pemon settlement sizes. The Adventist Pemon communities in the southern portion of the tribal territory had (1970–71) in some cases upwards of 100 persons per settlement. There were (1970) at least two communities in the eastern portion of the tribal territory which had populations of 80 or more — Peraitepui de Roraima and San Rafael de Kamoiran. Peraitepui de Roraima in 1970 was actually rather spread out on a hillside, and the community was largely held together by a school and a resident Pemon school-teacher. San Rafael de Kamoiran had around 80 people in the late

1960s, according to figures from the Malariologia Division of the Venezuelan Ministry of Health and Social Assistance (MSAS).

In the area of the Caroni upstream from Uriman, from the criollo settlement at Uriman upriver to Aripichi Falls, in June, 1970, my own
observations in conjunction with those of the Malariologia personnel
showed that settlement sizes were on the order of one to four households
for the most part. Yet in June, 1975, some two hours upstream from
Uriman there was a settlement of some 90-100 people. And even in
June, 1970, just above Aripichi Falls was a settlement known as
Cachimbo, which had probably 50 people or so at that time. What accounts for these terrific variations in settlement size, both over space
and over time? Even excluding for the moment the Adventist communities, the criollo settlements (Uriman, Santa Elena, Icabaru), and
the Capuchin mission sites (Kavanayen, Kamarata, Santa Elena Ma-
locas de Mision, the Uonken Old Mission) per se, we find the dispersed
pattern of small settlements broken at certain points.

We will not tackle this problem all at once, but will deal with the processes which influence the formation and duration of settlements as they
are conditioned and limited by kinship and marriage as a mode of integration. We shall see that there is good reason to believe that Pemon
kinship has a self-limiting tendency in terms of the number of people it
will hold together, and that an upper limit for Pemon settlements under
"normal" conditions appears to be about seven households. Even in
Koch-Grunberg's time (1911) the situation existed of a large communal
dwelling (a *waipa* or round house) which was surrounded by satellite
settlements (often some distance away) and used mainly during festive
occasions. We have already noted that the round house at Maikanden
was used in a similar way in 1970, particularly during the season of intensive Hallelujah dancing from October through December. The
waipa at Maikanden often drew people from as far as two and a half
hours' walk just for a day's dancing. But the people so drawn could not
be counted as residents in any sense.

We have already treated in some detail the cycle of household
development, and have discussed two settlements in detail. Two more
cases are relevant here, one looked at from the point of view of a single
individual, moving among settlements through time. The first example,
that of the settlement at Paraman, in the very south of the Uonken
region, shows a pattern which we recognize from the account of the Old
Mission neighborhood, that of the polygynous male whose offspring are
intermarried with the offspring of a co-resident sister (see Figure 11).
The head of settlement was a man of 55, born at the site. His sister
(about 50) and aged mother lived in the household of one of his sister's
sons. His present wife (his fourth; two died and he divorced one and is
living with one wife at present) is a sister's daughter of his sister's hus-

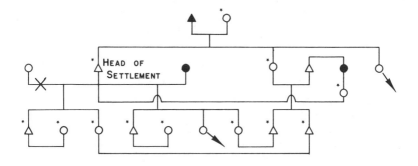

"•" indicates residence at Paraman.

Figure 11. Genealogical relationships at Paraman (1970).

band. His sister's husband resides in the Icabaru drainage with another, younger wife. Of his surviving adult offspring (numbering three males and three females), two males and two females are resident in the settlement. His two resident sons have both brought their wives to live patrilocally. In one of these cases the son's wife's mother is deceased and her father has remarried. His two resident daughters are married to two brothers, his sister's sons. The Paraman settlement consists of six households, but only five of these are connected to the head of settlement by close kinship ties. The sixth household is formed by a pair of brothers-in-law and their wives living jointly some five minutes away from the main portion of the Paraman settlement.

The head of settlement has other relatives nearby — a sister just downstream on the Caroni and a sister's son (son of the sister who is resident at Paraman) living on a nearby tributary of the Apanguao River. Even so, it is unlikely that his settlement will increase further in size, unless he successfully retains the younger offspring of his current wife in the settlement as they marry. His eldest son by his current wife is married out way downstream on the Caroni, outside of the Uonken region. Here, then, is the key to the limits of large settlement build-up by a single head of settlement — he must maintain his sons living patrilocally, in violation of the verbal ideal norm of matrilocal residence, while convincing his sons-in-law to stay on in accordance with the ideal. He can justify this if (1) the natal families of his son's wives are no longer intact or (2) the natal families of his son's wives have several daughters with resident sons-in-law, so that one of the daughters is in effect not all that needed. These are two conditions which are just the opposite of one another, one a function of the fragmentation of the families of his daughters-in-law, the other a function of their strength. The "strong" condition is seldom fulfilled, so the opportunity for maintaining the sons living patrilocally usually rests on the fragmentation of a daughter-in-law's natal family.

Of course, even in the event of the fragmentation of his daughter-in-law's natal family, as her siblings come of age they will attempt to regroup in their natal area and try to pull her back into that area.

Why, then, cannot a settlement in the normal course of events get beyond the six or seven household limit? In the main, because the senior male generation (35-50 and over) cannot maintain ties in its own generation which can be perpetuated in the 20-35-year-old generation, except by ties through a co-resident sister. Why not, then, the "solution" of two co-resident brother-sister pairs, the classic "sister-exchange" situation? The answer seems to be, as we shall see in our discussion of Pemon marriage and affinal relations, that the groom's obligations to his parents-in-law always overshadow his obligations to his wife's brothers; when his father-in-law is gone, his obligations to his own siblings are more important than those to his wife's brothers. The subordinate relationship of a son-in-law to his father-in-law means that he is subordinate to one man only, and when that man is gone he can abrogate his obligation to the remainder of his affines and try to realign himself residentially with his own siblings.

The complex of factors affecting the settlement through time becomes clearer upon consideration of the history of moves in which one individual adult male participated from the time of his first marriage.

In 1948, after his marriage to Felicia Fajardo, Jorge Fabregas came to Uakauyen, then the settlement of his father-in-law Alfonso Fajardo. Jorge had married a classificatory MBD, a regular marriage according to Pemon ideals. At Uakauyen at that time were: first house — Alfonso and his wife Tari; Alfonso's two sons Roberto and Cayo and their wives and children; Jorge and Felicia; second house — Miapok and his wife; Miapok's daughter Amanda and her husband Aurelio Carbonel and their children; third house — Wiachi, a classificatory parallel cousin of Alfonso's, and his wife and children.

After about three years the occupants of the first and second houses moved to a nearby location, Kusariparu. The reason for the move was fighting among the families. Wiachi stayed in Uakauyen with his family. After living in Kusariparu for about two years, Alfonso and his wife left and spent one year in Apanguao (about a half-day away), leaving Roberto and Cayo and their families, and Jorge and Felicia, at Kusariparu. Miapok and his wife both died at Kusariparu within one year of each other, the wife first. Roberto, Cayo, and Jorge and their families left for Apanguao after the death of Miapok; Aurelio Carbonel and his wife Amanda (Miapok's daughter) stayed with their family at Kusariparu.

After the second year in Apanguao, Alfonso, Roberto, Cayo, Jorge, and their families went to Apoipo, a newly forming Adventist settlement to the south, out of the Uonken region. This was in response to a request from the capitan of Apoipo that people get themselves together in a "town" at Apoipo. After three years in Apoipo, Alfonso Fajardo died. About one year after Alfonso's death Jorge's wife died in an epidemic. Leaving Roberto and Cayo Fajardo and their families in Apoipo, Jorge and his children came back to Kusariparu. Jorge subsequently married Linda Carbonel, daughter of Aurelio Carbonel and Amanda. During the first part of his three years in Kusariparu with Linda, Jorge went back to Apoipo for the space of nine months, returning with materials taken from his plot there to plant at Kusariparu. These were the first plantings at the newly founded (1968) settlement at Apauraitepɨ. The reason for moving from Kusariparu was that the harvest from the plots in Kusariparu was insufficient. It is about two hours' walk from Kusariparu to Apauraitepɨ. Jorge sometimes returns to Kusariparu to pass several months, then comes back to Apauraitepɨ.

Subsistence reasons forced a move only once in the 20-year span of the above narration. Recruitment (temporary in Jorge's case) to Adventism, disputes among the families in a settlement, and death were the other reasons for moving. Even so, Kusariparu and Uakauken are very close to one another (actually within sight of one another across the savanna), and this indicates another feature of site shifts of Pemon settlements—most moves of settlement sites are within a radius of about one-half hour travel time. Also, shifting a settlement site may or may not mean moving one's manioc plots away from a given area where one has been cultivating. Often a given individual will maintain settlements within a radius of 30 to 45 minutes' walk for much of a lifetime. A good example of this is the case of Lisandro Bernal, mentioned above, who lived at Kuaiparu, Uoctapa, and other sites not far from the Old Mission site from 1940 to 1970.

The relative continuity of occupancy of many Pemon settlement sites may be a function of both dispersion and relatively small size, since a larger population concentration in any one place would necessarily exhaust the nearby forest faster and promote shifts of settlements for environmental reasons. However, it should be noted that the relative sizes of settlements in the riverine forest area downstream from Otovanta Falls are for the most part in the same range as those in the savanna and gallery forest (Gran Sabana and Kamarata) areas of the tribal territory. Both the savanna portion and the riverine forest portion of the tribal territory support settlements of relatively large size (in the range of 100 persons). In all cases these large settlements are held together by forces beyond the kinship domain.

We have argued the case for a "natural" limit to Pemon settlements of about six or seven households, on the grounds that a single settlement head, even with the presence of a co-resident adult sister, cannot simultaneously maintain ties with brothers-in-law in his own generation and ties with his sons and sons-in-law in the upcoming generation. This is due to the asymmetrical quality of affinal obligation which binds individual males more to their fathers-in-law than to their brothers-in-law, and to two sets of contradictions within a single generational level: (1) the verbal ideal norm of matrilocal residence at marriage, which must be violated if the settlement head is to retain his sons about him (except if his sons marry a co-resident sister's daughters), and (2) the pull of ties to siblings as opposed to ties to brothers-in-law. The brother-in-law ties, given the nature of affinal obligations in general, eventually give way to the pull of ties to siblings. A system of direct exchange between two "lines" cannot maintain itself in Pemon society because ties between brothers-in-law (ZH/WB) and between sisters-in-law (BW/HZ) are "weak" ties, in the sense that a young man's affinal obligations focus mainly on his parents-in-law, and affinal ties in his own generation are correspondingly weak. Thus the basically cross-generational nature of affinal obligation in Pemon society spells out a fundamentally fragmentary tendency in the whole structure — once the senior (parents-in-law) generation is gone, siblings regroup at the expense of own-generation affinal ties. Ultimately, cross-generational affinal hierarchy and subordination give way to the relative equality (in extrahousehold relationships) of own-generation ties, which fragment along the lines of sibling sets. All this depends on the fact that most decisions about residence are taken with reference to primary relatives (F, M, B, Z, S, D, H, W). This gives rise to a paradox: by being with those who are "close" genealogically, one automatically lessens the broad inclusiveness of the system of kin classification. As we shall see in our discussion of marriage and affinal relations, there is only one exclusively affinal term in the whole of Pemon kinship nomenclature outside of the husband and wife terms, and that term is cross-generational.

The focus here has been on those settlements in the average or normal range of settlement sizes. We shall take up the other, larger settlements in Chapter IV.

Marriage: Ideals and Practical Concerns

Pemon marriage can be thought of from a variety of perspectives: as a bond between two families (those formed by the parents of both spouses), as a relationship between two individuals, as a relationship between either husband or wife and the primary relatives of the spouse, and as one intersection of two different sets of siblings. Pemon marriage cannot be thought of as a link between corporate groups (there are none to link) or as an exchange between two intermarrying "lines." There is a rule in Pemon society that one should marry a relative of a certain categorical type. This rule is as much a rationalizing device and a mechanism for making "close" those who are distant as it is a positive injunction. We will examine marriage from each of the above perspectives in turn, bringing together the ideal and the actuality and showing how Pemon manipulate their own rules and play one rule off against another in order to justify their choices.

The practice of childhood betrothal is recorded by Koch-Grunberg (1916–28, III: 95): "Children are often designated for one another in earliest youth by both (sets of) parents, although this promise is later not binding." The practice is not found today, and from the last half of Koch-Grunberg's statement we can conclude that it was not much of a force in marriage relations 70 years ago either. The initiation of negotiations leading to marriage is a gradual process, since young women may have a number of sexual partners before marriage, and neither party is much bound by the relations. The young man must, if he wishes to consolidate the relationship into a marital one, have his prospective wife sound out her parents. While her parents may be well aware of her relationship with the young man in question (they usually have an idea of where the small gifts she receives have been coming from), and they may let her know how they feel about him, the request for the daughter's hand in marriage must come from the young man.

There is not now, nor was there in the past, any ceremony accompanying marriage — the marriage becomes public when the groom takes up residence with his parents-in-law and begins his brideservice. Up to and even after that time the relationship may be broken off; indeed, some young men, when I queried them as to their liking for a particular woman whom they were known to be seeing, stated that the woman in question was *unopɨ manarɨ*, literally "my wife a little bit." This phrase indicates the more or less tenuous situation during the early time of the marriage relationship.

There is no word for "to marry" in the Pemon language, except a verb derived from the English missionaries of then British Guiana in the nineteenth or early twentieth centuries, *marima* (the Pemon corruption of the English "marry"). This word is used most often to refer to those Pemon who have been married in a mission. When discussing marriage, both males and females use the verb *apɨichi*, literally "to take." This expression is usually asymmetrically phrased, the male "taking" the female to wife. The marriage rule itself, however, which specifies what category of person one should marry, is phrased in equivalent terms for males and females. Both parents of the bride discuss the matter and, if they oppose the marriage, will simply try to avoid giving the young man the opportunity to contribute anything, directly or indirectly, to their household, thus fending off his potential claims.

The daughter has considerable say in the question, and the amount of discretion exercised by young Pemon women in this matter is considerable. Essentially, the daughter holds a trump card, in that she can, if she chooses, elope with a mate or flee and thus deprive her natal family of both a valued worker and the chance of bolstering the family by holding a new son-in-law in residence. While it is rare that grievous disagreements occur between parents and daughter on this score, they do happen and can have quite serious consequences. In one case, a young girl was scheduled to be married to a man who had returned to the Uonken area, after a considerable absence in the criollo world of Cd. Bolivar, looking for a wife. He was related to his prospective spouse through numerous genealogical connections. The girl (about 14 years old at the time), dissatisfied with the man (he was, by all accounts, something of a misfit) and unable to convince her parents and the man's mother (the girl's MMBD), who all desired the union, fled the tribal territory. More often, of course, the parents and daughter come to an understanding and the new son-in-law begins working on the plots of his parents-in-law, bringing to their household the fruits of his fishing and hunting trips, and slings his hammock at the opposite end of the family dwelling from his parents-in-law.

The importance of economic viability for the new couple cannot be overemphasized. Present-day informants relate that formerly a long series of protesting interchanges prior to marriage went on between the parents of the betrothed. Parents of the female customarily protested that she was, though nubile, not sufficiently steeped in the practice of household tasks, work in the fields, and the making of manioc beer. Parents of the male suggested that, though he was ready for marriage, he was not sufficiently proficient in the hunting, fishing, and building tasks that make up the male subsistence role. The customary protests over proficiency in subsistence tasks must be seen as reflecting the importance of marriage as an economic partnership.

Formerly, puberty rituals were held for both males and females, rituals basically aimed at ensuring, by magical means, proficiency at subsistence tasks. These rituals are no longer performed, though Koch-Grunberg (1916–28, III: 121–31) gives a good account of what they were like. He does not specify any exact duration for the ceremonies he describes and only says that, for the males, food prohibitions — all game animals, large fish, and large birds are forbidden — last about one year, dating from the start of the first ceremony. An old man, usually the grandfather, "gives him many blows over the whole body, beginning with the left leg and ending with the right foot, with a whip, a strongly-twined rope made of mauritia fibers, tied to a short stick" (1916–28, III:

121). To ensure success in hunting, the old man gives the young man cuts over arms, torso, and chin and spreads magical substances over the wounds.

The relations between father-in-law and son-in-law are crucial in determining the course of a marriage. It is a Pemon adage that one should "take care of his father-in-law" (bilingual Pemon will speak of *cuidar a tu suegro*, literally "look after your father-in-law"), and the son-in-law is supposed to aid his father-in-law economically. We will take these relations up in more detail below, in the discussion of affinal relations. When the verbal ideal norm of residence at marriage is with the wife's parents, the young couple will in fact spend a good deal of time moving back and forth between the households of the parents of both spouses, even after they have set up manioc plots close to the wife's parents' household. Visiting may involve travel over a considerable distance, but most young couples seem to enjoy it, and periodic trips to the natal family of the groom continue as long as his parents are alive.

Whom, then, does one marry, and how are marriages set up? The phraseology and import of the marriage rule are important in understanding the process of selecting a mate, its relationship to the idea of marrying "close," and the ways in which Pemon get around the rules. Recall that there is no category for "opposite-sex cross-cousin/in-law" or for "eligible spouse." All cross-sex members of one's own generation are classed together with siblings. This is not, as far as I can tell, a particularly recent development, and Simpson (1940: 537) recorded a crucial piece of evidence in Kamarata in 1939 which indicates that this configuration of zero generation terms is probably of long standing (see Thomas, 1971: 8–9). The "sweetheart" term *uyawasirɨ* can have a variety of meanings all the way from "boyfriend" or "girlfriend" to "mistress" (as opposed to "wife") or "sleeping partner." The ribaldry and joking which are associated with this term (I have heard wives chide their husbands with the assertion that the reason for their trip to such-and-such a place was their many *tawasirɨton* at that location) give no indication of its having been an "eligible spouse" category.

The marriage rule is phrased with respect to Ego's parents' generation. Both males and females are enjoined to marry someone in the category of *waʔnɨ mure*, literally a "child of" *waʔnɨ*. The *waʔnɨ* term can be succinctly glossed as "FZ/MBW/spouse's mother" for both male and female speakers. Both male and female speakers share three terms in their classification of members of the first ascending generation: *papai* (and synonyms), *amai* (and synonyms) and *waʔnɨ* (including the synonym *wyawopɨ*). They do not share a common term for "MB/FZH/spouse's father." The marriage rule phraseology thus specifies (1) a category which includes opposite-sex cross-cousins, but does so by reference to the first ascending generation, while the category of opposite-sex cross-cousin/in-law is eliminated in Ego's own generation and, (2) specifies marriage with a consanguineal relative. The *waʔnɨ* term cannot be strictly factored into consanguineal and affinal components, and it may be stretching things a bit to call the usage "consanguineal" in the marriage rule phrase *waʔnɨ mure*, but the Pemon preference is clear: marry a true MBD or FZD (male point of view) if you can. The prescription is categorical, the preference genealogical.

In order to give an idea of the ways in which the facts can be manipulated to fit the prescription, let us recall a few of the marriages discussed in our accounts of settlements. We said that Jorge Fabregas, whose first marriage brought him to Uakauyen as a young man in 1948, had married a classificatory MBD. The relationship between Jorge and his first wife Felicia Fajardo was actually FBWBD. Jorge's father had been a brother of Candido Rulfo, who had lived at Uakauyen in the 1930s but had moved to the Old Mission neighborhood in the early 1940s. Candido's first wife, Etinawa, was a sister of Alfonso Fajardo. Jorge Fabregas had been raised by his mother and her relatives at Kuaiparu, since his father died when Jorge was very young. Jorge's MFBS or "MB" Achikara had numerous offspring, but most of these had already married by the mid-1940s or were already contemplating marriages with the offspring of Lisandro Bernal, their MB. Jorge thus sought out Candido Rulfo's wife's brother, Alfonso, his "MB" (since Candido was Jorge's *papai* (FB), his wife Etinawa was *amai*, and her brother Alfonso *umui* = FZH, MB/spouse's father.) The wife of anyone classifiable as *umui* is *waʔnɨ*, whose daughter is, of course, *waʔnɨ mure*.

There are other ways of working with the multiple meanings of Pemon kin terms to produce the *waʔnɨ mure* outcome. The *yese* term, which can be glossed as "male cross-cousin/brother-in-law" for a male speaker, is a polysemic term which is also the greeting term for unrelated males. This is quite understandable, as the term connotes a quid pro quo relationship, balanced reciprocity, and obligatory hospitality. The mother of any *yese* is *waʔnɨ* and the sister of any *yese* can be *waʔnɨ mure*. Thus an exchange relationship (e.g. a trade partnership) between two males can be expanded into an affinal one if the circumstances warrant.

We have previously discussed one case (above, p. 67) in which a man, basing his own classification of kinsmen on the usage of his parents, produced a justification of his own marriage choice based on these "situational" classifications by his parents. His justification resulted in a categorization of his wife as *waʔnɨ mure*, in accordance with the ideal prescription. In some cases, however, what seem to be irregular marriages are made and go uncommented upon for the most part. I wish to examine a few of these cases in detail before considering the whole range of marriage types in Pemon society and extracting from that range some principles which are not apparent in the verbal ideal norm of *waʔnɨ mure* marriages. Recall the marriage of Jaime Portales to his second wife (he was polygynous), undertaken to solidify his relationships in his natal neighborhood after his first marriage to an outsider. This was a marriage to Jaime's FZSD, a woman who falls into the *upase* category. The *upase* category for a male speaker includes the sister's daughter in its denotata. It is significant that this marriage solidified Jaime's relationship with his FZS, Poyina, and put him in line to take up Poyina's leadership role in the neighborhood. Also, this marriage was within the neighborhood (both Jaime and his second wife were born in the neighborhood).

Now consider another marriage, also a FZSD marriage, in the Old Mission neighborhood. The marriage was between persons who were both resident in the neighborhood at the time, though the wife had been born outside the neighborhood (during the time spent by her father doing his brideservice in her mother's natal settlement). In this case, the husband's father-in-law was a prominent big trader in the Old Mission area, and, in fact, up until his death in 1965, a man who engaged in trade on behalf of a large number of people throughout the valley of the Karuai River. The husband subsequently took over the trading partnership of his deceased father-in-law, but did not continue to trade on the same scale.

A third marriage, also in the Old Mission neighborhood, was of the FZDD form, also falling under the *upase* term (male speaking). (Note that if the Pemon terminology were a regular "two-line" system, FZDD would be classified as "daughter" and hence unmarriageable.) In this case the husband's father-in-law was deceased at the time of the marriage. The husband was born at Tereyen, the approximate site of the present (1970) Old Mission, and the wife was born at Warmo, just outside the neighborhood but only some 40 minutes away on foot.

These three examples point up the importance of spatial proximity in marriage choices (marry into the wrong category if you must, but stay close to home) and, in the cases of Jaime Portales and the son-in-law of the big trader, the importance of a special relationship with the father of the prospective spouse.

The degree to which the *waʔnɨ mure* marriage prescription is actualized in the genealogical sense is not insignificant. Of the 35 unions (out of 100 unions in existence in the Uonken region in 1970) for which genealogical connections exist, 21 unions are genealogically horizontal and fall under the *waʔnɨ mure* categorical prescription. In apparent violation of the bilateral, horizontal prescription are the oblique unions, 14 of the 35 unions with actual genealogical links between spouses. Twelve of these 14 unions reduce to the *upase* or "ZD" term. Thus, in an analysis of genealogical connections between spouses in current Pemon marriages, three categories are easily discernible: (1) oblique unions, totaling 14, of which 12 are "ZD" or *upase* unions; (2) horizontal unions, the *waʔnɨ mure* or cross-cousin unions; (3) unions between genealogically unrelated spouses. The group of spouses who are genealogically unrelated may contain unions in which terminological manipulations are used to produce conformity with the *waʔnɨ mure* rule. Despite the oblique genealogical characteristics of the "ZD" unions, most of them show little age difference between spouses (see Thomas, 1979; 1973: 287–91). Data were not available on the relationships of the husband to WF for each of these marriages — all parties could not be interviewed directly. It is likely that, in cases where the WF is living, there may be a considerable age difference between the husband and his WF. But the husband and his WF are genealogically related, and genealogical reckoning normally takes precedence over age criteria in cases of close genealogical relationship. The husband and his WF in these "ZD" unions will be related as *uyese/uyese* or brothers-in-law.

We can think of the three types of unions (genealogically unrelated spouses, cross-cousins, and "ZD" spouses) as representing a continuum of affinal obligation. This continuum ranges from a maximum of affinal obligation in the cases of those WF to whom the groom is unrelated, to a middle point in those cases where the groom and his WF are related as ZS/MB or WBS/FZH, to a minimum in those cases where the groom and his WF are related as "brothers-in-law." These "ZD" unions are thus seen to be the interior end of a continuum manifesting progressive reduction in the amount of obligation due his affines by the groom. The desire to marry "close" and thus minimize the potential strain in the DH/WF tie by means of emphasizing prior genealogical linkage between DH and WF is consistent with the tendencies toward suppression of the quality of being an affine which we have already found in the terms for opposite-sex members of Ego's generation and in the phrasing of the marriage rule. The "ZD" unions, the elimination of a category for "eligible spouse" in Ego's own generation, the marriage rule circumlocution, all move toward a given end — the de-emphasis on the category of "affines" as a distinguishable social entity in Pemon society.

Herein lies a paradox, for while the quality of being an affine is suppressed, the *potential* for making marriage arrangements with virtually anyone who is not a sibling or parallel cousin is greatly enhanced by the broad use of the *yese* term, and the corresponding possibilities for entering into marital relationships via the expansion of an exchange (including simply an exchange of hospitality or small favors) with a "brother-in-law" into marriage with his sister. Affines are not primarily a category of people in Pemon society but rather specific individuals. The various usages, circumlocutions, and rationalizations which we have mentioned give extreme flexibility in choosing who these specific individuals will be. (Basso [1970: 409] has used the term "affinibility" to refer to the "potential for initiating or participating in an affinal relationship with ego." Here we will speak simply of the "potential for becoming an affine.") At the same time that Pemon usage suppresses affinality in favor of an idiom of cross-sex interaction as "brother-sister," it maximizes the potential for recruiting affines as individuals.

A sequence of priorities in Pemon thinking about marriage is evident:

1) On the most general level, marry within the *waʔnɨ mure* designation. Within that designation, marry a consanguine (traceable through known genealogical relationship via named individuals).

2) Marry someone from your own or an adjacent neighborhood. If necessary, marry a "ZD" *(upase)* to accomplish this. (The "ZD" unions have other functions for the individuals concerned, as will be detailed below.)

3) In any event, convert affines into consanguines by means of the application of the term *waʔnɨ* to the spouse's mother. The point here is that the categories *waʔnɨ* and *umui* (male speaker) or *uyawo* (female speaker) carry both consanguineal and affinal "loadings," and implicitly refer to common substance in the sibling set of Ego's parental generation.

The Pemon are employing here a technique of incorporating outsiders (who are feared) by implicitly asserting common substance in Ego's parental generation. Those from more distant places are feared, but they must be incorporated. Ultimately sorcery (Kanaima) always comes from somewhere "out there" (most often from the Makuxi, who are not even Pemon), or from a malevolent shaman to whom one is not related. The response to outsiders is not necessarily to shun them, however. In the Pemon situation the prudent (and affable) response is hospitality, trusting that the outsider, temporarily satisfied, will not harm one, and then, for those outsiders who don't move on, incorporation.

One author (Kaplan, 1975: 169–82) has talked of the "affine as kinsman" with reference to the use of teknonymy as a means for conversion of unrelated into related persons. While the Pemon do have a (somewhat attenuated) teknonymic system, it revolves around the use of kin terms in conjunction with (not to the exclusion of) nicknames, usually of children, and not around such phraseology as "mother of my son" (Kaplan, 1975: 171). Conversion of the more distant into the close in the Pemon system proceeds by asserting common substance not in the generation of Ego's offspring but in Ego's parental generation. This is understandable, since relationships in Ego's parental generation are the basic cues for Ego's kin term usage. To speak of "kin" versus "affines" in the Pemon case is misleading, if one is trying to explain the Pemon (not the anthropologist's) way of doing things. There are simply more and less distant relationships, and one strives to convert the more distant ones into less distant ones. We shall see below that the diffuseness characteristic of Pemon boundary concepts in terms of relatives (-*yombaton*) and the process of bringing unrelated persons into relatedness is quite adaptive in a vast regional system (the Gran Sabana and neighboring areas as a whole) in which marriage and sibling relationships can span huge distances.

Despite the ideal of concentrating sibling and marriage ties in one's own neighborhood, no neighborhood ever attains enough critical mass to involute, to turn inward upon itself and become a discrete unit, one to which the term "endogamy" would be applicable. Neighborhoods are composed of settlements, which are discrete but not endogamous. Each settlement is a focus of ties of relatedness which spread outward from it in several directions, sometimes skipping nearby locations to end farther away. While neighborhoods do center on a given river or section of a river system, the drawing of neighborhood boundaries is always a function of visiting and interaction patterns as well as of physical space.

Before considering affinal relations, one more perspective on Pemon marriage must be introduced: marriages as links among various sibling sets. Let us return to the neighborhood of Maikanden and the Makarupai River area. In the area of the Maikanden settlement, in the generation 20–35 years of age, we found:

Sibling set: *Solano*   *Portales*   *Castelar*

Jacinto Solano, Hu of Felisa Portales
Gerardo Portales, Hu of Jovita Castelar
Belisa Solano,   Wi of   Jorge Castelar
Lila Portales, Wi of   Javier Castelar

Sibling set members, resident, but married into other sibling sets:
Ardila Portales

Sibling set members, not resident, married into other sibling sets:
Abelio Solano   Paulo Castelar
⟵――― divorced ――――⟶   Armando Castelar
Abelia Castelar

We have already commented on some of the forces at work on these sibling sets, but here assessing the marriage links is important. The marriage of Belisa Solano to Jorge Castelar was, by 1970, an exceptionally solid one, and the couple was in the process of establishing a home site at Wuruwarai, close to Maikanden. This strong connection between the Solano set and the Castelar set was counteracted by the divorce of Abelio Solano and Abelia Castelar (there were many allegations throughout the region that Carlos Sandoval, Abelia's new husband, had "stolen" her from Abelio Solano). Javier Castelar was constantly journeying to the settlement where Armando Castelar (and his wife) and Abelia Castelar (and her new husband) were located, a half-day to the east on the Apanguao River. The connection between Lila Portales and her half-sister (different mothers) Felisa was not very strong, and the bridge formed by the Portales set which might have been expected to combine with the strong marriage of Belisa Solano and Jorge Castelar to paper over the disruptive effects of the Abelio/Abelia divorce, was weakening markedly by late 1970. In early 1971 (see above, p. 79) Jacinto Solano and Felisa Portales left Maikanden to live in the settlement of Jacinto's brother Abelio, a half-day or so to the south.

By 1975 the Portales set had more or less dispersed. Gerardo and his wife Jovita Castelar were living away from Maikanden at a site south of the Makarupai River. Lila Portales and her husband Javier Castelar remained at Maikanden, as did her sister Ardila. With this dispersal the Castelar set had also thinned out, though Jorge Castelar remained near Maikanden and took on a son-in-law (a man from outside the region, not a local man). Marriage links can only serve to bind multiple sibling sets as long as (1) there are several ties among the sets which parallel each other, that is, each set is connected to each other bound set by more than one marriage tie; and (2) none of these ties are disrupted by divorce or death. It is not necessarily the case that the sibling bonds of a given individual will take second place to the marital tie as the individual ages and the marital tie strengthens. In some cases this happens (e.g. the Jorge Castelar–Belisa Solano union) but in others it does not (e.g. the Javier Castelar–Lila Portales union, where Javier maintained very strong ties to his elder brother and elder sister and continually took his wife to visit them).

In some cases a sibling set will remain relatively localized, even though marriages have been contracted with members of as many other sibling sets as there are members. An example of this is a group of half-siblings, offspring of a common mother, resident in the area near Maikanden in 1970–71. The eldest, a male, had married a woman from Apoipo whose parents were long deceased and who had come to live with him in the Uonken region. His half-brother and half-sister lived at a site about 20 minutes' walk from Maikanden. The half-sister's husband was living matrilocally and continued to do so even after the death of his wife's mother. The eldest's half-brother had married a woman from the Uriman area (outside the region) and brought her to live at the site near Maikanden. A third half-brother had married a daughter of Ciro Paciano and set up a household near Ciro's house at Maikanden.

The nonexistence of a class of "eligible spouses," the individuation of affinal relations, and the maximization of the field of potential affines by means of the exchange possibilities in the *yese/yese* relationship allow a terrific amount of individual maneuvering in arranging a marriage. Pemon often regale themselves with jokes about sister exchanges which fell through when one of the sisters ran off with someone other than the intended. Individual choice is limited, however, by the need of the individual to strike a balance along a whole series of dimensions: own parents' versus spouse's parents' wishes, own siblings' versus spouse's siblings' locations, own parents' versus parents-in-law's priorities. In the final analysis, it is not the bounds placed on individual choice by the ideal marriage rule or even by the ideals of obligation to parents-in-law (on the part of the groom) which are the major constraints on individual choice in seeking a mate. Ultimately it is the pragmatic necessity for support in time of need which impels the individual to narrow the field of prospects. Too far afield can be out on a limb. If you are a shaman or a master of *taren* (magical invocations) and can ward off the potentially malevolent spirits which exist at great distances from one's natal area, or if you are a trader who can cement ties with partners in distant places, you may (if you are male) venture into a distant area in search of a mate.

The single household can, and sometimes does, go it alone, but never for long. Likewise the individual can go it alone, but must possess both the practical and spiritual skills to do so. Personal autonomy in Pemon marriage choices is relatively little constrained by the ideal rules, which ultimately can be rationalized into place ex post facto. The more pressing constraints are the pragmatic rules which mean that an individual should not be linked to persons who will either (1) not support him because of their own obligations to others opposed to him (as, for example, in the lack of solidarity between Jacinto Solano and Javier Castelar because of the acrimonious divorce of their respective siblings), or (2) not support him because he can be defined as "other" (for example, the general lack of support for Maria Solano's husband, referred to as "one of those Kamarakoto," in his efforts at reconciliation).

Affinal Relations and the Interior Limits of Sex and Marriage

We have seen that Pemon thinking about marriage involves a bilateral, horizontal prescription which embodies an ideal of direct exchange. This ideal of direct exchange is one of exchange between individuals, and Pemon do refer to sister exchange as such in some cases. On the ideal plane the only return for a woman is another woman — a reciprocal, symmetrical exchange. In actuality the "giving" of the female is done by her parents, and by her brother only in the case of a deceased or divorced father. The groom pays off his father-in-law with brideservice and the promise to care for him in his old age.

We have also seen that there is a substantial proportion of "ZD" or oblique unions. The importance of the father-in-law/son-in-law relationship, and the quid pro quo characteristic of the relationship between brothers-in-law taken in combination help explain these "ZD" unions: from the point of view of the groom, marriage with the ZD means that WF = ZH, the father-in-law is a brother-in-law. The prior brother-in-law relationship, with its relatively smaller load of obligation, is maintained and precludes the formation of a fully asymmetrical father-in-law/son-in-law relationship. The groom may be working in the fields of his brother-in-law even prior to the marriage, but such work is considered in the light of an ongoing reciprocal tie, and return favors will be given when the need arises. For an individual male, relationships with his future brothers-in-law are not as important in influencing his marriage choice as are relations with his future wife's father. The relative age difference (the generational difference) between the son-in-law and father-in-law is seldom present in the brother-in-law relationship. In Pemon society relative age colors the totality of all social relationships, and one is necessarily more equal with a member of one's own generation. The elder/younger distinction found in the sibling terms is not present in the cross-cousin/brother-in-law term. Even if there are age differences between the groom and the wife's father, the "ZD" union means that these can be papered over with the use of the brother-in-law classification for the wife's father. Essentially you can never fully pay back your affinal debt to your father-in-law — you owe him for his daughter as long as he lives. In the case of a "ZD" union, however, the father-in-law is essentially eliminated, and the prior brother-in-law relationship, with its relatively lesser load of affinal obligation, can be emphasized.

The "ZD" unions give us an insight into two aspects of Pemon sexual and marital relations. On the one hand, their presence points up the theme of the absent father-in-law, the idea that the emphasis on a prior tie can serve to lessen the potential strain in the father-in-law/son-in-law relationship. This solution of resolving potential strain in affinal relations through the "ZD" unions (-pase term) works only up to a point. That point is the actual ZD union itself, which meets with negative comments from informants. They say that such unions are "too close," that "something odd is going on here."

The actual ZD unions demonstrate the second aspect of the significance of these oblique marriages — they represent the interior limit of what can constitute marriage (or the possibility of sexual relations) at all. The actual ZD unions are not, strictly speaking, incestuous, but they provoke many of the same reactions that occur in actual cases of incest — verbal scorn, plus the statement that they (the offenders) keep to themselves and are too far away to do anything about anyway. The actual ZD unions do not provoke the comments which brother-sister incest does – in one such case of incest, the offenders were said to be "just like dogs" and were assiduously avoided whenever they happened to appear away from their settlement (hidden deep in the forest, some two to three hours' walk distant from any other settlement).

To understand the quasi-incestuous significance of actual ZD union, we must go back to the notions of common substance underlying Pemon kinship. Our designation of affinal relationships as implying common substance in Ego's parental generation is important here. The oblique unions merge the parental (father-in-law) generation with that of Ego or, rather, transform away the father-in-law into a brother-in-law. Since a brother-in-law is implicitly related to one by common substance through the parental generation (whether or not the sister's husband is actually so related to Ego), the actual sister's daughter represents a combination of Ego's own substance (in theory identical to that of the sister) and the substance of Ego's brother-in-law (common substance through Ego's parental generation). The appearance of common substance through the parental generation is a desirable quality in the intended spouse (the *waʔnɨ mure* category includes MBC, FZC). What is incestuous is the joining of one's own substance with itself. From this point of view, it is easy to see that father-daughter, mother-son, and brother-sister unions are incestuous. The actual ZD union, in line with this thinking, should be incestuous. Though it does arouse a considerable degree of unease, it does not receive the same opprobrium that actual incest does. Why is this? The answer lies in the fact that the sister's daughter union emphasized the prior brother-in-law relationship with the sister's husband. The actual ZD, by this emphasis, is removed to the lesser proximity of a MBSD. No one is fooled by this cover-up, of course, and the unease remains. An attempt to question the husband in an actual ZD union about genealogical matters met with a flat refusal to discuss anything and a very considerable amount of openly expressed hostility to boot. Such overt expression of hostility is completely contrary to Pemon etiquette and testified to the extreme sensitivity of the subject.

That the potential strain in father-in-law/son-in-law relations is embodied in Pemon tales is not surprising. I choose one example here, for illustrative purposes – some of its themes will also be taken up subsequently (example taken from Armellada, 1973: 37–39; translation my own, from Armellada's Pemon text; my translation differs in some places from his Spanish translation of the Pemon).

JAGUAR WOMAN

There was a Pemon, an unlucky fisher and hunter, whose arms were bad with open sores. One day he went to his manioc plot, and there met the daughter of a jaguar. "Let us go to my house," said the jaguar woman. Then they went to the house of the jaguar, in the mountain tops. "I have brought you your son-in-law" (*payɨnu* term, see below), said the jaguar woman. "Yes, but if he is unlucky at hunting and fishing, I will eat him," responded the jaguar father.

Another time his father-in-law said, "Bring me *auyama*" (a crop plant). Then the Pemon went to find *auyama* but didn't find any. Without any *auyama* he returned; his wife came to meet him. "Wait here," his wife told him. Then she brought her husband the *auyama*, but he saw them not as *auyamas* but as agoutis.

Another time his father-in-law told the Pemon to find *auyama*; he went, and killed the elder brother of the jaguar, believing that it was an agouti. As he was carrying his kill to the house he met his wife crossing the river. His wife said, "Why did you shoot it? We should take it back." "Wait, let us think," they said. "Let's put a stick through the innards." Then they returned to the house. But the father-in-law saw that they killed a jaguar and asked them, "Who killed my elder brother?" "I," said the Pemon, even though his wife told him not to say so. Then the jaguar jumped on his son-in-law and ate him. (The story continues.)

Leaving aside for the moment the symbolic import of the story (the jaguar theme, and the particular confusing transformations, *auyama* = agouti, jaguar = agouti, which occur in the eyes of the Pemon and result in his demise), let us examine the social relations portrayed, the words used to portray them, and the affective tone embodied in them. The son-in-law is a misfit, he can do nothing right. When his jaguar wife introduces him, she uses the *payɨnu* or son-in-law term, not the "ZS" term *poitorɨ*. He is a Pemon, a complete outsider in the world of the jaguars, and thus is given a maximally distant term. His father-in-law is peremptory, giving orders (something which is almost never done directly, in Pemon etiquette), making demands. The wife is protective, attempting to shield her husband from his father-in-law, but ultimately the son-in-law's lack of caution and failure to heed his wife's advice result in his being eaten by his father-in-law.

The father-in-law is fearsome (a jaguar), demanding, and prepared to consume the son-in-law if his demands are not met. The son-in-law is inept, confused, and lacking in caution, overbold with respect to his father-in-law. Myths can be simultaneously warnings, injunctions, and justifications, aside from their functions on the level of symbolic meanings. In line with Levi-Strauss's statements that myths serve to perpetuate social systems (as well as to mediate symbolic contradictions), the portrayal of affinal relations in the story emphasizes several warnings and injunctions: be cautious in your relations with your father-in-law, use your wife as a buffer, be proficient or pay severe consequences.

Finally, of course, this portion of the story involves retribution, not for failure to meet demands for economic support of the father-in-law but for the killing of his elder brother. From the son-in-law's point of view, the asymmetry of his relations with his father-in-law represents a kind of dangerous hierarchy, one based on fear. This is not only the fear of lack of connection (no common substance at any degree of remove), which goes both ways, but the fear of arbitrary and continuing demands which cannot be, in the last analysis, balanced out. The disruptive nature of these "top down" relations derives from the nature of a generalized debt which can never be fully repaid.

Cross-generational affinal ties seem particularly likely to cause disruption, while own-generation affinal ties, despite disruption, may eventually reach an equilibrium. The deliberate doing away with one's affines seems to be characteristic of the cross-generational affinal relationships portrayed in the myths. For example, in the story of Chirikavai (Armellada, 1964: 70–78) Chirikavai does away with his mother-in-law in the following sequence of events: Chirikavai complains of hunger, and his mother-in-law brings him many fish in a gourd. He later finds out that she obtains the fish by "sitting on the gourd and filling it with fish" (Armellada, 1964: 70; Armellada does not provide the Pemon text, and the original version has probably been expurgated, so that the passage remains ambiguous). He subsequently refuses to eat the fish which she brings, enmity heightens, and he sets up a trap for her in the forest and kills her. Later his wife avenges her mother by killing Chirikavai.

In the Chirikavai story the mother-in-law is helping her son-in-law by means which are repugnant to him. Her help is a reversal of the normal relationship in which the son-in-law gives fish to his wife who in turn gives them to the mother (this occurs both in actual Pemon daily life and in myth). In a story titled "The Old Woman who only wanted large fish" (Armellada, 1964: 134–36) we see almost the reverse of the Chirikavai story. A mother-in-law demands only large fish from her son-in-law, who tricks her by bringing home an anaconda (quite large!) which chases her out of the settlement. In each case an inordinate demand is met by means of a trick of some kind (Chirikavai complains to his mother-in-law about being hungry, she feeds him by means of a trick; the old woman demands only large fish, and is tricked by her son-in-law), which brings either disruption or disaster. The cross-generational affinal relationships provide the context for inordinate demands, which are disastrous.

That these situations are not confined to myth is evident from the following account, taken from my field notes, of a dispute between a father-in-law and a son-in-law. Anton was married to his deceased elder brother's former wife, Maya Bernal. Benigna, her daughter by her former husband, was married to Uslar Campos. One Saturday evening Anton came to me with the following story: some time ago Uslar had loaned him a pair of barber's shears. Somewhere along the line Anton lost this pair of shears. During the day on Saturday, when both Anton and Uslar had been drinking *cachiri*, Uslar demanded payment in cash for the shears. Anton, angered, paid him (amount unspecified). According to Uslar, Anton owed him Bs. 5.5, given the following: Uslar said he owed Anton for a small file, Bs. 3 at the mission store price, and for a pack of cigarettes, Bs. 1.5 at the mission store price. Uslar put the value of the shears at Bs. 10; thus 10 minus 3 minus 1.5 leaves Bs. 5.5. Anton argued that he had no intention of collecting for the file or the cigarettes, and demanded to know why Uslar demanded to be paid for the shears. Uslar grudgingly admitted that he needed the money. Anton then charged that Uslar was here living with his "daughter" (Pemon *uyensi*; Spanish *hija*, which Anton changed to *sobrina* or "niece" later in the conversation; Uslar's wife was Anton's BD and WD, simultaneously, and Uslar and Anton were son-in-law and father-in-law in Pemon classification), and not doing anything at all.

Earlier, Uslar's account of Anton's anger had included the assertion that Anton was not really his -*kuipɨnɨ* (= MB, FZH). In fact, Uslar had no prior connection with Anton genealogically, and was emphasizing this lack of genealogical relatedness in his account to me. Anton was obviously very angry with his son-in-law, on several counts. Uslar was, according to Anton, lazy and contributed little if anything to the support of Anton's household, which included Benigna. Uslar was also attempting to introduce the idea of strict reckoning—characteristic of the relationship between brothers-in-law—into their relationship. This would abrogate the hierarchical and subordinate relationship which is supposed to characterize the son-in-law/father-in-law tie. Uslar's strategy was to do just this, and to justify his actions by invoking the lack of prior genealogical ties between himself and Anton. In this case Uslar was able to convince Benigna to leave with him for a settlement over a day's walk away, in the south of the region.

There are several other actual patterns of relationships between an in-married male and his wife's primary relatives. A man in his thirties headed a household which included both his wife's parents and two of her brothers (aged 16 and 12 at the time). His 16-year-old brother-in-law was a major help in clearing fields for the household, and the two often went on fishing trips together. On longer hunting trips, however, the head of the household most often went with two brothers (related to him as MBS, WFS, and, in the case of one, also as ZH) who stood in the -*yese* (cross-cousin/brother-in-law) category to him but who were older, more experienced men. His parents-in-law were older people, and his father-in-law (also his MB) was inactive economically and depended on the son-in-law for support.

We have already noted one household at Paraman where two married brothers-in-law were co-resident in the same household. This is somewhat exceptional, but the co-residence of a wife's brother or sister's husband in the same settlement is rather more common. At Maikanden the ties between Ciro Paciano and his wife's brother Anibal were quite close. Their houses were placed right next to each other, some distance from the remaining houses in the settlement, and both families often ate in each other's houses. The younger children (three to ten years of age) from both families were constant playmates. Whenever Ciro or his sons brought in any meat, some of it was soon sent to Anibal's house, and Anibal and his sons reciprocated often with the good-sized fish which they were proficient in catching. The manioc plots of the two households were separate, and Anibal had obligations to his wife's mother which compelled him to limit somewhat his exchanges with Ciro. Nevertheless, Ciro was much more closely aligned with Anibal that he was with his own elder brother, Placido, who lived to the south across the Makarupai River near their father's old homesite. Examples of a man and his wife's brother being co-resident in the same settlement could be multiplied. In none of these current cases, however, were they partners in a sister exchange.

We should not think of relationships with the spouse's parents only from the male point of view. The visiting patterns of the young couple usually mean that there will be some interaction between a young wife and her husband's parents. This is portrayed in myth (see Armellada, 1964: 172–74) as a conflict between mother-in-law and daughter-in-law over that now familiar theme of Pemon affinal relations, accusations of laziness by the elder same-sex in-law. There is some symmetry in the potential strain in affinal relations for men and women — for men the principal problem is the father-in-law, for women the mother-in-law. This is not exclusively the case, of course, as we have seen in the problems of Chirikavai with his mother-in-law. There are no wholly affinal terms available for use by the parents-in-law to refer to or to address their daughter-in-law — the -*pase* term has both consanguineal and affinal referents. This contrasts with the situation for the son-in-law, since the wholly affinal -*payɨnu* term is available to the parents-in-law.

We have emphasized the tenor more than the explicit content of affinal relations because the content, in everyday life, varies quite a bit more than the underlying themes. Affinal relationships are, as we have noted, relationships between individuals, and in some cases — for example, that of Ciro and Anibal — the continuation of balanced reciprocity over a long period of time (since the early 1950s) has resulted in an easygoing equilibrium which has muted all traces of rivalry or hostility. The asymmetrical and demanding relationship of the father-in-law to a son-in-law can in practice be muted by prior genealogical connection, (the father-in-law is an actual MB or FZH), the graceful retirement of the father-in-law from the head of settlement status, or the designation of the son-in-law as heir to the father-in-law's trading relationships. Or the relationship can be polarized, as we saw in the case of Anton and Uslar.

We have already spoken of the kinds of cooperation manifested in sibling relationships, and affinal cooperation most often applies to different activities. Brothers-in-law may clear plots together – if they are in the same household – or hunt or fish together. They are seldom found working together on household construction. Though siblings and offspring inherit trade items, and trade occurs between various types of kinsmen as well as others, trading relationships are frequently passed on from father-in-law to son-in-law. In times of illness or injury one will call on a specialist (owner of *taren*, or a shaman) regardless of kinship connections, but one will look to one's elder brother's household (or in some cases the father's younger brother's household) to keep the family supplied with manioc and other everyday necessities.

For every individual, relationships with his or her spouse's primary relatives represent a kind of balancing act, requiring just the right degree of commitment and tact. Most are reluctant to press their spouse's primary relatives for aid, since to do so would be a sign of weakness. Most are also reluctant to give too much to them, since one loses one's own sustenance by so doing. Retaining one's autonomy, then, involves a proper judgment as to when to define obligations to the spouse's relatives in strict terms and when to cut people a little slack. Strict reckoning may be used to precipitate a break. By the generalized nature of the norm of aid to one's parents-in-law, Pemon leave much room for maneuver and for the negotiation of the amount of support to be given a spouse's relatives. "Wife givers" are always superior to "wife takers," but the open-ended debt which is incurred can be very onerous if it is not properly fended off at times. The most common means of so doing is simply the intensification of visiting ties with the relatives of the husband. Common reasons given are: (1) need to help a sibling in the clearing of fields, (2) need for the husband's parents to see their young grandchildren, (3) need to return to the husband's home area to obtain a particular type of plant for cultivation (usually one of an enormously large number of types of peppers), or (4) need to provide the husband's relatives with a specific trade item.

The importance of the ideals of direct exchange which permeate Pemon thinking about marriage and relations with the spouse's relatives (at least the own-generation ones) is that they provide a starter for entering into relationships as well as a norm of balance for perpetuating them. If they are invoked too strictly, things fall apart. If one gives too much, one becomes a servant of one's spouse's relatives; if too little, a laggard and an ingrate. As Colson (1974: 49) has remarked, people give as much out of fear as out of generosity or reciprocity. She was referring specifically to the fear of sorcery, but there is another fear which keeps one from giving to the point of giving away — the fear of loss of autonomy. In Pemon society, to be unable to give is not the same as to be unwilling to give — in the former case one is *iwomɨn*, unlucky, and in the latter, *amunek*, stingy, tight-fisted — and both are bad. But to give too much is to admit that one is subordinate. Ultimately, then, Pemon are not only balancing allegiances to their spouse's relatives and their own parents and siblings in the course of deciding how much they owe their affines, but they are deciding how far they will divert their skills — technical, interpersonal, and supernatural or spiritual — to someone else's purposes. By giving too little, one is stingy and unlucky; by giving too much, one lets go of the autonomy which skills (*ipuninbe*, the "state of knowing how") ensure.

The Limits of Kinship

We have seen that there are some rather pronounced limits in the normal size range of Pemon settlements, imposed by the following characteristics:

1) The settlement head finds it difficult to hold both sons and sons-in-law at home without violating the verbal norms of matrilocal residence at marriage. If he manages to keep both sons and sons-in-law in the settlement, it is usually through the expedient of contradicting the norm and in addition marrying his sons or daughters to the offspring of a coresident sister.

2) Conflicts among the sibling sets of those individuals in the 20–35-year-old generation are centripetal forces pulling at their allegiances to the members of the 35–50-year-old generation. That is, as head of settlement accumulates sons-in-law who remain with him, there is an increased probability of conflicting allegiances, given the obligations of those sons-in-law to members of their own sibling sets.

3) The "sister exchange" situation doesn't endure because often an individual's brother-in-law is not the one who has given away the bride (the father-in-law is). Debts are to individuals, and when they are gone, the debts do not necessarily get transmitted to the next generation.

4) Residential decisions are always taken with respect to primary kin, thus allowing maximum play for the conflicting obligations to siblings and to affines to exercise centripetal force on a fair number of individuals in any given settlement.

The double bond that results when an affinal tie is reinforced by a consanguineal one (when one marries a consanguine) is limited in practice to first- or second-cousin range by the truncated genealogies of the Pemon. This increases the scope for negotiability and reassignment of people into categories (*uyese, uyeruk*) which are maximally negotiable in terms of the content of the relationship, but limits the potential for mobilization of sizable numbers of relatives on a basis other than that of strict quid pro quo transactions.

We shall see in the next chapter that leaders who occupy sociocentric statuses — capitanes, shamans, etc. — are mostly unable to build a bounded followership on the basis of extrakinship ties, and must depend on such egocentric ties for links with other leaders and with partners or clients. We shall see that coupled with the vast area of negotiability in the egocentric status domain are variable means of transmission of the sociocentric statuses.

Dole (1966: 85) has remarked, "I have suggested that the lack of effective political authority in primitive societies can be traced, at least in part, to the absence of exclusive channels through which leadership may be exercised and through which authority may be transmitted from one generation to the next. . . . A more extensive investigation might establish a functional relation between cognatic structure and the absence of central political authority." Dole's statement can be adjusted to take genealogical depth and manipulation into account. Where the requisite depth for producing large numbers of potentially overlapping ties (among which selections can be made by the individual) at higher genealogical levels (above the second ascending generation) is lacking, as it is with the Pemon, either potential mobilization must be limited in scope, or non-kinship mobilizing devices (e.g. devices based on sociocentric age-related statuses or solidarity in terms of "place") must be present. It is noteworthy that while relative age is a component of almost all Pemon social interaction, absolute age reckoning or age statuses are quite limited. Pemon recognize *chiriki* (infant), *mure* (child), *wuri* (woman), *kurai* (man), *nosanton* (old woman), and *aeketon* (old man), and have no finer absolute age reckoning.

Mechanisms of incorporation, such as the wide use of the *yese* greeting term and its potential for engendering an exchange relationship, the elimination of affines as a class while maximizing the potential of choosing specific individuals as affines, the conversion process whereby all wife's mothers become *waʔni* if they are not already such before the marriage takes place, all are somewhat fragile. When necessary, Pemon will invoke very restricted definitions of relatedness in order to justify their actions, particularly in a conflict situation which they wish to get out of. In the absence of conflict, people accept the conversion of genealogically unrelated persons into persons with whom relatedness is asserted (with the assertion of common substance having existed in the parental generation of both parties). However, when conflict occurs, the net is drawn very tight indeed, and the realm of relatedness contracts markedly. In order to maintain support and necesary social interaction outside the nuclear family (of orientation or of procreation), the realm of balanced reciprocity, the negotiable middle-distance social relationships epitomized by own-generation affines, must be maintained.

In Chapter V we will see that in conflict situations there is a marked tendency for Pemon, including both allied and opposed individuals, to fragment along lines dictated by the most restricted definitions of relatedness. The domain of kinship, then, is anything but a constant in Pemon life, and only by attention to the ways in which it is limited can we understand it.

CHAPTER IV

Leadership

Conventional definitions of leadership center around the relationship between leaders and followers and the quality of directed action under the leader's influence (see Gibb, 1968: 271; Schmidt, 1933: 282). As Kracke (1978: 5) notes, leadership is "one phenomenon which mediates between the individual psyche and the social system." In Pemon society leaders are recognized persons, persons out-of-the-ordinary, who exercise influence over varying constituencies through time. One of the foremost characteristics of Pemon leadership is that it is not possible to define precisely a bounded group of followers or the limits of influence of a particular noted individual. This renders the study of the leader-follower relationship difficult, and a social psychological or "small group" approach inapplicable to the Pemon. A leader in Pemon society is a person who can exert more than ordinary influence on the course of events but who does not necessarily maintain a defined followership. Ultimately we are talking about persons of renown rather than bounded groups encompassing leaders and followers.

Our own notions of leadership focus on the leader as a person who mobilizes people in some common endeavor, on the one hand, or on the leader as an arbitrator, on the other (see De Jouvenel, 1957: 50–53). While Pemon leaders do perform both of these functions at certain times, the basis of Pemon leadership status lies for the most part in another direction. We will not neglect the interpersonal skills, personal attributes, and social structural positions of Pemon leaders, but it is clear that for the Pemon knowledge is an important basis of leadership. This can be either secular or sacred knowledge, knowledge of ritual formulae (e.g. the owner or master of *taren*), knowledge of trade routes and alien ways, knowledge of the Spanish language or of the Yekuana language, knowledge of the history of a particular local area — there are many varieties of knowledge which serve as necessary conditions of leadership. To be sure, knowledge is only a precondition of leadership, and other things are requisite, including the demonstration of the effectiveness of one's expertise. To cite knowledge as a principal basis of authority may seem just a platitude ("knowledge is power"). I hope to show that the Pemon themselves view the basis of leadership as a kind of expertise, and that the fund of knowledge drawn upon and developed by leaders is essentially conceived of as a reservoir which must not be misused.

It may seem odd to include shamans and masters of *taren* in our treatment of leadership. While these statuses are not overtly political, there are many implications which the actions of *piasan* and *taren esak* have for the community at large beyond their services as curing or preventative specialists. We shall contrast leadership in the secular domain — capitanes and big traders — with leadership in the sacred domain — shamans, *taren esak*, rezadoras (women Hallelujah prophets, leaders of the ceremonies) and prophets. This should not be thought of as a hard-and-fast division, since capitanes, at least, must deal with the conflicts arising from sorcery accusations and ostensible misuse of shamanic powers.

Weber (1961: 4) defines authority as "the probability that a specific command will be obeyed." Specific commands are rare in Pemon society, and the utterance of a command most often occurs in a situation of direct confrontation, when conflicts are being openly aired. As we have seen in our discussion of "Relatives, Residents, and Neighborhoods," the principal relationship of authority outside the nuclear family in the domain of kinship is that of father-in-law and son-in-law. This asymmetrical relationship carries the obligation of economic and political support on the part of the son-in-law. We have also seen that considerable attention to the marriages of siblings and of own offspring is necessary for a man to build up a relatively large settlement.

Authority in Pemon society is always personal, even when the holder is occupying a recognized status. There is no such thing as the power of an office — there are only more or less influential holders of specific statuses. Any attempt to parcel out Pemon authority patterns in line with Weber's tripartite division (Weber, 1961), as Fock (1971) has done for the Waiwai, would result in a caricature. Leaders in Pemon society, and the authority they hold, can most fruitfully be thought of as resources, guides to be turned to when the occasion calls for it or the need arises. Meggitt (1973: 202) has emphasized the difference between periods of compression, when one must follow a given leader, and periods of relaxation (of tension between segments in a segmentary lineage system), in which individuals are free to choose and factionalism can arise. He emphasizes the need for diachronic analysis to interpret leadership patterns. Following Meggitt's lead, we can say that the authority of a given leader is in evidence when called forth by the situation. In this sense it can be thought of as a reserve, to be tapped both by the leader himself and the community at large. This perspective seems to beg the question of how authority is legitimated when it does come into play. To speak of "traditional" legitimation leads us only to the oft-repeated and unilluminating "our forefathers did it that way." There is an aspect of legitimation which is often referred to but seldom analyzed (outside of the context of bureaucracies) — expertise held by one actor and recognized as such by another *in itself* constitutes a basis for legitimate authority. The clearest expression of this type of legitimation is found in the realm of knowledge of the spirit world. Knowledge in this sense is active knowledge: it must be applied and manifested in practice. This is less apparent in the secular leadership statuses of capitan and big trader.

The approach taken here, of looking at authority and leadership as resources to be tapped by the community at large and by specific individuals, would seem to neglect somewhat the motivations, character, and personality of leaders, to focus on the level of the social structure. While this is true to a certain extent, we will examine the careers of individual leaders in some detail, not with an eye to discussing their relationships with specific followers (see Kracke, 1978, for this approach) but to see how they respond, successfully or not, to the challenges posed by the social environment. Our approach is in a sense a reverse of the so-called "resource mobilization" approach (see Oberschall, 1973) used by some sociologists to discuss social movements in contemporary societies. They look at the ways in which leaders and organizations put together resources and a following, the way in which a movement or leader is created around a given issue. What I wish to do is to find out how situations bring about leaders, as well as how leaders attain and hold leadership positions.

Clastres (1977: 27), basing himself on a text by Lowie (1948), talks of the "chieftainship" in lowland South America:

> It is surely by four traits that the chief is distinguished in South America. As chief, he is a "professional pacifier"; in addition, he has to be generous and a good orator; finally polygyny is his prerogative.

> A distinction is called for, however, between the first of these criteria and the following three. The latter define the set of prestations and counter prestations which maintain the balance between the social structure and the political institution: the leader exercises a right over an abnormal number of the group's women; in return, the group is justified in requiring of its chief generosity and talent as a speaker.

Clastres sees the relationship leader/group of followers as a kind of balanced reciprocity. The group allows the leader certain prerogatives, while he renders services to the group as a whole. The idea of balanced reciprocity which Clastres expresses is attractive as an explanation for the proverbial lack of authority of the leader in lowland South American societies. It is true that both capitanes and male shamans in

Pemon society tend to be polygynous, and that the capitan is expected to be a good orator and the shaman an articulate and masterful performer. Capitanes are supposed to be generous, at least in the provision of bountiful supplies of *cachiri* for guests; shamans, on the other hand, get some return for their services. Pemon leadership comprises more than just males — female shamans exist, and have existed in the past, and a number of prophets have been women — and polygyny also fails as a criterial attribute of leadership for male prophets, who are pretty strictly monogamous. Big traders may or may not be polygynous and are always males (though women are very active participants in the trade system). In short, Clastres's theme of balanced reciprocity between leader and led is a little too restricted to encompass the spectrum of Pemon leadership types. We shall not abandon it, however, but will return to it after examining leaders in detail. Just as we were unable to understand Pemon kinship without reference to both balanced reciprocity and hierarchy, so we must allow for the interplay of multiple principles in the domain of leadership.

It might be argued that our application of the term "leader" is too broad, that it is unwise to conjoin secular and sacred statuses under one rubric. In a commentary on a recent symposium E. Colson (1977: 385–86) states: "The papers in the symposium . . . can be seen as falling into two groups, depending on whether they focus on secular or spiritual power." She contrasts the two foci:

> Elsewhere in the world, however, men conceive of power over men as derived from contact with spiritual forces. Success or failure is evidence that men have gained or lost spiritual force. For those who look at life in such a fashion, it is nonsense to talk about consent or consensus as underlying political power, since the very essence of spiritual force is that it takes precedence over the wills of human beings. Men and women neither consent to the working of the supernatural nor successfully dispute with it.

Colson's separation of these two power domains is rather overdrawn, for the simple reason that holders of both sacred and secular power often interact, and their power, from whatever sources, is ultimately contingent on its impact on the community at large. Colson would have us believe that spiritual power is totally of the mechanistic variety. That this is not the case is attested to by the fact that a given individual is often judged on how he channels and directs the spiritual forces which he contacts. Pemon do speak of the will of God (most often with the platitude, in Spanish, *Si Dios quiere*), but individuals are responsible for being *kanaimaton* (sorcerers). The prophet in Pemon society is not only a person with access to the spiritual world but also the head or representative of a movement.

The separation of leaders into sacred and secular is helpful in understanding Pemon society, and will be adhered to here. This separation does not mean that shamans and *taren esak* are exclusively ritual curing specialists, or that prophets do not have to exhibit considerable organizational skills. Capitanes will intervene or participate in matters having to do with the spiritual. Concern with the spirit world is shared by all Pemon, and all serious illness and death are believed to be caused by Kanaima, the spirit of evil in all its forms and manifestations. The welfare of the community is a concern for Pemon leaders, whether secular or sacred, and malevolent use of spiritual forces or of secular influence must call forth a response from them. Butt (1965–66) has detailed the legal and political role of the shaman, and the use of the shaman's séance as a forum for the airing of grievances and discussion of personal transgressions, among the Akawaio, eastern neighbors of the Pemon. Her account emphasizes the role of the shaman in moderating disputes rather than in fostering them. She (1965–66: 176) states: "Although the shaman's accusations, expressed during the course of his seances, may not only state but exaggerate tensions, they are in fact the beginning of a process whereby these tensions will eventually be reduced and even, perhaps, eliminated." Pemon seem to be more ambivalent about shamans and their use of spiritual forces than the Akawaio. There is much fear of shamanic power, as well as desire for their curing services. The knowledge possessed by shamans in Pemon society is very much seen as a two-edged sword. We shall explore this characteristic further in this and the following chapter; for the present, it is best to keep in mind that, while a source of influence by shamans, *taren esak*, and prophets-rezadoras is spiritual knowledge, and a source of influence of capitanes and big traders is secular knowledge, the separation of leadership into these two categories should not be overemphasized.

All Pemon leaders are part of a regional system which encompasses the tribal territory as a whole and extends beyond it. What happens in one river valley can have major repercussions in the next valley over, and beyond that to the next. We shall see the implications of this diffusely bounded system as we discuss particular conflicts.

Big Traders

The trade system which operates in the Gran Sabana and neighboring areas has at its base an ideal of balanced reciprocity, both in material goods and in the social relations of exchange. The extension of the ideal of balanced reciprocity into the activity of intertribal trade serves to perpetuate a system which extracts labor-intensive goods from the Yekuana in return for capital-intensive goods from the Pemon. The Pemon are not exclusively middleman traders, since they do trade considerably in the *oin∔* bowls manufactured in the Uriman and Kamarata areas, in cotton hammocks which they manufacture themselves, and in some other items of their own manufacture. Even so, it is clear that an ecologically poorer zone, the Gran Sabana, is to a certain extent extracting energy (in the form of labor embodied in canoes and manioc graters) from an ecologically richer forest zone to the west. This system has been sustained by an influx of non-Pemon goods from British Guiana (now Guyana) and from Brazil, but the rules by which it operates are indigenous ones. These rules are clearly differentiated by both Pemon and Yekuana informants from buying and selling as practiced by the bearers of Western culture.

Here I want to focus not on the material relations of exchange (types of items traded, exchange rates, etc.) but on the social relationships involved in the transmission of goods, and on the careers of several big traders. A basic concept is the word *pawana*, meaning "in a trading relationship." Thus *pawanaton*, trading people, usually refers to the Yekuana but may also refer to big traders who operate in the middle Caroni and middle Paragua. *Pawanabe enin tesen*, being in a trading relationship, is used to describe a trade partnership or a more casual trading relation. The trade partnership is usually described as a one-to-one relationship of exclusivity — "I trade only with so-and-so" — whether or not this always holds in practice. The establishment of a trade partnership can occur variously: in some cases, on the death of one partner, his end of things will be taken up by a son or son-in-law. In other cases, a big trader who is grooming a younger man to become a big trader will propose that one of the people accompanying his own trade partner on a given visit become the trade partner of the younger man. At other times people with goods on their hands simply go looking for an outlet (see Thomas, 1972: 25) and strike up a partnership with someone who has desired items.

The careers of two big traders in the stretch of the Caroni near and upstream from Uriman provide insights into the ways these brokers operate and the sources of their influence. Fabian Ortega is a man in his mid-forties who resides (1970) at Avikara (Cachimbo) just above the confluence of the Icabaru and Caroni rivers upstream from Uriman. Fabian's parents died in the Antabari drainage (the Antabari is a rapids-strewn, swift-running tributary of the Carun, which in turn flows into the Paragua), and he has been going on trading journeys through the Paragua drainage as far as the Erebato, a tributary of the Caura River, since he was a young boy. He speaks the Yekuana language but does not know Spanish. He is married to a daughter of the leader of the Chochiman cult, which has its main center at Avikara. His father-in-law is rather old but has numerous daughters who are located in the Uriman area. Three of Fabian's wife's sisters survive and live with their husbands near Uriman. Fabian has only one surviving sibling, who lives at Kunken, Tirika. He has thus invested much in his affinal ties, both in his own generation and that of his children.

Fabian's married offspring are somewhat dispersed: one daughter lives with her husband in his natal area, Kamarata. One daughter lives with her husband at Avikara, and another daughter, divorced, also lives at Avikara. A fourth daughter, Mariana, is married to Lucas Gentil and lives at Kamadak, in the northwest portion of the Uonken region, just east of the headwaters of the Tirika River. In addition, Fabian and his wife raised Herrera, his WMZS, who was orphaned at an early age. Herrera made several trips with Fabian to Parupa, a Yekuana settlement on the middle Paragua, when he was a young boy. Herrera is married to a woman who was born in the Uonken region; his wife's sister is married and resides at the Old Mission settlement. Herrera's wife's parents are both dead and she resides with him in his natal area, Tirika.

Fabian trades principally in shotguns, manioc graters, and canoes, and journeys often to Kamadak to obtain shotguns and bring in manioc graters. His daughter Mariana is living patrilocally at Kamadak, but this serves Fabian's purposes quite well. His ability to tap sources of shotguns in the Uonken region stems from the strategic ties of his daughter's husband and daughter's husband's parents with the Old Mission settlement in the central part of the region. The Old Mission neighborhood is dominated, as was discussed above, by the offspring of Lisandro Bernal. Lisandro is Lucas Gentil's MMB, and Lisandro's adult offspring are cross-cousins of Lucas's mother. Thus there is a channel for the routing of shotguns and graters from Fabian through his DH to his DH's mother's cross-cousins. Likewise, since Fabian in effect raised Herrera as a son, he has other ties into the Old Mission area through Herrera's wife's sister. Fabian does not need to depend only on his own trips westward to obtain manioc graters, since he can call upon his WZH (he has several) in the Uriman area for graters. Uriman is a principal end-point for Yekuana expeditions from the west (see Coppens, 1971). Fabian and his wife often travel together between Avikara, Kunken, and Kamadak, and their daughter Mariana, her husband Lucas and Lucas's sisters often make return visits from Kamadak to Avikara. For a depiction of Fabian's affinal trading relationships, see Figure 12.

Fabian is a respected source of information on the state of the trade with the Yekuana. Some have wondered, though, if his predictions of an imminent decline in the system (because of an alleged increasing unwillingness to trade on the part of the Yekuana) might have been self-serving. One of the Old Mission people had discussed with Fabian the fairness of the trade rates when Fabian told him that his Yekuana partners were no longer accepting *kasuru* (glass beads, which come in from Guyana) in return for manioc graters. The man maintained that the

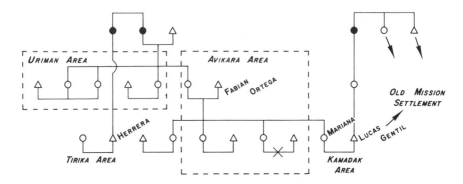

Figure 12. Fabian Ortega's affinal trading relationships.

rates were the same as they had always been (not quite true) back to the time of the grandfathers when muzzle-loaders had been an article of trade. Fabian agreed, but pointed out that the Yekuana were being given "everything" by the missionaries at Santa Maria de Erebato, and that the missionaries seemed to want to stop the flow of goods.

Fabian's broker role depends on his ability to use his affinal ties. The marriages of his daughters, several of whom are living patrilocally in contradiction of the verbal ideal norm of matrilocal residence, and his connections with his wife's sisters' husbands near Uriman provide the necessary channels. His intimate knowledge of the trade routes and of the Yekuana is in the process of being passed on to his adopted son Herrera, who started out trading as a boy, as did Fabian. Fabian will not pass on his own trade partnership to Herrera, since they currently make combined journeys and Herrera already has a Yekuana trade partner. Herrera's own affinal contacts (WZH) in the Old Mission area will perpetuate the connection to the central part of the Uonken region. We shall see that this dispersion of affinal ties and the constant journeying represent an opposing strategy to that of a capitan, who must have a concentration of affinal ties in his own area to build a base of support.

Valerio Ojeda is another broker who lives to the north of Uriman, not far away from the overland route that goes through the mountains to Kamarata. Kamarata is the source of the best clay for making the *oini*-type bowls, which are highly desired by Pemon and Yekuana alike. Valerio's wife has learned the art of making these bowls, and Valerio and his sons occasionally make trips to Kamarata and actually haul clay overland on their backs for the manufacture of *oini*. Valerio thus has an edge on the bowl trade. He also trades in canoes, graters, and shotguns. Valerio seldom deals directly with the Yekuana but travels frequently to the Antabari, where he has Pemon trade contacts. Valerio's trading is less long-range than that of Fabian, but he is perhaps the second most noted trader in this stretch of the Caroni. Valerio's wife is from Kamarata, as is one of his sons-in-law, so that his access to clay and to additional sources of *oini* is assured. Valerio has no siblings in the area except for a man whom he calls "elder brother" who lives at the foot of the mountains north of Uriman. This man, Gaspar, is a shaman, now old and semiretired, and neither Valerio nor Gaspar could demonstrate any genealogical relationship. Valerio depends more on casual trading and his Antabari trade partner than he does on his own kinship contacts, and by 1975 had constructed a house near the Pemon section of Uriman (a mixed criollo-Pemon community) and was known in some quarters as the "capitan segundo" (assistant to the capitan) of the Uriman area. He has managed to keep some of his sons and his daughters either in his own settlement north of Uriman or close to Uriman, and has not dispersed his affinal relationships after the fashion of Fabian Ortega. He has pursued what might be called a middle way between an emphasis on trading and a commitment to building up a stable settlement to the north of Uriman.

Another major broker in the western area of Pemon territory is Tirso, who resides in the middle Antabari and who journeys with his Yekuana trade partner as far as Isla Casabe, on the lower Paragua, to obtain Venezuelan goods. He trades mainly in graters, shotguns, canoes, and bolts of cloth. Tirso's Yekuana trade partner makes his home at Parupa, on the middle Paragua. During a single visit Tirso may take away as many as 30 or more manioc graters, to be distributed to settlements along the Antabari and to his Pemon trade contacts who come from the Uriman and Tirika areas. Tirso is bilingual — he speaks Spanish but not Yekuana. His Yekuana trade partner speaks some Pemon.

The following example serves to show the extent to which a broker may be a funnel for goods from a rather extensive hinterland. Baco Bandino was a resident of the Old Mission settlement in the Uonken region. Up until his death in 1965, Baco used his trade partnership with a Pemon from Kuyumeru, Antabari, to supply both his own kinsmen and neighbors in the Old Mission neighborhood and those living at Maikanden and south of Maikanden along the Makarupai. Baco's Pemon trade partner would come to the Old Mission settlement via the Tirika River when in need of shotguns. Baco would then gather shotguns, hammocks, and beads from people at the Old Mission settlement and to the south, and trade them on their behalf. Baco's Antabari partner spoke Yekuana and had a Yekuana trade partner at Santa Maria de Erebato. Baco's own visits westward never went any farther than Antabari, and Baco was monolingual. His Antabari partner was frequently referred to as *Muyungon*, the Pemon word for the Yekuana, simply because he knew the Yekuana language. The origins of Baco's trade partnership were not known to my informants, but the relationship was of sufficient importance both to the Antabari Pemon and to the people of the Old Mission settlement for a renewed affirmation of the partnership by Egberto Palacios, Baco's son-in-law, upon Baco's death.

Some insight into the workings of Baco's broker role can be gained from an account of the continuing relationship with the Antabari trader, Pizarro. In October, 1969, Pizarro came to the Old Mission from Antabari and collected five shotguns. Egberto, his brother, his FZS, his WZH, and one man from south of the Makarupai each provided one shotgun. Egberto's mother, his father's sister, and his father's second wife each put one hammock into the trade with Pizarro. Egberto's FZS and another man from south of the Makarupai gave him several bunches of bead necklaces to trade. In September, 1970, Egberto was in the Caroni at a mining camp downstream from Uriman, and received word from Pizarro to come to Antabari and collect the manioc graters due from their trade of October, 1969. Egberto and a friend (the man from south of the Makarupai who had participated in the 1969 dealings) brought 26 graters with them upon their return, in near full payment for the shotguns, hammocks, and beads. The scheduling of the trading is clearly not all that regular, and when one or the other partner has the need to obtain or to dispose of some items, he sends a message to his counterpart, suggesting the necessary visits in either direction. Usually it is the seeker after goods who bears the travel costs.

Baco served as a port of entry for Pizarro's graters, and simultaneously as a funnel for people without their own trading relationships. To one side of the broker, whoever he is, is a unitary relationship with a trade partner, someone in the Paragua drainage (either Pemon or Yekuana) who has access to manioc graters and canoes. On the other side of the broker is a pool of kinsmen and neighbors, a regional hinterland which constitutes a many-to-one relationship of persons to the broker. Even in the case of Valerio Ojeda, whose family produces many of the bowls he trades, his affinal relations in Kamarata provide access to a hinterland for the obtaining of bowls and the disposal of small graters received for them. The broker does not have as his objective the stockpiling of items, the accumulation of wealth, since the system operates at relatively fixed rates (see Thomas, 1972: 13–14; Coppens, 1971: 49) which preclude rapid short-term accumulation. He serves as a channel for the movement of items considered necessary in the day-to-day activities of Pemon households. The fixed rate aspect of the system means that the broker does not often build up a huge inventory, but that he must constantly renew his ties with his hinterland — his estate, if such there be, is this set of relationships with people in a given area.

We have seen that Fabian Ortega is preparing to pass on his knowl-edge of the Yekuana to his adopted son Herrera, who has affinal connec-tions in the center of the Uonken region which potentially will allow Herrera to create for himself a hinterland there. Fabian is not passing on either a specific trade partnership (as Baco did to his son-in-law) or a specific followership (a set of affinal ties) to Herrera. Herrera himself, if he chooses to, will develop into a broker on the basis of his experience, his many trading journeys with Fabian. The achievement of the status of big trader may come about either through direct transmission (of both a trade partnership and a hinterland), as in the case of Baco and his son-in-law, or less directly, as in the case of Fabian and Herrera. There is an indefinite quality to the transmission of this status, and in no sense can we speak of any kind of inheritance. In the case of Baco's son-in-law, Egberto himself informed me that he had to reaffirm the trade partnership with Pizarro and show that his word was good before the relationship could be consolidated. In Herrera's case the potential for his development of the role is there, but it may or may not be taken up.

As I have pointed out elsewhere (1972; 1973: 242–48), the trade sys-tem of the Gran Sabana and neighboring areas has an ideal of balanced reciprocity at its core. Even in the material relations of trade (customary equivalences and actual rates as manifested in observed ex-changes) an ideal of one-for-one exchange prevails in many instances. Likewise, on the plane of the social relations of trade, ideally one trades in a relationship of exclusivity with one's trade partner. The broker role alters this, substituting a regional hinterland of relationships, derived from relatives and others, for one pole of the nominally one-to-one trade partnership. What advantages does the broker get for his many journeys and negotiations with those in his own hinterland of relationships? First, in the process of delays which characterize trade between known and trusted partners, the broker always has on hand items for the use of his own household and settlement. His role thus guarantees items on hand for those immediately dependent on him, and precludes the possibility of being without these items. In the case of canoes, at least, this lack could be very detrimental to the welfare of a settlement or ex-tended family. Thus one objective is a kind of security. But this is countered by the need for long trips, often over difficult terrain, sometimes at substantial risk (rapids and the like) on swift-flowing tropical rivers.

More important, perhaps, is the new set of social relations which the broker can create outside of his own river valley area. In many cases persons active in the trade system, even if they have not quite achieved the status of broker, enjoy a much wider set of visiting ties than other persons in their own neighborhood. A man from the Maikanden neighborhood who lives south of the Makarupai but who was active in trade to the east (with partners in the Yuruani River area, east of the Apanguao River drainage), where he obtained large quantities of *kasuru* (beads), maintained much closer ties to the Old Mission neighborhood than did others in the Maikanden area. Because of his entree as a trader, he was often found at the Old Mission settlement drinking *cachiri* and socializing with friends, even though his kinship connections with persons in the Old Mission settlement were less close than those of many others in his home neighborhood. Likewise, Fabian Ortega was a welcome visitor anywhere in the northwest portion of the Uonken region, even if he brought only news and had no goods to trade on a particular visit.

The broker in no sense controls or monopolizes a given hinterland, and the fixed-rate ideals by which the system operates mean that anyone in need can get into the act on his own by simply searching out someone with goods on hand who is willing to let go of them. However, when an individual does not have the time, energy, or desire to search out his or her own contacts, the broker is available. There is no continuing obligation on the part of those who utilize the broker always to move goods through his auspices. Some women from the Maikanden area who wished to trade hammocks for graters would customarily go to Baco Bandino in order to find an outlet, rather than undertake seeking their own contacts, but others would use his auspices only when they could not obtain things through their own kinship ties. In short, the broker's hinterland is a potential pool of sources of goods and of needs for goods, one which turns into an active trading resource when the broker mobilizes it or when those in need mobilize the broker. In spite of the one-to-many relationship which the broker maintains with this constituency, there is no element of hierarchy or control involved. The broker can induce people to trade through him only if he proves that his lines of supply are reliable.

Rumors to the effect that the trade with the Yekuana would soon cease were rife during 1970–71. There may be some truth to allegations that some brokers (e.g. Fabian Ortega) used these rumors to attempt to speed up the flow of shotguns, which were already at that time becoming increasingly difficult to obtain. One informant stated that Fabian's claims about the cessation of trade with the Yekuana had been made in much the same terms three years before and things had remained pretty much the same anyway. Others stated that even if the supply of shotguns were to dwindle away, they could always go back to the old ways of trading hammocks for graters (the rates for hammocks and graters were one to one, while those for shotguns and graters were one shotgun for four, five, or six graters). Some informants even went so far as to say that the Pemon themselves might be able to make graters in a pinch (the wood for manufacture of graters was to be found in the western part of Pemon territory, as well as in Yekuana territory, and by 1970 all grater teeth were made of small pieces of tin cans pounded into the face of the grater board). The point made by most informants was that trade with the Yekuana would continue, in some form or another, with or without the brokers. That anyone who had the initiative could get into the trade was convincingly illustrated by the account of one old woman who had purchased a shotgun (a strictly male item in daily use), gone overland from the Uonken region to Tirika and found someone to exchange with, returning with four manioc graters which she used herself and with which she supplied her daughters.

Brokers, then, have a certain renown, a wide-ranging set of social relationships which extend well beyond their home neighborhood, and a knowledge of the trade routes, and possibly of the Yekuana language. The status usually requires the cultivation of relationships with spatially distant affines and the dispersion of the marriage ties of one's offspring. The individual broker can maintain his pool of sources (his hinterland) only by a process of constant cultivation in which he is responsive to the needs of various individuals and households who come to him for aid. He has little freedom to manipulate the rates of exchange, and the relative fixity of rates serves as a kind of guarantee of proper dealing for those who trade through him (see Thomas, 1978). In short, the big trader in Pemon society is a broker, but not a patron with a set of clients. He mediates between a shifting set of constituents and his own trade partner but cannot monopolize exchanges in a given area, or give people a better deal — except in terms of the time required for them to get what they want — and still play by the rules.

Capitanes

No overall unitary political organization exists among the Pemon. As Koch-Grunberg (1916–28, III: 92) noted: "An actual tribal organization does not exist among the Taulipang, or perhaps does not any longer." This merely means that political institutions are not formally differentiated among the Pemon and that political problems are dealt with, insofar as they occur, by the society overall. We would call the capitan a regional political leader, but I doubt that our sense of the word "political" would convey much to the Pemon. Politics as either the art and organization of administration or as a domain which involves a monopoly on the legitimate use of force is foreign to the Pemon.

The Pemon capitan *(teburu)* is not a mobilizer of group labor. As in some other lowland societies, such as the Kuikuru (Dole, 1966: 78), an individual who wishes to have settlement mates or others aid in some endeavor, usually barbasco fishing or plot clearing, will throw a work party with *cachiri* and food provided by the host for those participating. Such events are rare, however, and the emphasis on the nuclear or extended family as the cooperative work group is paramount. The capitan will only, at most, mobilize his own settlement to produce enough *cachiri* to provide for a party or upcoming visitors. This is nothing more or less than any head of settlement would normally do. In no sense are any of the component households of a settlement or a region dependent on the coordinating or mobilizing efforts of either the head of settlement or a capitan for ensuring their subsistence.

What, then, does the capitan do? How can we define his status as a political one, when he has no recourse to coercive sanctions outside of those (of self-help) available to any individual of the society? As Simpson (1940: 525) noted for the inhabitants of Kamarata, "The authority of the cacique [read capitan] over the various homes *[hogares]* is almost exactly the same as that of the to'esa' [head of settlement] over the members of a single home. It rests on prestige, custom, and consent more than on force or any formal legal base or religious theory or practice." He (1940: 526–27) goes on:

> The cacique is respected and can have first choice in the division of benefits, but does not receive any emolument in work or in goods, and in the eminently democratic and individualistic society which is the tribe, is considered as one additional person, though outstanding. His duties are as vague as they are light. He arbitrates the few differences which arise among families, represents the tribe in negotiations with other [tribes] or with Venezuelans, directs the affairs of the community and generally acts as father of his people. We did not observe any case of disobedience to his orders, and were told that this never occurs; but it is well to note that the orders of the cacique do not have a threatening tone, being rather a persuasive exposition of his desires and opinions.

There are many who would define the political as simply the ability to produce an effect on public affairs (see Kaplan, 1975: 46n), preferring this broad definition so as to preclude prejudging the issue of what is political in a particular society. The problem then becomes "what constitutes public affairs?" and we are back with a difficulty. Some rather domestic enmities and disputes may end up with far-reaching implications for large areas of the tribal territory, and there is no Pemon conceptual distinction corresponding to our public/private dichotomy. We might be tempted to characterize the Pemon as Sharp (1958: 7) does the Yir Yoront: "There are roles, and rules for the roles, and a system of law with specified kin serving as public agents with authority to act in defined circumstances, and provision for changes in the roles and rules through public action or inaction. But all of this is simply kinship. In the field of conduct, there is no distinguishable social organization for economics, for religion, or for government." Interestingly, while the last sentence holds quite true for the Pemon, not all of Pemon society is kinship. There is no distinguishable social organization for economics, religion, or government in Pemon society either, but there are non-kinship statuses which pertain specifically to these areas of social life. How can we speak, then, of a political status — capitan — without a political organization?

The answer lies in the mediating, counselor role of the capitan. Not only is the capitan a mediator in interfamilial disputes, but he is also the representative of some regional grouping of Pemon, in the face of Pemon from other areas who have no kinship ties in his area, and in the face of non-Pemon. All of these functions have in common the function of mediation, particularly mediation between persons who stand in potentially or actually hostile relationship to one another. We are back to Clastre's (1977: 27) designation of the "professional pacifier." The two aspects of the role of capitan which place it in the political domain are those of mediation and contact with outsiders. This in spite of the fact that there is no comprehensive organization of capitanes, no agreed-upon hierarchy of capitanes (though some are definitely better known and more prestigious than others), and that each one, outside of his own area, may or may not be recognized as a leader.

There is little question that the role of capitan in relating to non-Pemon has been of principal importance in determining who can achieve the position. This has undoubtedly been true for the time span we are concerned with, the last hundred years. Significantly, Simpson (1940: 525) comments: "Actually, the cacique of the Kamarakotos is Alejo Calcaño, a pure member of the tribe, even though he is one of the two or three who speak Spanish and have spent some time in Venezuelan cities." In recent years there has been discussion of the need for a "capitan general," and some informants in the Uriman area referred to Alejo Calcaño as having been such. Despite the recent pressures on the Pemon from the national society (see Chapter VIII), there has been no widespread agreement on such a personage, nor in my opinion is there likely to be.

Before going further into the actions of the capitan, his role as a leader, the means of achieving the status may be examined. One account was given by a capitan of the Uriman area as follows:

There was Alejo, who was "capitan general," everything. He was first. There were two, placed by Alejo to represent him here — Eduardo Landaeta and Esteban. Esteban is now in Kamarata. And there was the father of _____, the old man Eladio. In Uonken, there was the old man Candido (see above, account of the Old Mission neighborhood). In Santa Elena, Amado. . . . They were the beginnings, the capitanes. But when Alejo was directing, those who were placed by Alejo much deceived the people around here. They spoke much, but it was fraud. They did not speak as Alejo spoke. Here they said that there would come many *racionales* (criollos), to take away our women . . . but this was lies, so that people would become frightened and in order to get another woman. They said, "If you give me the girl, I'll talk to these people so that they won't take away the woman." And then you had to give him your daughter, or your sister. They spoke thus, to create trouble, to get another woman, to have two women. And then Alejo found out, since he was "capitan general" and they went — those who went to make a complaint — to Kamarata and asked "Is it true that these people, placed by you, should speak in this way?" He told them no, that it was bad that they spoke thus. Then, people, all the people, looked for another capitan, but they had no one. Here were only Landaeta, Esteban, there was no one. There were some here, but they were not recognized as capitan, they couldn't do it. Then they saw that I was here. I was working the mines, I was around here. I never thought of directing (*mandar*), being capitan. But they gathered together, they called me, all the people, even the *racionales* voted (*votaron*) for me. They called Landaeta, they called Esteban, they called Ruben Monagas (from Icabaru). In front of them, those who spoke lies, it was said that they could not go on directing, because they were speaking very bad things. They did not want Landaeta, nor Esteban. Monagas neither. A sergeant spoke to me, "When they name you capitan, don't turn it down, because they're going to name you capitan." When they called me to the gathering they asked me if I could be capitan; I said that these people could not go on directing (*mandando*), that they spoke many lies. Then they named me capitan of the indigenas. I knew nothing of command (*mandar*), but if you are going to vote for me, I will accept, I said to them. Everyone voted, including the comerciantes (store owners), miners, everyone.

The events described in this account took place around 1958–59. The acculturative aspects of the account are quite clear: the use of terms from the current Venezuelan idiom (*votar, mandar*), the influence of the criollos in the Uriman area on the process of selection, and the "they drafted me" bias in the narrative. More important, perhaps, is that the incumbent capitanes — Eduardo Landaeta and Esteban — were censured for two things: speaking lies and attempting to obtain too many wives. Their abuses set the stage for the entrance of Raimundo Losada, as we shall call the author of the account.

Raimundo was separated from his mother on the death of his father and spent several years as a young boy on a ranch in the flatlands west of the lower Paragua, working for criollos. His mother remarried and settled with his half-brother in Uriman after the death of her second husband. Raimundo returned in his mid-teens to find his mother and half-brother, took up residence in Uriman, and went through two wives before finally settling down with a third woman. His present wife, like Raimundo in her late 30s, is the daughter of Justo Isorio. Justo's sister's husband is Eduardo Landaeta, one of the men whom Raimundo edged out in becoming capitan. Justo had married two sisters, and had lived in the Uriman area until about 1960, when he left his two wives and married a "ZD," a daughter of Landaeta. Many of Justo Isorio's offspring by his first wives live in the Uriman settlement or close by, and Raimundo's marriage to Justo's daughter brought him numerous wife's brothers and sisters (Justo had 12 offspring by his first two wives). His own half-brother and his brothers-in-law and their families formed the core of his support. Raimundo had not broken with Landaeta after becoming capitan of the area, however, and his eldest son by his present wife is married to one of Landaeta's daughters. This son and his wife live in Raimundo's house cluster in the Uriman settlement. Landaeta and Justo Isorio now live far upriver from Uriman, just below Aripichi Falls. Justo's separation from his first two wives (around 1960) left them in Uriman with their offspring, and Raimundo's household contains both his own mother and his wife's mother.

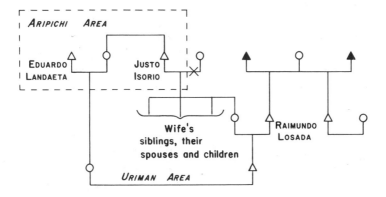

Figure 13. Principal kinship relationships of capitan Raimundo Losada.

The kinship relationships shown in Figure 13 formed the core of Losada's support in the Uriman area. He had no antecedents in the area (his mother was born in Uonken, and had lived much of her life in the Paragua drainage before coming to Uriman). His third marriage, with a member of the large sibling set of Justo Isorio's offspring, provided the basis for his accession to the status of capitan. Landaeta, the former capitan referred to in Losada's account, was married to Isorio's sister, and after his divorce from his first two wives Isorio moved upriver to Landaeta's settlement near the Aripichi Falls. Losada, however, was still allied with Landaeta as late as July, 1970, and Losada's son's marriage to Landaeta's daughter was an important link in this ongoing relationship. Though Landaeta was in eclipse as a leader in the middle Caroni after Losada's accession to capitan in 1958–59, many people along the river still referred to Landaeta as a capitan in 1970. Since Landaeta's home settlement was many hours upriver from Uriman, and Losada seldom went that far upriver, there was no necessary conflict of spheres of influence between the two. Landaeta's reputation, though tarnished by the accusations during 1958-59, remained relatively intact, and he still was sought out (in 1970) by people to give advice in interfamily conflicts and adultery cases. The competition between Losada and Landaeta is not a clearcut opposition, and both of them are careful not to make it such. On a trip to Isla Casabe in July, 1970, Landaeta accompanied Losada to a meeting of Pemon leaders from the middle Caroni, Paragua, and Chiguao river areas, where both participated on an equal basis in the discussions.

If one asks how many capitanes there are, the answers one gets depend very much on how the respondent views the current alignment of leaders in his own river area. Losada and Landaeta had overlapping constituencies in the middle Caroni during the 1960s, even though Losada had more or less unseated the older man. Patterns of accession to the status of capitan are far from well defined. In Losada's case, a series of abuses by the incumbent allowed him to move into the position, given the large number of supporters he was able to marshal among his wife's numerous siblings and their families.

The pattern of succession of capitanes in the Uonken region was rather different. As was mentioned in Chapter III, Candido Rulfo, in competition with Paulo Plaza, had moved into the area of the Old Mission settlement in the late 1940s, following marriages of several of his children to people there, and established himself as capitan. When Candido died in 1965 (Paulo Plaza had died in 1962), the position passed to Baco Bandino, a big trader at the Old Mission settlement who also died in 1965. Throughout the decade of the 1960s Justo Fabregas, a man not related to Candido or Baco, was known as "capitan segundo," a position which most people regard as a kind of stop-gap or stand-in when the capitan himself is not around. He did not become capitan after the deaths of Candido and Baco, and the position remained vacant until 1969, when Jaime Portales of Maikanden was (apparently rather half-heartedly) acknowledged as capitan by the people in the valley of the Karuai River (the Uonken region). Many people in the region were not particularly enthusiastic about Jaime's accession to the position, and there had been little importance attached to the fact that there was no capitan in the area. There was no move to install a capitan in the Uonken region until Raimundo Losada (whose mother's siblings and parallel cousins and their offspring lived in the Old Mission area) came from Uriman in 1969 and urged upon the people the necessity of so doing.

Simpson (1940: 527) records that Alejo Calcaño was grooming his ZS to become his successor in the position of capitan in the valley of Kamarata (in 1939). From Raimundo Losada's account, Alejo Calcaño was still capitan in Kamarata in the mid-1950s. The MB-to-ZS transmission of the status clearly did not obtain in the Uriman area in 1958-59 or in the Uonken area in 1965 and 1969 (though Losada and Landaeta are related as WBDH/WFZH, which is terminologically equivalent to ZS/MB in Pemon classification). In the case of Baco Bandino, Baco was simply a prominent man in the same settlement as Candido, the deceased capitan, and took up the job. In some areas, for example the middle Paragua, the position seems to require only a suitable location. The head of the settlement at the mouth of the Carun River was known as capitan, largely because of the traffic up and down the Paragua past that point and because of his hospitality. Likewise, the example of Justo Fabregas shows there is no reason for a person who has been "capitan segundo" necessarily to become capitan on the death of an incumbent. Justo, a mild-mannered man who often expostulated to me on the intractability of the people in the Uonken area, was never able to count on the backing of a large personal kindred or a large group of his wife's relatives (his wife was from outside the Uonken region) and thus remained a man who filled in when others were absent but exerted little further influence on events.

What kinds of interventions does the capitan make in the life of a particular river system or a particular neighborhood? We have mentioned (Chapter III) Jaime Portales's intervention in a divorce case, and the circumstances of that case point to a principal reason for seeking out a capitan: the absence of any available ties through relatives which can be mobilized in a given situation. This can occur in a variety of situations, not all of them involving conflict. In cases where individuals lack a trade partner but have an urgent need for some trade system items, they may call on a capitan to intercede for them and find an outlet for their goods or find the goods they are seeking (see Thomas, 1972: 31). Persons arriving in Uriman from Kamarata who had no kinsmen in the Uriman area would seek out Raimundo Losada in order to try to arrange transport upriver, for example, for trading or attendance at ceremonies.

The contrast of the mediating and facilitating functions of the capitan with the lack of any organizing functions in economic life is somewhat striking. This was nowhere better illustrated than at a mining camp on the Caroni below Uriman in September, 1970, when Losada's attempt to organize a stretch of streambed "for Pemon only" failed almost immediately. Many Pemon were in partnership with criollo miners, and even those in partnership with other Pemon preferred to stick with their own square of diggings wherever they had set down originally. The helter-skelter nature of the alluvial mining camp was probably a major factor in this failure, but traditional economic life confirms the inability of the capitan to mobilize more than the totality of his own settlement mates (and even that infrequently) for a barbasco fishing party or the buildup of a food and *cachiri* supply for a party.

The capitan may call an assembly of persons from throughout his river area (e.g. the Karuai River valley area, the Uriman area including the Caroni upstream and downstream from Uriman proper for the distance of a day's canoe travel, paddling) to discuss problems or air grievances. I have only been present at one such gathering (in Maikanden in early 1971), which will be discussed in detail in Chapter V. These gatherings are infrequent, and only those attend who have some interest in the proceedings. From informants' accounts, there is no formal sequence of events during these assemblies, though individuals generally speak in turn and without interruption. The capitan may summon the gathering but after it starts it may take its own course. If it is an airing of grievances and accusations are being made, peripheral conversations occur on the fringes. The capitan may attempt to sway opinion, but no action other than verbal is usually taken by those assembled. The assembly dissolves after several hours and, as in the case of Raimundo Losada's installation as capitan, may simply have expressed the results of a long process of getting rid of those who have been deceitful (*kaimayek*, or lying).

In instances where a capitan wishes to take action against a specific individual, he must do so by mobilizing his own settlement mates and members of his own and his wife's personal kindreds (usually members of what we have called the core kindred). Or he may be able to recruit those from his own neighborhood who have a similar animus against the person. In any case, if he goes to the extent of attempting to do away with his enemy or to damage seriously that individual's home or settlement, he runs the same risk of retaliation as anyone else (see Chapter V). His prestige as a capitan will not allow him to mobilize individuals who wish to remain apart from a conflict. This may include even fellow residents of the same settlement, who refuse to take part on the grounds that they themselves have not been prejudiced by the actions of the people aligned against the capitan. This is not simply a "mind your own business" mentality, since those who dissociate themselves from a capitan's efforts to force out an opponent (either a leader of some kind or just an ordinary person) from his local area may be quite adamant that if they or their family are done any harm by the opponent, they will take action against him on their own. The capitan may well be ranged against an opponent and get help from a distant river area (in one case to be considered in Chapter V, a capitan from the Karuai River valley sought the aid of a prominent man in the Uaiparu area, a tributary of the upper Icabaru, some three of four hard days' travel away), at the same time that members of his own settlement refuse to participate in the dispute. The capitan, then, if he wishes to mobilize support against an individual beyond that of his own personal kindred, must successfully convince people of abuses by the individual he opposes. We have seen the place of "speaking badly" or "speaking lies" by incumbents in Raimundo Losada's account of how he came to be capitan. It was only the connection of this "speaking badly" with the attempt to obtain an inordinate number of wives which enabled Losada to push forward, however.

A man who ends up in the status of capitan must not only have the requisite backing of numerous wife's relatives and own relatives but must also be able to demonstrate the infringement of some crucial values (justice in the marriage system, speaking well and truly) on the part of the incumbents, if they are still alive. The situation in Uonken in which the area was without a regional leader for about four years indicates that there is no immediate need necessarily felt to fill such a position. Landaeta still exercised some influence and was considered a capitan by some at least 11 years after Losada's installation. This shows that there is no clear demarcation of spheres of influence — there is no competitive exclusion going on, and old capitanes may hang on with a few adherents, fade away, or even maintain considerable influence after the accession of a new capitan. Losada's relationship with Landaeta is one of half-distance, half-alliance (with his son's marriage to Landaeta's daughter as cement). We shall see that competition among leaders only really becomes visible when multiple domains of leadership are involved and the supernatural comes into play.

Taren Esak

Taren, or magical invocations, are verbal spells with creative or prophylactic efficacy. There are numerous *taren* for specific situations, such as to aid in the birth of a child, to counter the bite of various snakes, against headaches, stomach aches, and so on. *Taren* are held or owned by individuals, who teach them to others at their own discretion. A large number of *taren* pertain to safeguarding the welfare of small children, either by preventing their parents' activities from having ill effects on them and causing the loss of their souls or by directly preventing such things as fevers, diarrhea, and other infant maladies. Armellada (1972: 17) classifies *taren* as those which do good versus those which do harm. Under the first category he lists four subcategories: those used to prevent something bad from happening, those which cause the evil to rebound against the evildoer, those which cause the evil to go back to wherever it came from, and those used to acquire desirable qualities or skills. The actual saying or performance of *taren* is accompanied by ritual blowing (see Butt, 1956, for a description of the "blowing" procedure used among the Akawaio of Guyana, eastern neighbors of the Pemon). In almost all cases the actual performance of *taren* is as private as possible, and in many cases the person performing *taren* will remove himself to the forest, or at least outside the house. The transmission of *taren* from teacher to learner is on a strictly one-to-one basis, and privacy of the interaction is paramount. One man, whom I had known for some time but whose knowledge of *taren* I was unaware of, never made any move to discuss any of this knowledge with me (though I had discussed many aspects of community life with him previously, including talk of spiritual matters) until one day when we found ourselves walking together along a deserted stretch of savanna for an hour or so. At that point he told me that it was unwise to be without at least some knowledge of *taren* and recited some for me, with the intention of continuing the instruction in private at a later time.

The *taren esak* is a practitioner who knows a large number of *taren* and who may be called in by others to practice them for a sick or needful individual. Many Pemon know a few *taren* (some of the more common spells against recurrent ordinary maladies), and, as Armellada (1972: 21) notes, Pemon shamans are principal repositories of *taren*. Nevertheless, there are individual *taren esak* who are not shamans but who are known as practitioners. *Taren esak* may be men or women, and the only criteria for the status is the extent of one's knowledge. Both of the *taren esak* whom I have known were not particularly prominent men, and one of them was rather withdrawn though well respected for his competence. One of these men had married into the Old Mission settlement from his natal area three days east on the Kukenan River. He stayed on in the Old Mission settlement long after his father-in-law had died and many of his wife's siblings had drifted away. His place in the settlement was assured by his ritual knowledge, and the lack of any members of his own personal kindred other than his wife's siblings in the area was not a problem for him. Given the value of his knowledge of *taren*, this outsider was fully a part of the Old Mission settlement.

In one case which occured during my stay in the Uonken region, a young man was bitten by a snake and was brought in to the Old Mission settlement. During the three days before the man died, a *taren esak* from the settlement worked with him (in private), but to no avail. The *taren esak* told me rather bitterly that the *taren* were of no avail and that this was not an ordinary case of snakebite but that Kanaima (the spirit of evil) was involved. His statements cannot be dismissed as mere papering over of a failure, since all of the dead man's relatives and his fellow residents of the settlement concurred that this was the case (others from elsewhere in the Karuai River valley were also adamant that the man's death was attributable to Kanaima: see Chapter V).

The *taren esak* may be a principal actor in a diagnosis of Kanaima, with the attendant consequences that this diagnosis entails. While ultimately all death and serious illness are due to Kanaima, the nature of the specific Kanaima which caused an individual's death is very important for his or her relatives and fellow residents of the settlement. If the Kanaima is judged to be an individual from another ethnic group (the Makuxi, southern neighbors of the Pemon, are often so designated), suitable reasons for this "distancing" of evil beyond the bounds of Pemon society must be found. If the affected (or deceased) individual had any contact with Makuxi, Ingariko, or Akawaio in the past, this contact will probably be invoked to explain the origin of the Kanaima which "got" (Pemon *apiichi*, literally to take or to grasp) him.

The *taren esak* will reach his diagnosis in accord with other members of the settlement. In the case mentioned above, for example, the *taren esak* and other people, especially the dying man's brother, his brother's wife's relatives, and another Old Mission resident spent hours discussing the case outside the room where the dying man was lying in his hammock. The final version which came out found the origin of the Kanaima to be a Makuxi man who had had a dispute with the dying man several years before in the southern part of the territory (near Santa Elena). The dying man's wife reported that some three or four days before her husband was bitten, a Makuxi man had come to the house asking after her husband. When she told him that her husband was not around, he disappeared and was not seen again. In this case, the final diagnosis that this Makuxi had been responsible for the death was made by an Old Mission resident (not the *taren esak*) who remembered that the dead man had had an altercation with a Makuxi in Santa Elena several years before.

The *taren esak* initiates the process leading to the assigning of responsibility to an outside party, but does not attempt any divination (which is not in the province of the *taren esak* to do). The *taren esak* is a technical specialist who will not go beyond the limits of his technical knowledge. In particular, if he does not know a particular *taren* for the malady or the remedy sought, he will generally recommend that another person be sought out to perform *taren*. There is no notion of a trial run, or experimentation, in the application of *taren* — either you know it or you don't, and if you don't you had better not enter in and muck around. Once the practitioner has learned the formula, he must be careful and strict in its application, but there is no latitude for applying a formula that doesn't fit the case and hoping it will work. There are both more generalized and more specific *taren* — for example, some *taren* will work against the bite of any kind of snake — but most *taren* (see Armellada, 1972: 27-38) are quite limited in scope (e.g. *taren* "to be able to cut down bananas, when one's child is just recently born").

The *taren esak* is limited by his medium, then, and may seek to augment his stature by an additive increase of knowledge. *Taren* are mostly thought of as a kind of security for the individual, as my friend indicated when he told me that it was unwise to be without at least some knowledge of *taren*.

Shamans

Pemon shamans are primarily curing specialists, but their contact with the spirit world makes them inherently political actors to some extent. Their interventions in affairs which have implications beyond their own settlements can be quite complex and have ramifications far beyond their curing role.

The spirit and soul concepts which are the basis of shamanic power and influence relate often to the *mawari*, or spirits who look like people and live in the tops of mountains. The *mawari* are shadowy folk who look just like Pemon and who spend their time singing and dancing in their mountaintop houses. The white blazes on the high faces of the mesas and mountains of the Caroni and Gran Sabana are the windows of these *mawari* houses. *Mawari* are dangerous, since they may steal souls and cause illness. One of the three principal souls, the *kamong*, or shadow soul, leaves a person's body upon death and goes to the mountaintops, adding to the number of the *mawari*. The *mawari* are stealers of the *tyekaton* soul (heart soul or breath soul), and it is the loss of the *tyekaton* soul which can cause illness. If the *tyekaton* soul, which can be stolen or go wandering from the body in dreams, is not recovered in time, death will result. One old shaman averred that people have at least three principal souls: the *tyekaton* soul, the *kamong* soul, and the *enuto*, or eye soul, which can be seen as a very small man deep in the pupil of the eye. He said that the *tyekaton* soul normally goes to the sky, or to God (he used the Spanish word *Dios* at that point) when a person dies, while the *kamong* soul goes to the *mawari*.

Shamans must possess knowledge of how to marshal their various helper spirits, ascend the ladder (*yekatɨ*) to the sky, and communicate with *kawai*, the tobacco spirit (also *kawai tamo* in some informants' accounts, literally the "grandfather of tobacco") and head of the other helper spirits. During a curing ceremony the shaman mixes up various plants in a kind of thick soup which he uses to intoxicate himself by taking it through the nostrils. In Pemon thinking the plants in the mixture are the helper spirits and are very potent forces which the individual shaman must be able to control. In the course of his trance the shaman

must encounter the *mawari*, as well as the spirit helpers of other shamans, and must be able to fend off and manipulate both the *mawari*
and the spirit helpers of other shamans in order to accomplish the cure.
While *kawai tamo* is the head of the helper spirits, the shaman usually
contacts *kawai tamo* in order to have him direct the plant spirit *ayuk* to
bring about the actual rescue of the soul from the *mawari*. In a séance
the shaman will actually call certain *mawari* and interact with them, in
order to determine the location of the missing soul and how best to go
about getting it back. The four plants most frequently mentioned as
spirit helpers are *ayuk, saraorai, araradek*, and *alichai*. These all go into
the mixture taken by the shaman. *Ayuk* is described as the "director of
all the *mawari*. The *mawari* can control sicknesses. *Ayuk* is the capitan
of the *mawari*."

There are no prerequisites for becoming a shaman other than the desire to do so and the ability to find a suitable teacher among currently
practicing shamans. Some informants claim that certain shamans have
learned their craft directly from the *mawari*, bypassing human
teachers. In any case, the use of the proper plants and their corresponding helper spirits is deemed to be fundamental to the process of learning
to be a shaman. In the case of Gaspar, a shaman from the Uriman area,
an interesting pattern of transmission of the status occurred. Gaspar
married into the Antabari River area west of Uriman. His father-in-law
and his mother-in-law together taught him to be a shaman. (Other informants said that his mother-in-law was his most important teacher.)
Gaspar's son's wife Agnes was also a shaman though it was never clear if
Agnes learned all of her knowledge from Gaspar or through people in
her natal area, Kamarata. In all cases the description of the training
period emphasizes that the novice learns from the *mawari* to a greater
or lesser extent, but in most cases there is some practicing shaman guid-
ing the novice. Multiple teachers are not uncommon for a single individual. Gaspar mentioned that he had learned from a man in the Uriman
area and beyond. One informant, describing the workings of shamans,
expressed himself this way about their abilities:

> There are some who learn only in order to cure. Not to kill others, only to
> cure people. There are others who learn in order to do evil. But they learn
> with the same plants, with the same leaves of trees. And there are others
> who do not like to do bad things, they undertake curing, and the people give
> them a fee. Sometimes they cure one for free. For example Gaspar, he is an
> old man, and he learned much, and people are saying many things about
> him, that he is going bad. One doesn't know what he is doing, at least we
> don't know what he is doing. When he does his work, one doesn't know. But
> some others who know what he does, they say that he is doing bad things,
> killing people, that he is a danger to other people. They themselves (the
> shamans) do their work. But if I do not know how to work like they do then I
> don't know what they are doing. One doesn't know. For this reason other

people are saying, why nowadays should one learn what Gaspar knows . . .
this should be stopped, they should quit working, they should not work.

Abel Portela, a shaman from the Avikara area, traveled much more
widely than Gaspar (Gaspar was quite old when I met him in 1975, probably over 60) and was in close contact with the settlements in the lower
Karuai River and its tributary, the Makarupai, in the Uonken region.
Abel was known in Uonken and in Uriman as a "curing" shaman, but
many alleged that his knowledge was much less than that of Gaspar and
Agnes. Raimundo Losado, capitan in the Uriman area, stated at one
point that he was a good shaman but capable of being overpowered by
those like Gaspar and Agnes with superior knowledge.

Some shamans, like Flavio Mateos of the Aripichi Falls area upstream
from Uriman, are placed in virtual exile in a certain area (which may be
called an area of asylum for them) and seldom travel outside of it. The
range of movement of a particular shaman is often an indicator of his
current standing as either welcomed or feared, as well as of his connections to clients in river areas other than his own. Flavio, for example, is
closely connected (by kinship ties) to residents of the Old Mission settlement area in the Uonken region, as well as to other settlements to the
northwest of the Old Mission, yet has not been able to travel in that area
since 1971.

Connections between shamans and other persons who are in leadership statuses may be quite direct. Valerio Ojeda, the big trader who in
1975 was considered a kind of "capitan segundo" to Raimundo Losada
in the Uriman area, claimed that Gaspar was an "elder brother,"
though neither of them could show any genealogical relationship to
each other. These kinds of connections can best be visualized through
the charts in Figures 14 and 15, which show the relationships among
several well-known shamans and other leaders in the Uonken and Uriman areas during the period 1970-75. Both genealogical and nongene-
alogical relationships are shown. Two of the shamans, Abel and Flavio,
have multiple ties to present and past leaders in both areas. Flavio resides close to Eduardo Landaeta, the former capitan, while Abel is called
"brother-in-law" by Losada and has one wife who is the daughter of
capitan Jaime Portales's wife's sister (Abel is a WMZS and a WZDH to
Jaime; the latter tie makes Abel a "DH" or son-in-law, while the former
tie makes Abel a "brother-in-law," which is the relationship which actually obtains). Gaspar, as previously mentioned, is "elder brother" to
Valerio Ojeda; he is tangential to the set of relationships linking Justo
Isorio, Landaeta, Losada, Flavio, and Abel. However, his SW Agnes is
perhaps the most renowned shaman in the areas of Kamarata and
Uriman, and her influence extends much farther than any of the other
shamans mentioned.

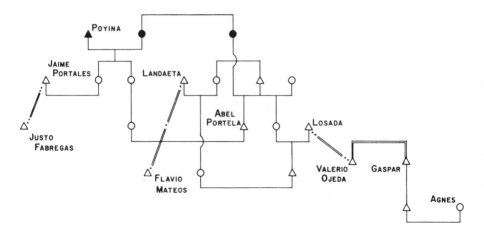

Figure 14. Relationships of capitanes and shamans in the middle Caroni and Uonken regions.

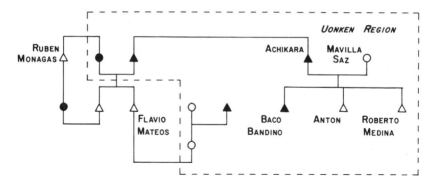

Note: Some members of sibling sets omitted for clarity.

Figure 15. Selected genealogical relationships of shaman Flavio Mateos.

These interconnections among shamans and past and present capitanes cannot be construed to form some kind of "power elite" or core leadership group in the central portion of the tribal territory. Valerio Ojeda's position is that of relative outsider. Though he has built up a group of active sons-in-law over the period 1965-75, he is limited in his influence by his lack of siblings in the area and the fact that his wife's relatives are three days' walk away in Kamarata. This means that Gaspar cannot count on a capitan for support, and thus his reclusive and retiring habits are his only security against potential accusations. His isolation, of course, simultaneously provides his accusers with seeming support for arguments that he is up to no good.

Over the period 1970-75 the following configuration of relationships among shamans and capitanes in the middle Caroni and Karuai River areas (Uriman and Uonken regions) obtained:

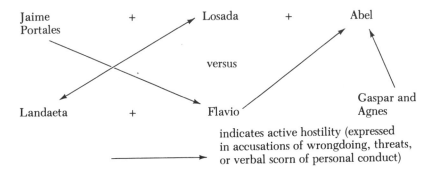

Each of these individuals depends on a fluid group of siblings and in-laws (usually wife's siblings, their spouses and children, and own sons-in-law and daughters) or (for shamans) clients for support. In any conflict people will have in mind the set of interrelationships among the shamans and other leaders as a principal consideration. Whether or not any shaman or capitan can mobilize his own settlement mates, sons-in-law, and wife's (or husband's) relatives depends as much on these interconnections among leaders as it does on a particular interpretation of who did what to whom. This is not only because of the "cross-cutting ties" which form such a prominent part of anthropological discussions of conflict (Losada's son's marriage to Landaeta's daughter is such a tie), but because each leader's supporters may split up and individual supporters back out if they feel that the potential for harm to their own immediate family (primary relatives) is too great. In Chapter V we will amplify the above diagram and show how various supporters of each of the individuals in the configuration responded to conflicts and why.

Prophets

Prophets are a phenomenon of the times since the advent of the Hallelujah movement among the Carib-speaking peoples of the Guiana Highlands in the latter part of the nineteenth century. Since that time there have been men and women Pemon prophets of the Hallelujah movement, of the Chochiman cult, and most recently of the San Miguel movement (see Thomas, 1976). Prophets, as Butt (1960; A. Colson, 1971) has shown, appropriated the techniques of the shaman and transformed the shamanic soul flight into a flight of the soul to heaven in search of redemptive contact with the Christian God. After their visionary experience they become ceremonial leaders who direct chants and dances, praying and purification. The current (1975) San Miguel movement provides an example of the prophet phenomenon which is immediately accessible to study.

On December 8, 1971, an old woman in Icabaru, in the extreme south of the Caroni drainage, had a vision while working in her manioc plot. She was visited by a white-clothed figure (later identified as San Miguel) who identified himself as "angel, archangel" and who announced the forthcoming end of the world. Much impressed by her story, a man recorded songs made up by the old woman praising San Miguel (on a cassette recorder), and spread them about on his travels in the Caroni area upstream and downstream from Uriman. This man had a long history of association with the Capuchin missionaries and with Roman Catholic religious doctrine. He proselytized for over two years, spreading the word of the old woman's vision of San Miguel and her songs. He did not, however, have visionary experiences himself during this period.

During Easter Week, 1974, the proselytizer was celebrating the Holy Week in a settlement now known as San Miguel upstream from Uriman. One of the inhabitants, a young man who had taken the songs of the old woman particularly to heart, by dint of praying and dancing himself into a trance state, achieved a vision — this time a soul flight into the sky, not a "visitation" after the manner of the old woman — in which his spirit ascended to the "door of heaven" and spoke with San Pedro, San Miguel and other figures of the Roman Catholic religious cosmos. On this journey his soul was accompanied by two angels (analogous to the shaman's helper spirits); in one of his subsequent visions (over the following few months) an angel gave him a plan of the cosmos, which he codified into a drawing. The drawing is truly syncretic, incorporating shamanistic elements and elements from past religious movements as well as Roman Catholic imagery. The prophet includes in it a "paradise of the shamans" which contains Kanaima, the tobacco plant, and other plants associated with the shaman's helper spirits. Upon awakening from his initial vision, the young man stated, "What San Miguel asks of us is to build a church." He thereupon began gathering his kin and affines from the immediate area into a large settlement centered on a church, built in the same oblong style as a Pemon dwelling but much larger.

By June, 1975, the settlement, now known as San Miguel, comprised over 30 structures and an estimated 80-90 people, about twice the normal maximum for a Pemon settlement. Prayer and preaching services were held in the "chochi" (church), and ritual dances, of the same form as those of the Chochiman cult but incorporating new songs in honor of

San Miguel, were held in a small structure near the church. This young man, his authority legitimated by the fact of his vision as well as by its content (he had spoken to San Miguel and interpreted the archangel's wishes to the people), immediately became the leader of the San Miguel movement, entering into a kind of joint leadership with the proselytizer previously mentioned. The latter acknowledged the validity of the prophet's vision and leadership. The proselytizer continued his recruiting on behalf of the movement in his travels in the Uriman and neighboring areas.

The prophet maintained sexual abstinence for a year after his initial vision, for the purpose of self-purification. He continually created new songs to accompany the Chochiman-type dances which were incorporated into the San Miguel religious observances. With the aid of an outboard motor provided by a parallel cousin, he undertook trips up- and downriver to distant settlements for the purposes of preaching, proselytizing, and settling disputes among followers. He also undertook to cure the illnesses of followers by means of soul flight and the rescue of souls in dreams. In these curing efforts (which apparently did not occur with earlier prophets of the Hallelujah and Chochiman movements), the San Miguel prophet would seek out the places where evil shamans had hidden souls, battle the spirits of the evil shamans with his own spiritual strength (derived from the figures of the Roman Catholic cosmos), and rescue the soul of the ill person.

The bases of the San Miguel prophet's leadership include his large personal kindred (the sibling sets depicted in Figure 16 are huge), his successful achievement of ritual purity, his mobility up- and downriver, the fact that he speaks only Pemon and thus emphasizes traditional qualities, his soul-flight cures of followers, setting of the forms of prayers, and continual invention of new chants to accompany the San Miguel ritual dances. Situational determinants of his emergence include the ever-deepening hostility between capitanes and shamans in the Uonken and Uriman areas, and the spatial position of his natal area (now the site of the San Miguel settlement), which lies almost midway between the home areas of Landaeta on the one hand and Losada on the other. Losada became an adherent of the San Miguel movement, and the San Miguel prophet actually performed prayer ceremonies in Uriman in the course of his voyages up- and downriver.

The larger than normal settlement at San Miguel represents a coalescence of people formerly spread up- and downriver from the San Miguel site. While many of the inhabitants consider themselves permanent in the place, they also maintain their old residences farther afield, and return to them to harvest manioc and perform other subsistence tasks at times. This is in keeping with a long-established pattern in Pemon society in which a central location is used as a ceremonial center but may not be a

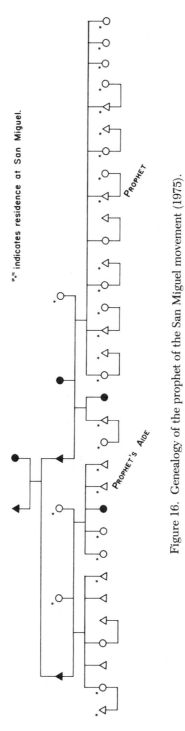

"•" indicates residence at San Miguel.

Figure 16. Genealogy of the prophet of the San Miguel movement (1975).

permanent place of residence over a long span of years. The San Miguel prophet is a young man, moves about a lot, and has taken an active role in settling disputes among followers of the movement as far away as three and four days' travel downstream from the San Miguel settlement. A large part of the successful spread of the movement can be attributed to his youth (he is about 22 years of age) and spatial mobility.

A somewhat different role is found in considering the leader of the Hallelujah ceremonies in the valley of the Karuai during the year 1970. An older woman who had lived much of her life in the upper Karuai drainage not far from the present mission site of Kavanayen, she was in her mid-60s in 1970, head of a large household which included her eldest daughter (then widowed) and granddaughter and her granddaughter's husband. The household formed part of a settlement that included her elder daughter's sons and their wives. Surprisingly, though the woman herself was venerated by the people in the valley of the Karuai, her descendants were not popular in the area. Her eldest daughter, who was in a sense an understudy to the prophet, was said by many not to have the ability to learn the chants, stories, and ceremonies. The prophet, whom we shall call Consuelo, had learned the Hallelujah religion as a young woman in the area of Kavanayen in the 1930s; she had a vision after a violent separation from her husband, and eventually came to be acknowledged as a *santa* (saint).

In the valley of the Karuai there was no fixed congregation for the Hallelujah ceremonies, and people would come from as far as two or three hours' travel (on foot or by canoe) to participate in the ceremonies on Saturday and Sunday afternoons from October through December, when the ceremonies are most intense and most regularly held. The ceremonies are long rounds of dancing, accompanied by chants, and when the prophet is present there is an interim period in which the prophet recites aloud a Christian story (e.g. the story of Noah and the flood) and the congregation joins in at the end with an antiphon. Families bring *cachiri* by the gourd, people come in and out, fall into trances after dancing, all with an informality which makes our word "ritual" seem somewhat inappropriate. The prophet's role is central in all this (though dancing does go on on days when she is not present, since everyone knows the steps and the chants) and she may, if she wishes, prohibit outsiders (e.g. criollos) from being present.

Her status cannot be passed on to her daughter except by acknowledgment from participants in the ceremonies that the daughter in fact knows enough. (A frequent comment about the daughter and another woman who was an understudy was that neither one of them knew enough to become prophets). It is interesting that, in the case of this Hallelujah prophet (who herself had had a vision early on), there was no talk of the necessity for the understudies to achieve a vision, but only to know the content of the stories and ceremonies and chants in utmost detail. The prophet herself had presided over ceremonies in different areas (including the Kamarata area, the area near her natal settlement south of Kavanayen, and the Uonken region) and changed homesites often with the successive moves of her children and grandchildren. Here was no fixed base of operations, as in the case of the San Miguel prophet, but only a strong reputation which allowed her to preside over different congregations in areas far removed from one another during the course of many years. The Hallelujah religion dates from the late nineteenth century and was still in the process of spreading among the Pemon when Consuelo learned it in the 1930s; a comparison with the San Miguel prophet is somewhat difficult since we are looking at two different movements and two different prophets at varying points in their trajectories. Some differences stand out, since the San Miguel prophet is more closely tied to a strong base of support among members of his own sibling set and his parallel cousins who form the core of the San Miguel settlement. Consuelo's prestige makes her the unquestioned head of the ceremonies during times set aside for them, and during ceremonial periods she is in effect the center of the Maikanden settlement, and of the people who come from other settlements to attend. The capitan is much in awe of her and is a follower in this situation.

A parallel exists in the relationship between capitan Losada and the prophet of the San Miguel movement. Since the advent of the San Miguel prophet in early 1974, Losada has set aside a former dwelling in his settlement as a place for San Miguel observances, and the prophet leads prayers and chants there when he stops by on his way up- or downriver. This does not mean that the prophet exercises influence in everyday affairs in the Uriman area, or that the prophet is involved in any direct confrontations with shamans (except in soul flights in dreams), as the capitan himself may be.

The major point about prophetic leadership is that it requires only the acceptance of the prophet's vision as a valid revelatory experience (this acceptance is conditional on the prophet's personal purity, sexual abstinence for a time, eschewing the acquisition of numerous wives, and knowledge of ritual). In Pemon society it is not necessarily related to any particular organizational base, but we will argue in the following section that it may well be contingent on a particular type of conflict, which is recurrent in Pemon society.

Coexistence and Contests among Leaders

The types of expertise and the organizational support which different Pemon leaders require to maintain themselves as leaders are overlapping but not congruent. There are mutually exclusive requirements which make it difficult for one individual to unite in himself the necessary qualities to be accorded several leadership statuses simultaneously. The tendencies toward polygyny exhibited by capitanes and shamans are incompatible with the stringent need for ritual purity characteristic of the prophet, and the shaman and capitan are different from the prophet in this dimension of purity. In secular affairs the nearby support which the capitan needs in the form of siblings and wife's relatives close at hand contrasts with the need for far-flung affinal ties which must be maintained by the big trader if he is to be successful. While some individuals have combined elements of both statuses, as in the case of Valerio Ojeda, success in one means ultimate relinquishment of success in the other. Ojeda, for example, as he becomes more involved in his role as "capitan segundo" in the Uriman area, must gradually let go of the long-distance connections which have been his mainstay as a trader.

These incompatibilities among the requirements for various leadership statuses occur even in cases where one status can be thought of as incorporating elements of another. The rather mechanical magic of the *taren esak* is often a tool used by the shaman (shamans are repositories of *taren*), but the shaman must go beyond this kind of knowledge to an interactive stance with respect to the spirit world. If one proceeds additively, accumulating more and more *taren*, one can be a good *taren esak* but not a good shaman. The knowledge possessed by the shaman is thus different not only in quantity but also in quality and is based on a different technique, a different kind of training. While the *taren esak* can initiate the process of determining the origin of sorcery, the shaman can actually combat its effects. There is thus a contrast between the mechanical knowledge possessed by the *taren esak*, which is potentially additive, and the interactive knowledge possessed by the shaman, which is also potentially additive but which involves a much greater degree of personal responsibility for outcomes.

Likewise the two principal leaders in spiritual affairs, shamans and prophets, exhibit different requirements as to the kinds of knowledge and organization which they must command. The prophet is a representative of generalized, redemptive power which is arrived at through self-purification, and his knowledge is directed toward helping himself and his followers to achieve that purification. To that end he must be able to demonstrate through knowledge and conduct that purification is possible. The prophet may disgrace himself, but then is no longer a prophet (one competitor of the San Miguel prophet, who had achieved a vision, disgraced himself by abusing a woman and slunk away). Prophetic knowledge is by definition a single-edged sword, which can only be employed for good, and that mostly in collective manifestations aiming at purity. Shamanic knowledge, on the other hand, is a two-edged sword, which contains all the potential volatility of the individual shaman, his personality and situation. It is also highly personal, as is prophetic knowledge, but much more private in character. The outlines of how shamans work are known to all, the details only to the shamans themselves. It is this control of technique, not just of information, which provides the shaman with his power.

The shaman is almost always tied to a capitan, either in support or in opposition, while the prophet subsumes the capitan as a participant in a movement. Prophetic leadership is, in relation to the capitan, limited to ceremonial observances, but the prophet as leader of a movement must maintain some of the organizational bases of leadership which also characterize the capitan. The San Miguel prophet, for example, appropriated techniques from the roles of shaman and capitan. From the shaman's repertory he took the acquisition of spiritual power by means of the soul flight and the appropriation of the role of "good" shaman by rescuing souls during soul flight in dreams. From the repertory of the capitan he took the function of settling disputes among followers (a takeover of the capitan's "father of his people" role) and the gathering of a large kin-based settlement around him as a launching pad for his proselytizing efforts.

Neither the shaman nor the capitan normally operates before a large congregation, with the rare exception of a convocation called by the capitan to air grievances. By comparison with the prophet, they are not often public performers. The shaman and the prophet deepen their spiritual knowledge over the years, while the capitan (despite whatever increase in personal acumen and interpersonal skills he may attain) is continually forming and re-forming his settlement mates and affines into a base of support. As we have seen by the comparison of the San Miguel prophet with Consuelo, the Hallelujah prophet, a prophet may, as the years go on, substitute ever-increasing personal prestige for the original local support group of settlement mates, siblings, and affines. That is, the prophet may successfully trade on increasing knowledge and still be able to count on a variable and changing constituency in different locations over the course of a lifetime. The same holds true, to a certain extent, for shamans. Knowledge may substitute for organizational skills in the sacred realm, but it cannot do so for the capitan and big trader.

Likewise, kinds of knowledge are, to a certain extent, incommensurable in practice. The prophet, though adopting shamanic techniques, must combat malevolent shamans with such symbols as the Holy Trinity; angels are substituted for helper spirits, but the San Miguel prophet said that it was extremely exhausting to have to combat malevolence and retrieve the souls of the sick, and that he could not carry it out often, since it required a deep trance state which sapped his strength. The shaman, as we have seen, commands *taren* as well as other knowledge of helper spirits and the *mawari*, but cannot invoke the force of purity or the Christian God to back up this kind of knowledge. Again, similar techniques, but with different content, result in different power types — incommensurability is found in content and intent (good and evil versus only good), not only in technique.

The problem of the advent of prophets has been a central interest of anthropologists for some time. While we don't propose a solution here, some portions of the Pemon experience indicate that the need for and potential accessibility of certain forms of generalized power on the part of the community at large may contribute to the rise of prophetic leadership. The rise of the San Miguel prophet and the San Miguel movement came at a time in which conflicts between capitanes and some (if not all) shamans in the central portions of the tribal territory were becoming very grave. We have seen the statement of one informant to the effect that young persons should not learn of shamanism, that this kind of knowledge was too dangerous and should be allowed to die out (see above, pp. 143–44.).

The conflicts between capitanes and certain shamans (Flavio, Gaspar, and Agnes) can best be thought of as the product of several forces which ranged one alignment of capitanes, together with the shaman Abel, against another alignment of the former capitan Landaeta, together with his settlement mates and the shaman Flavio. Ojeda, who is a "younger brother" of Gaspar, falls somewhere in the middle of this conflict. The conflict was a continuation of long-standing personal differences. We have noted that Losada edged Landaeta out of a principal leadership position in the period 1958–60, while Landaeta retained much of his influence along the middle Caroni through the middle 1960s. Flavio, meanwhile, had married into Landaeta's settlement in the Aripichi Falls area while also, in the late 1960s, marrying a woman from the northwest part of the Uonken region (like most shamans, Flavio is polygynous). His attempt to marry a third wife, a young woman who lived in a settlement at the mouth of the Karuai River, was defeated by both the woman herself and her father in 1968–69. The people at the mouth of the Karuai were aligned against Flavio on several counts (we will detail the structural relationships below), and by 1970 Flavio was more or less a refugee in the Aripichi Falls area, since the Karuaiken people threw in their lot with Jaime Portales against him.

If, as Burridge (1969b: 5) notes, religion is concerned with "the systematic ordering of different kinds of power," the current (1970–75) hostility toward shamans among the Pemon, particularly on the part of the capitanes, becomes intelligible. When the general welfare of the community is threatened (for example, in a time of widespread sickness as in 1970–71), the capitan as a secular prestige figure is looked to for some response. His "scapegoating" of the shaman seems a reasonable alternative, but he cannot condemn all shamans, only those against whom he can make a case. The prophet solves this problem by using shamanic techniques in an idiom of only "good" supernatural power, taking over the role of the "good" or curing shaman. In a sense, in contemporary Pemon society the prophet is the dialectical synthesis of the opposing forces of the capitan and the shaman, through which control over the supernatural is reasserted in the name of the *benefit* of the *entire* community (in fact of the whole tribe, ultimately). The secular leadership of the capitan is to some extent taken over by the prophet (though only temporarily, in most instances). The capitan becomes a follower of the movement, acceding to the need for this kind of intervention, and this kind of leader, in the crisis. Later, as things quiet down, the secular portion of the prophet's role diminishes, and the capitan, together with his sometime ally/sometime opponent the shaman, comes back into prominence to handle the affairs of everyday (small-scale conflicts, disease, and so on). Pemon prophets emerge in the interstices of the traditional leadership statuses, and create a new position (the prophet phenomenon keeps coming back, though particular prophets come and go) which cycles through time in accordance with conflicts between the incumbents of the other principal leadership statuses.

The prophet, despite his advocacy of syncretic religious forms which are heavily Christian in content, is a more traditional figure than the capitan in terms of contact with criollos. Many capitanes have spent considerable time outside the tribal territory in essentially criollo environments (witness Losada's personal history, as well as that of Alejo Calcaño; many other cases could be adduced). The prophet, by contrast, has adopted the Christian religious forms for Pemon use while remaining by and large apart from contact with criollos.

Control of one leader by another, either of the same type (as in the case of capitanes of greater or lesser relative prestige) or of different types (as of a capitan by a prophet), is temporary. This is the best characterization of what may be called "situational" leadership; the control of one leader by another can only obtain as long as there is a specific situation which calls such control into being. Usually this situation involves more than just the leaders themselves: if it is a sorcery accusation, multiple families are involved and the capitan comes to the fore; if a ceremony, the prophet. The situations which may allow one leader to be in control for a specific span of time do not necessarily relate to an external threat, as is the case with many segmentary systems. Once a conflict has spread beyond a single river area (region), it will involve several capitanes, whether or not the contending parties are all in one river area.

The reasons for the coexistence of various leaders in contemporary Pemon society are mostly functions of the different types of expertise that they represent. Their contests, on the other hand, occur because there is no way in which power, either of the organizational, secular variety or the manipulative, supernatural variety, can be strictly parceled out in walled-off compartments. There are some basic ideals of types of power in Pemon society (see Chapter VI), and they are distinguishable. But people persist in juggling boundaries and invoking one type of power in a situation in which another type is called for by normative convention. (A principal example of this is the attempt on the part of shamans and capitanes to obtain inordinate numbers of wives using threats of some kind of outside power — usually related to criollos in the case of capitanes, as we have seen in the case of Losada's accession to the status, and to direct supernatural threats in the case of shamans, as in Flavio Mateos's effort to obtain a third wife from the settlement at the mouth of the Karuai.) Thus one type of leader can control another only so long as he can contain that other within the bounds of his own expertise and his own definitions of applicable types of power. There are correspondences built in to the connections between various power types at the ideal level (e.g. "*Ayuk* is the capitan of the *mawari*") which seem to presage the attempts by different actors to encompass all types of power under their own aegis, even if only for a short time. This can never hold for long, of course, since an attempt to do this immediately engenders the countermeasure of invoking the traditional views of the propriety of each kind of power "in its place."

Leaders alternately co-exist and attempt to contest the leadership of others in a continual come-and-go between different definitions of applicable kinds of power. There can ultimately be no complete agreement on the specific kind of power to be invoked or looked for in a given incident. For example, whether or not a Kanaima is involved and, if so, what its origin is and what action should be taken are all up for grabs in terms of the personal history of the injured party (or the deceased). Many times (as in the case of the diagnosis of death resulting from snakebite in our account of *taren esak*) the availability close at hand of a particular individual determines the course of the remedial action taken at the time. Over a longer time span, however, the existing configuration of relationships among leaders will make itself felt as specific incidents are placed in the context of the welfare of a particular settlement, neighborhood, and river area. Contests among leaders must recur as an individual leader attempts to gerrymander past incidents into a reality supportive of his own definition of the proper type of power and the

proper type of remedy to be applied when he is dealing with disharmony. There is no finality to the configuration just as there is no finality
to Pemon procedures for remedying personal misconduct, for redress,
for disease, or for evil in general. In a sense, old capitanes never die,
they just fade away (this is certainly the case with Landaeta). We will
find in Chapters V and VI that the same is true for conflict in general,
and that the failure to mobilize which places a limit on conflict extension and generation is both a social structural fact and an ideological
one.

CHAPTER V

Forces of Disharmony

In Pemon life social and personal harmony are intimately connected, and it is impossible to understand the one without the other. There is no public/private distinction which corresponds to our own, but simply more and less widely known happenings, opinions, and personalities. There is no abrupt division but rather a continuum in the number of people, or number of settlements, or number of neighborhoods affected by some piece of knowledge or behavior. To understand conflict, one must understand how small events, domestic squabbles, marriage negotiations between settlements and individuals become larger events, problems which affect other settlements and possibly the region and beyond. Seemingly domestic events can easily be catapulted into what we would consider the public realm without the mobilization of institutional mechanisms such as we find in our own society. An analysis which focuses on levels of violence would omit the bulk of potential sources of dispute which more often than not are "nipped in the bud." Conflict must be explored through Pemon concepts of personal and social harmony, and particularly through the concept of abuse, of what constitutes undesirable conduct and an undesirable personal way of being. Ultimately, illness and malevolence come from outside the individual and outside one's circle of close relatives. The concept of the individual as normally existing in a state of harmony is coupled with the assignment of malevolence to those who are distant (in both genealogical and physical space), quite often to those who are outside the tribe altogether. This distancing of forces of disharmony or malevolence can take several forms, and includes the tendency, described in Chapter III, to define relatedness very narrowly when conflict is at hand.

Illness and Personal Well-Being

Pemon believe that illness is a manifestation of social and personal disequilibrium, and that violations of proper conduct, the failure to observe proper food taboos or restrictions, and intrasettlement or intra-household dislikes between individuals can result in illness. They are of course quite clear that many maladies are of natural, not supernatural, origin, and they practice many secular and practical remedies for specific ills. For example, a tree bark (the tree is known as *kuari*) is cut from the trunk and an infusion made from the sap which is used to treat cuts and wounds. Remedies for specific maladies are referred to in Pemon as *ipik*. Thus *kwasu ipik* means "remedy for diarrhea." The question of personal and social disharmony comes up principally when a person is indisposed or ill for an extended period of time, or when the illness or injury is quite clearly severe. When a person is ill, the person will describe the illness with one of a number of statements, such as the following: *enepe edai* = "I am sick," simply referring to the whole person. A second level of description is embodied in such phrases as *uyevan enepe ichi* = "My stomach (belly) is sick," which refer to specific parts of the body. Finally Pemon refer to specific illnesses, e.g. *Aton pɨk edai* = "I have a cold" or *kwasu pɨk edai* = "I have diarrhea."

Pemon are perfectly well aware of a variety of common maladies and do not attach great importance to them unless they show signs of worsening. If parents of a sick child (and it is recognized that infant maladies such as diarrhea and whooping cough can easily be fatal) do not undertake proper food restrictions (which include in their mildest form refraining from consuming *cachiri* and peppers — the peppers are thought to be "hot" and will thus aggravate the child's "hot" condition; see A. Colson, 1976, for "hot" and "cold" conceptions as related to disease among the neighboring Akawaio of Guyana), then the parents will come in for censure from other persons in their settlement or neighborhood, particularly if the child worsens. Proper care of an infant includes protecting the infant's soul and combatting illness with the proper food restrictions. Pemon will seek out Western medicines if they are available, and have no qualms about being eclectic in the treatment of illness, either their own or that of their children. Pemon will simultaneously undertake dietary restrictions on behalf of an ill infant and administration of whatever physical remedies are at hand.

Ultimately all serious illness and death are thought to be the result of the action of Kanaima, the spirit of evil in all its forms and manifestations. This is perhaps the most difficult Pemon idea for an outsider to grasp, but the following are important dimensions of the concept:

1) Kanaimaton (plural of Kanaima) are beings which can manifest themselves in human or animal form; in addition they may take control of a living person and make that person execute their will. Thus given individuals within the tribe or local area (as well as outside of either of these) may be designated as Kanaima. As Koch-Grunberg (1916–28, III: 92) noted: "The inhabitants of another village on the upper

Surumu . . . were considered by all the other Taulipang as feared poison-mixers and especially their chieftain Dzilawo was notorious among his fellow tribesmen as being Kanaima (a stealthy murderer and wicked sorcerer)."

2) Kanaimaton are the actual or final cause of all serious disease and death. Disease and death are the intrusions of the spirit of evil into a world essentially good as it is constituted.

3) Kanaima can refer to a purely spiritual entity or to an embodiment of that spirit in human or animal form.

4) Individuals of non-Pemon provenience are often imputed to be Kanaimaton. Thus Simpson (1940: 556) states: "Some Maquiritares are Kanaimaton for the Kamarakoto."

5) Kanaimaton can be ordered about by a Pemon shaman. In some cases shamans themselves are reputed to be Kanaima.

6) Kanaimaton are particularly likely to be found in the forest (as contrasted with the savanna) and at night.

Pemon do not recognize the intervention of Kanaima unless disease or mishap takes an untoward turn. They will say, for example, "We don't die of snakebite," and if the bitten individual recovers (using, for example, the application of *taren*), there is seldom any discussion of Kanaima. When things go badly, however, and a person dies from snakebite (or other mishap), discussion begins immediately as to the origin of the Kanaima responsible. It should not be thought that the Kanaima concept is merely a kind of "scapegoat" notion, invoked when all else fails to account for events. Kanaima is a real presence in the lives of the Pemon, a continuing force, and even when no immediate events serve to bring Kanaima into focus, the Pemon are still aware of the potentiality of the spirit of evil (we shall have more to say about the generalized power represented by Kanaima in Chapter VI).

Less potent than Kanaima, but also of grave importance, are *muran*, or charms, magical plants which are thought to have enormous powers, including the power of some plants to grow instantaneously and kill onlookers merely from the sight. Some informants characterize *muran* as "bandits," "things which make an end of us." The primary meaning of *muran* is charm, usually referring to a plant which is rubbed into cuts in the arms or legs to ensure success in hunting (*muran* were formerly used at puberty rites for the purpose of ensuring success in hunting and fishing). However, the magical plants are, particularly by association with the various plants used by shamans (see above, Chapter IV), often thought to be involved in evildoing, and those who use them or acquire them may be suspect. *Muran* have potentially beneficial effects (unlike Kanaima) and must be procured from those who are familiar with the effects of a particular plant. Using them without proper instruction is potentially fatal.

The importance of *muran* for conflict is that their use by a person can be used to impugn the motives and actions of that individual. They are not assumed to have direct effects projected by the user onto another person. That is, *muran* are personal charms which can enhance the power of the user, but are not thought to be like plant spirits which can be sent by the shaman to do his bidding. Their power inheres in the *muran* per se, and cannot be projected by a human being, who can only absorb (with either good or bad effects) the power emanating from the *muran*. *Muran* can be thought of as reinforcers, augmenters of the strength of the individual in particular tasks (mostly hunting, but others as well).

There is somewhat of an overlap between *muran* and *ipik*, with *ipik* pertaining more to the secular realm than *muran*. The fact that an individual employs *ipik*, however, cannot be used to impugn him, nor can it be used in the course of an accusation of wrongdoing. The distinction here is important despite the overlap, since the possession of spiritual efficacy by *muran* is the basis for their importance in accusations of wrongdoing. The more secular *ipik* are not seen as having the potential for evil.

Personal Qualities and States

The powers represented by the various forces of Kanaima, *muran*, and *ipik* are only brought into play when various abuses, deriving from personal qualities which are undesirable, occur. In order to understand the nature of these abuses, it is necessary to understand concepts of desirable and undesirable moral qualities as the Pemon work with them. Most important among these are three notions, those of *kaimayek* (literally "lying"), *sakorope* (literally "angry"), and *amunek* (literally "stingy").

Kaimayek refers only to direct misleading of someone by another (an active lie as opposed to a passive one), and not to the withholding of information which results in detriment to another. Pemon, when discussing an incident which is under dispute, will often preface their statements with the almost ritual *kaimayek eserumɨ neke* (literally "Lies I speak not"), averring the truthfulness of the statements to follow.

Sakorope refers to two distinct, though related, personal characteristics or states. The first is that of being angry and manifesting it. Manifesting anger, to the point of shouting, blows, or other actions directed at others, is extremely strongly reproved in Pemon society. The expected reaction in the face of an insult is that the injured party withdraws and begins to mobilize others in support of the recognition of the injury done him and his vindication. Hence the term *sakorope*, meaning manifestation of anger, also means withdrawn, removed from social interaction. The term refers not only to these states but also to anger and being withdrawn as personal qualities. Thus there are angry persons who habitually get involved in contention and fisticuffs or who are habitually withdrawn and antisocial. The latter form of *sakorope*, while not esteemed, is nevertheless not an object of public comment and demands for action. The withdrawn type does arouse suspicion but little direct action, while the *sakorope* "fighter" (bilingual informants will sometimes use the Spanish *peleador*, literally "fighter") arouses much indignation.

The usual response to those who habitually end up in confrontations of fisticuffs is strong avoidance by nonsettlement mates and, after repeated admonitions by the capitan have failed, much discussion as to how to get the person to remove himself from the territory (into another river area, or at least out of the immediate neighborhood). This is usually attempted by bringing pressure on the primary relatives of the offender, cutting them in ceremonial gatherings or excluding them in rounds of stops for *cachiri* drinking within the neighborhood. In some cases this can bring about fragmentation of the set of primary relatives of the offender and changes in their place of residence. They may, if remonstrating with the offender proves unsuccessful, simply remove themselves to the residences of their spouses' siblings or their spouses' parents. In one prominent case in the valley of the Karuai, two individuals of this type became involved in fisticuffs resulting from drinking at a party after a hunt in which several peccaries had been killed and in which the division of the meat had left some disgruntled. Two men, one of whom had the reputation of *peleador*, and both from up valley (the northwest neighborhood, some six hours on foot from Maikanden), got into a fight on a Saturday night after the hunt, leading to blows and to one of them, Franco, being bloodied and battered. Pancho Sandoval, the aggressor, was from a settlement near that of Franco, but there were no real ties between the two men, as Pancho's relatives had only recently moved into the region. In addition, both were some six hours from their home settlements, and Franco's family were much the longer-time residents in the region.

On the morning after the fight, which was said to have broken out after drinking had loosened both men's tongues regarding those people in the neighboring settlement, Franco's father came from two hours north of Maikanden, where he had been staying, to show the capitan his son's bloody shirt (Franco's mother's brother's relatives had brought him away from Maikanden to recuperate the night before) and to attempt to compel the capitan to take action against Pancho. Pancho had by this time removed himself to a settlement some distance north of

Maikanden, about 20 minutes' walk away. Franco's father remonstrated with the capitan at length about the assault on his son by the *peleador*, but the capitan did not attempt to go after Pancho. Upon hearing this, a man living in the same neighborhood as Franco's mother's brother, and to whose settlement Franco had come to recuperate, took up the cudgels. This man, also a noted *peleador* whose several half-brothers living in the same settlement had failed to curb his actions, set out for Maikanden on Sunday morning, intending to go after Pancho. This second man, Andres Plaza, found Pancho's "yB" at the ongoing ceremonies in the round house at Maikanden on Sunday afternoon. Andres then proceeded to chase Pancho's "younger brother" outside and around the circular dwelling, failing to catch him in a run through the savanna. At this point the capitan advised Andres to cool down. He refused to do so and he and Pancho, who had entered the fray by this time, exchanged blows some distance out on the savanna away from the round house, with no conclusive result.

Without going into further detail at this point, it is clear that there were no effective curbs by the capitan on either of the two *peleadores*, and that Franco's cause was taken up by one against the other not so much because of the kinship relationship between them but because the chance presented itself. Andres's intervention on Sunday afternoon was directed at the first available target, the "younger brother," a young man of about 18 years of age who happened to be at the Hallelujah ceremony at Maikanden. The capitan was successful only in diverting this first random intervention of Andres, but not in preventing the further inconclusive confrontation between Andres and Pancho.

The confrontation between Andres and Pancho could not escalate because of the large gathering at the Sunday afternoon ceremony. Even had Andres's brothers (half-siblings) decided to escalate matters on behalf of Franco and Andres, they confronted a large group of people who were effectively "neutral" and would have prevented them from taking on those of Pancho's siblings who were present. Pancho's siblings were at this time aligning themselves with relatives of Jaime Portales, the capitan at Maikanden, and they rather quickly maintained a strict neutrality, avoiding siding with Pancho in his aggression on Franco or in his confrontation with Andres. Andres, however, maintained a solid front with his half-siblings, and some months later it was Pancho, not Andres, who left the valley of the Karuai for Kamarata. This example gives the clearest picture of the lack of ability of the capitan to exercise effectively any police power. He could parry an initial charge, but could not avert a confrontation between two partisans who had "drawn the line." These two *sakorope* types embodied the unconstrained aggression which is so strongly reproved by the Pemon.

The withdrawn type of *sakorope* can exist over a long period of time in a given community without arousing comment. (We do not refer here to being simply taciturn, or given to few words. Such silent types are often noticeably present at gatherings and, though not "out front," are anything but withdrawn.) They are in a sense limited to interaction within their own household and settlement, and often socialize, if at all, only with one other household in their settlement. One such man was well known for his peculiarity in this direction in the valley of the Karuai in 1970. He had a sister and brother-in-law in his own settlement, as well as a half-brother less than an hour's walk away. He had brought his wife from the Uriman area and interacted mainly with his sister and her family in his own settlement. Outside of his brother-in-law's household, the man's social contacts were nil. Nevertheless, comment about him was nonexistent, and the classification of his condition as *sakorope* was only forthcoming upon extended discussions with his elder half-brother.

The third important moral category, phrased again in the negative, is *amunek*, stingy, tight-fisted. The rule is that if something is available and is requested, it should be given. Although according to Armellada (1943–44, II: 210) there is a Pemon word for generous, it is not generosity but its lack which causes comment. (Missionaries, particularly certain individual priests, are the most frequent focus of charges of being *amunek*, at least in the areas immediately proximate to the mission.) This quality is most often attached to persons rather than states or specific actions, and particularly centers on heads of settlement who fail to provide *cachiri* with sufficient frequency during the rounds of "movable feasts" that course through the neighborhood. More than the other two terms described above, it is a long-term judgment which relates to the production capabilities and hospitality of certain households, their household heads, and heads of settlement. The equivalence of reciprocal interaction and *cachiri* drinking which is sought is over the long term, and judgments are likewise rendered with reference to a span of years rather than shorter stretches.

The significance of the term *amunek* is not that it is ever brought up directly in disputes or contention, but that it represents a significant lack if used to label a particular individual, whose reputation and stature suffer as a consequence. It is a kind of reference which reflects stature in the subsistence domain, but only indirectly. Since generosity is never measured in any strict sense and subsistence production of a specific household is not widely known beyond the confines of the settlement, the *amunek* label is only a vague way of indicating those who cannot keep up, as well as those who are not hospitable.

The label *amunek* can have more important implications when attached to an aspiring leader or head of settlement. Any of the three above-mentioned labels would be enough to disqualify a person from leadership, but the *amunek* quality is more fundamental than the others. We have mentioned in the account of the Maikanden settlement, the oft-commented failure of Jaime Portales to live up to standards of generosity in providing *cachiri* for visitors. This failure led to statements like "Why is there never any *cachiri* in their house?" and "This is no capitan." Clearly the failure was basic, and was viewed as *amunek*, since Jaime in fact had a sufficiently large household and nearby brother- and sons-in-law to call upon for a considerable production of manioc.

The negative phraseology so often characteristic of the Pemon is important in interpreting these three principal qualities of Pemon moral evaluation. The normal state of things is that one is not lying, not angry, and not stingy. But there is no premium on or exaltation of the positive aspects of these virtues — one does not exalt truthfulness, equanimity, or generosity as in our own frame of reference — rather, these are the expected state of affairs and the negative deviations from them are commented upon. This is not a "Thou shalt not" canon. Pemon expressions regarding moral qualities emphasize a lack, an absence of the expected, real, or true values. Moral breaches are not so much things which are specifically prohibited as disesteemed qualities which manifest the absence of normal reactions and sentiments. The real or true is not something outstanding or exceptionally virtuous but the expected outcome. If something has gone wrong, then particular bad qualities, representing both the lack of true values and the intrusion of Kanaima into a world essentially all right as it is constituted, must be at work.

Other moral imperatives stem from the realm of kinship, and were treated in Chapter III. Here it is sufficient to note that abuses relating to marriage form a large part of causes for dispute. In fact, when questioned at length about territorial and fishing rights as sources of conflict, one informant brushed the question aside, saying, "No, none of that — the fights are about women and lying gossip." We have seen (Chapter IV) how accusations of trying to obtain too many wives helped unseat a capitan in the Uriman area. Usually such accusations center not only on the fact of too many wives per se but on the use of improper means (threats of supernatural sanctions or sorcery, threats of outside — i.e. criollo — intervention, etc.) in a specific marriage transaction. Wrong category marriages, with the exception of the actual ZD unions mentioned above (Chapter III), arouse little opprobrium, particularly given the ex post facto manipulations which we have shown are invoked as justification for past choices. The major charges relating to marriage negotiations center on threats against the woman or her parents and nonfulfillment of obligations to the prospective spouse and her parents. Infractions of the marriage relationship — desertion, adultery, wife-beating — are harshly thought of, though procedures for dealing with them are diffuse (see below).

Conflict Incidents and Cases

The following accounts cover a range of disturbances, not all of which resulted in conflict outcomes. Those which did are approached with several questions in mind: (1) How did the conflict break out? (2) What actions were taken by the parties involved and "onlookers"? (3) What, if anything, limited the conflict in the final analysis? The cases include illness and injury, perduring friction between neighboring heads of settlement, fighters and angry men, incest, adultery, homicide, and sorcery. All include events which surfaced during 1970–71 in the central portion of Pemon territory.

Illness and Injury

Anibal Montano and family: During the latter part of the dry season Anibal and his wife, living some 20 minutes' walk north of Maikanden, were both stricken with fever. Both took to their hammocks, and their three small daughters were also indisposed. Though Anibal's wife's brother was in the settlement, principal aid was rendered to the family by Anibal's father's brother's family, who took manioc and other food to the sick family for the duration of the illness. In spite of the fact that Anibal and his wife were ill for several weeks, no *taren esak* or shaman was sought out. In this case mild food prohibitions and the solidarity of the father's brother's family were deemed sufficient action.

Snakebite case no. 1: A young man (aged 23, married with three small children) was bitten in the hand by a snake in his manioc plot and brought to the Old Mission settlement. Antisnake serum was administered by a mission nurse, and a resident *taren esak* was called in immediately. The stricken man's foster father and family were summoned from their settlement four hours' walk away. After three days the man died. The *taren esak,* along with the entire population of the Old mission neighborhood, averred that Kanaima was involved. However, given that the young man was universally popular in the valley of the Karuai, no accusations were leveled. One man recalled that the dead man's wife had been asked by a stranger, apparently a Makuxi (from Brazilian territory), about her husband's whereabouts some four days before he had been bitten. She had given no reply, and the Makuxi had moved on. It was then remembered that the dead man had had an altercation with a Makuxi four years previously, in Santa Elena near the Brazilian border. The consensus in the neighborhood was that the Makuxi who had accosted the dead man's wife was in fact a Kanaima, seeking vengeance for the fight of four years before. The fact that the

Kanaima had chosen to reveal itself as the Makuxi before being embodied in the snake (the snake was killed and brought in to the settlement, then discarded in the bush) was not considered anomalous by anyone but, rather, confirmed the judgment that Kanaima was involved.

Snakebite case no. 2: The foster father of the young man who died in case no. 1 was bitten on the heel while on a hunting trip (May, 1971) and taken back to his home settlement at Kamadak, four hours' walk northwest of the Old Mission. Relatives from the Old Mission were summoned as soon as he arrived at Kamadak. He had been slung in a hammock and carried back unconscious to his home settlement. Meanwhile, Pancho (the noted *peleador* mentioned above), who resided at a nearby settlement, came in and performed *taren* against the *sararaipu* snake; after three days of ministrations by Pancho, the bitten man began to revive. His eventual recovery took some time, but his relatives from the Old Mission settlement attributed his recovery to the performance of *taren* by Pancho. No accusations of Kanaima or connections with the prior death mentioned above were made.

Local Rivalries

In the Uriman area, a long-term conflict between neighboring heads of settlement shows the extent to which physical separation is utilized as a means of terminating conflict.

Jorge Guerra was a well-liked and industrious man who, together with his several sons, had lived to the north of Uriman for many years. In the mid-1960s he obtained some small domestic pigs and began to raise a substantial number of the animals near his home settlement. The pigs, although fed from Jorge's own fields, were loose and roamed about the nearby savanna and forest. A neighbor, Valerio Ojeda, was a classificatory brother to the nearby shaman Gaspar and also had a large family, including sons, daughters, and sons-in-law, at his settlement some half-hour's walk from Jorge's home. Valerio's relatives, other than those in his own settlement, were several days away in Kamarata, and Valerio in his younger years (late 1940s and 1950s) had spent much time in middle-distance journeying as a big trader or broker. In the mid-1960s he had established himself some distance north of Uriman and was concerned with gathering his sons and son-in-law about him and building up a large settlement.

These men exchanged visits at each others' settlements, though often only in passing on the way to the criollo center at Uriman. Valerio, when out hunting with his dogs, would sometimes run on to Jorge Guerra's bunch of pigs, scattering them. Jorge complained of this but Valerio replied, "The open savanna is free, why do you let your pigs out there?" Though complaints were aired to third parties repeatedly, Jorge and Valerio visited each others' settlements and, toward each other at least, maintained an outward calm.

At one point Valerio's sons (this was around mid-1972), on a visit to Jorge Guerra's place, got extremely drunk ("falling down drunk") and were led homeward by one of Jorge's sons. On the trail home words were spoken, a fight broke out, and Valerio's sons arrived home bloodied as well as drunk. The next day Valerio came to Jorge's house to complain. Jorge told his son (who had gone with Valerio's sons on their way home the previous day) to maintain silence if they came to complain. Valerio came and protested, attempting to provoke Jorge's son, who maintained silence.

Following this incident, one informant stated, Jorge Guerra began to contemplate moving away. "The land is wide, it's been a long time that I've been enduring these complaints from Valerio. I'll take my bunch of pigs downriver, set them up there, and I'll sell what I can in that area." So, sometime in 1973 Jorge went downriver on the main course of the Caroni, prepared a temporary dwelling, brought his family, and left his former homesite north of Uriman for good. After his second year in the new location Jorge died (the informant went on to document the intervention of Kanaima, of Brazilian provenience, in Jorge's death).

While the incidents described are mainly illustrative, several things may be noted. Valerio, in the process of building a large settlement and a reputation in the area just north of Uriman, in effect forced out a competitor. By 1975 Valerio was becoming recognized as a capitan segundo in the Uriman area. Valerio's link with his classificatory brother, the shaman Gaspar, may well have been a strong consideration in Jorge's move, since the latter felt himself increasingly unprotected (in the supernatural sense) as time went on. The overt conflict regarding the pigs and hunting disguised a more fundamental competition in which Valerio gradually increased his influence in the area. Jorge Guerra was known and liked in the area, with a reputation for being strong (*meruntope*, an esteemed quality connoting both physical strength and well-being and strength of character.) That the conflict came to a head when it did, after a long time simmering, is best understood as a result of the changing leadership configuration in the Uriman area. As noted in Chapter IV, the alignment of leaders there was such that Valerio was in the middle, halfway between the positions of his "brother" Gaspar and Gaspar's daughter-in-law and fellow shaman Agnes, on the one hand, and the actual capitan Losada and the "curing" shaman Abel Portela, on the other. Valerio was "in the middle" but close enough to a powerful shaman on the one hand and a powerful (though opposing) capitan on the other that he was difficult for Jorge Guerra to oppose. While Valerio's relationship with the feared shaman Gaspar cannot be thought of as the whole cause of Jorge's disposition to move away from the area, the realignment of leaders which was coming about, with Valerio moving closer to capitan Losada, must have influenced him to some extent. It is only when the overall level of support for one becomes minimal that moving is contemplated.

Fighters and Angry Men

The incident described above concerning the two "fighters" Pancho Sandoval and Andres Plaza gave a brief idea of the lack of power of the capitan to do anything when confronted with such personalities. Though complaints in the valley of the Karuai regarding both men were widespread during the period 1970–71, only the confrontation between the two of them, coupled with other factors, eventually forced Pancho to remove himself from the area. There is always much talk that such men should be sent to prison, handed over to the criollos for internment in the prison located at El Dorado, and so on. My feeling is that such talk, while largely on the level of griping, is important in that it indicates the Pemon feeling that they cannot cope well with such a person, and that possible measures against him, short of outright physical beating or assassination, do not exist. Ultimately, as long as a fighter can maintain the support of his settlement mates, he can go it alone along with this small group. Some whole bunches of settlement mates become known as more or less "roughnecks," and Andres Plaza and his half-siblings were so known in 1970–71. Andres's isolation was considerable, aside from this group of his brothers, and his rebellious bent was coupled with a substantial amount of hauteur in the face of this isolation.

The mobilizational failures of Pemon society come to the fore in the case of the fighter. Unless there is another man of comparable disposition who will go up against him, the fighter can continue his ways for long periods of time with no sanctions brought to bear. Short of killing another, he can do a fair amount of damage with impunity. While Andres forced another fighter, Pancho, out of the area, Pancho's victim Franco also left the area some months after the above-mentioned fights took place. Andres's fisticuffs, since they took place only sporadically (he was limited by others' assiduous avoidance of him), could not really be limited as long as his sibling set held together. As we have shown in our discussion of kinship, the sibling set provides the basic identity of a Pemon individual, the basic cohort with which the individual moves through life. In a certain sense, as long as those primary ties hold, even the fighter cannot be sanctioned. We have previously related the story of a man who was widely known and feared and disliked for his wife-beating. However, his own siblings would take no action against him and his practice continued, to the detriment of his wife and children.

The presence of these types in the community, and the semi-tolerance which is enforced by the difficulties in mobilizing others against them, all point to a cardinal characteristic of the Pemon system of social control — if the prospective or actual damage done by a given individual can be tolerated by his sibling set, and the sibling set holds together, it is very difficult to bring any sanctions other than avoidance to bear on this individual. He will usually be labeled *sakorope*, avoided and tolerated until he comes into conflict with another of like disposition. If his own siblings fail to support him, he usually has little recourse except to move away (to his affines, if they will have him) or to moderate his fighting. If the minimal units (nuclear family, sibling set) are solidary, the higher levels and statuses (neighborhoods, capitanes) cannot effectively breach this solidarity. Since the initial response of an individual who is injured, insulted, or wronged is to withdraw and attempt to mobilize support against the offender, the failure of such a mobilization attempt is a failure of redress. Redress can only be obtained by convincing people at the lower levels (nuclear families, individuals) that their interests are affected by the offender. The higher levels (neighborhoods, mediating statuses) do not exist except as assemblages of the lower ones — they have no autonomy or influence on the lower levels except insofar as these lower levels move themselves. In any conflict between individuals, whether or not actual fisticuffs, destruction of property (e.g. purposely damaging some piece of equipment or household item), or personal injury has occurred, the routing of tactics for redress goes from the wronged party out to various individuals in the immediate settlement and neighborhood, then back down to the individuals who compose the nuclear families — there is no building up of oppositions as in a segmentary system; rather, all oppositions decompose to the individual level, and opposing groups can only be built up when *all* units of one group are simultaneously threatened by the actions of a given individual. This type of buildup is extremely difficult to achieve, and hence "bad lots" can be extremely perduring in Pemon society, provided they are mobile enough.

Incest

That localization of damage can preclude virtually all sanctions other than avoidance is nowhere better illustrated than by a well-known and widely reproved case of brother-sister incest in the Uonken region. The brother and sister in 1970–71 were co-resident with their parents, the brother's wife, another sister, and that sister's husband. They lived in a remote settlement two and a half hours' walk through dense forest from the nearest other settlement. They seldom visited other settlements, and the only time I saw the brother away from this home settlement was during his short stint of mission labor at Maikanden.

According to several informants, both of the sister's offspring were by her brother, and the woman was reputed to be something of a wanton. Except for their elder sister's husband and the brother's Makuxi wife (an older woman about whom I could learn little), the brother-sister pair in question were surrounded only by their nuclear family of orientation. Their father and mother were very old, minimally mobile, and had no surviving siblings. Whether or not the lack of parents' siblings had any influence on the failure of the daughter to marry was not known. Several men from other settlements claimed to have partaken of the daughter's sexual favors over extended periods of time. The brother in question, a surly and ill-regarded man, was seen as dangerous and *sakorope* by the residents of Maikanden. Though he was given shelter in the capitan's round house, his hammock and that of his Makuxi wife were slung at the farthest remove from the few others then present in the house. They maintained a completely separate hearth and were not invited to other houses in Maikanden for *cachiri*.

Scorn, often vehement, was heaped upon this brother-sister pair when I asked about them. The almost universal response was "Those people are dogs," coupled with "They live way up on the mountainside, away from everyone, so what can you do?" I have described the ambivalence and unease attached to evaluations of actual sister's daughter marriages (Chapter III). The incestuous brother-sister pair, however, aroused only scorn and disgust on the part of informants, coupled with evident frustration at not being able to do anything about the situation.

The failure or inability to bring any sanctions to bear on these individuals testifies graphically to the unbreachable character of the nuclear family, its relative imperviousness to outside pressures, and to the failure of the neighborhood as a solidary unit. Even though the offense was universally recognized and excoriated, the inviolability of nuclear family affairs which had no repercussions outside of it held strong. Pemon do not consider that incest will bring on disasters or supernatural retribution for the community at large. It is an offense which places the offenders into the "nonhuman" category but does not provoke supernatural sanctions. This ultimate turning inward is nonhuman, even anti-human, but it is not a strike outward at another individual or family unit.

The fragmentation of the neighborhood into its component families and sibling sets is nowhere better shown than by this case. Since there were no members of this particular family outside of their own settlement, and only one affine was resident with them, they had no external links to the rest of the neighborhood. In both of the adult generations there were no siblings in other settlements on whom pressure could be brought to bear. We have shown that Pemon life can be thought of as the interaction of linked sibling sets and nuclear families. The concomitant of this form of life is that particular offenses which do not serve to threaten multiple individuals and families prove difficult to control or to sanction. This brother-sister pair produced the ultimate isolation of their nuclear family of orientation. Nevertheless, since there was no threat — other than the general moral threat of such a heinous violation of Pemon norms — to particular individuals, nuclear families, and sibling sets outside of this single family, no one was willing to move against them in any way other than avoidance.

Adultery and the Mobilization of Gossip Networks

An example of the way in which gossip networks can be mobilized by a particular individual to force action by an offender is provided by an incident which occurred in the Old Mission settlement in early 1971. Justo Fabregas, then living with his wife and married and unmarried children at the Old Mission settlement, was caught one night by his wife *in flagrante delicto* with a widow from the northwest part of the region. Justo's wife, upon finding them some distance from the house, shined a flashlight on them and was reported to have beaten both of them with a stick. Justo's wife, instead of keeping the matter to herself, went immediately the following day to Jovita, a neighbor, close friend, and the widow of the former capitan Baco Bandino. Jovita had, in addition to her co-resident daughter in the Old Mission settlement, a son and son-in-law and their families in two settlements just to the south, not far from Maikanden. Upon hearing Justo's wife's story, she not only informed all of the women in the Old Mission settlement but also undertook a trip to her son's house, near Maikanden, to recount the story of infidelity and the rather ludicrous circumstances of its discovery. Within a week Justo's humiliation was everywhere and the subject of not a few rather hilarious jokes. In reaction, Justo and one of his sons undertook a trip south, out of the region, ostensibly for purposes of trade, as far as the Brazilian border. Within a month after the incident Justo had removed himself to a settlement southeast of Maikanden, out of the Old Mission settlement.

While it is not possible to detail the exact pattern of mobilization of the gossip network, Justo's wife's close friendship with Jovita, a much-respected woman with many close relatives in the Old Mission settlement, was crucial. Justo's wife had no relatives in the area; her only surviving relative, a brother, lived in Apoipo, two days' journey to the south and outside of the Uonken region. Jovita, through her children and sons-in-law, was able to spread the word widely and rapidly. That Justo could no longer afford to remain in the Old Mission settlement and bear the scorn of his neighbors was evident from his rapid exits, first temporary and then permanent. Though his eldest son and the son's wife stayed on at the Old Mission settlement, Justo's and his family's move was permanent.

The marriage, though buffeted by the incident, survived both Justo's actions and his wife's retaliation via the gossip network. The incident provides an example of the availability of some measure of redress through the regular means of withdrawing and mobilizing others to rally around one's cause. Justo's wife had the sympathy of the entire neighborhood, and though the move did not effectively remove the of-fending widow and Justo any farther from one another (the widow lived far to the northwest but frequently spent time near Maikanden), the moves occasioned by Justo's discomfiture were sufficient public demon-stration of her anger. In this incident, of course, there was no fourth party for Justo to contend with.

It is not my intention here to go into a detailed treatment of adultery, other causes of marital discord, or disputes over women in general. Such disputes usually arise in two instances: initial marriage negotiations, and the taking of a woman from her husband—i.e. a divorce caused by an adulterous relationship. The latter case can result in permanent schisms, as mentioned in Chapter III in the discussion of Abelio Solano's divorce. In all of these types of incidents, the injured party attempts to force a desired outcome or a return to the status quo by means of gossip pressure on the immediate near kin of the guilty party, or on the guilty party himself. If these kin give aid to the guilty party rather than re-monstrating with him or her, they may often successfully resist such pressures from the gossip network. In one case in early 1971 a young woman married to an older man was found in an adulterous relation-ship with his son (the son at that time was married to another woman). Though most people agreed that the woman had initiated the adulter-ous relationship, she removed herself from her husband's house to her elder sister's house some hours' walk away, and neither she nor her hus-band were interested in reconciliation. She later left the Uonken region altogether and took up residence in the Uriman area (whether or not she remarried after this de facto divorce I do not know). The woman was supported by her elder sister and her mother, both of whom sheltered her at their house for a considerable length of time, along with her chil-dren. Again, the crucial importance of ties with near siblings in seeking redress or succor is illustrated. Even though the young woman was deemed to be at fault, talk was circulated by her sister and mother that she had been deprived in the house of the older man, that he was no longer a good provider, and that he sponged off his in-laws (the house-hold of the elder sister and her mother). Needless to say, this countergos-sip was put out by the elder sister and mother to justify their actions in not forcing the woman to return to her husband, since the young woman was, by all rumors, totally at fault in the matter. The response was (much as in the case of Maria Solano, cited in Chapter III) that the adultery was in effect justified, and only an indication of the bad state of affairs reigning between the couple.

Gossip is resorted to as a pressure mechanism principally in cases of rather clear-cut misconduct related to marriage, or in marriage negotiations. It is mainly a means of throwing the blame and depends greatly on the ability of the wronged party to convince a pivotal close friend or relative to go to bat for him/her. The individual cannot defend himself/ herself directly, as this would contravene the norm of withdrawal upon injury.

Homicide

The following story was related by an old man in the northern part of the Uonken region. One night in early 1961 Eugenio, son of Takisha, then living at Karinakon in the far northwest of the region, and Hipolito Landaeta, son of the capitan Eduardo Landaeta of the Aripichi Falls area upriver from Uriman, were drinking heavily at the Uonken settlement just north of the Old Mission. First, very drunk, they assaulted Curcio, teen-age son of Mawai, beat him to death with sticks, tied stones around his body, and threw his body in the Karuai River. The body was later recovered, partially eaten by crabs. They then returned to the Uonken settlement and sought out the old man Mawai, whom they threatened and cursed, then beat and punched to death. Leaving his body, they fled into the night to the west, to Tirika and the middle Caroni region outside the valley and disappeared.

Subsequently Moises Garcia, a man living at Karinakon, went after Eugenio's father, Takisha. Moises and his son found Takisha in a canoe somewhere on the stream Aravak, where they beat him up; he died shortly thereafter at Karinakon. The informant said that the missionaries, who at the time of Mawai's killing were at the Old Mission, called the guardias from Santa Elena, who came to Uonken but who never got the culprits. Both Eugenio and Hipolito are still at large. The informant, when questioned as to why no one had avenged Mawai and his son directly, said that it was because Mawai's other offspring were very young at the time and living far away, in the Kukenan area. Also, Mawai had no living brothers who could take up pursuit of the culprits. The informant was in tears of rage as he completed the story, and said that it was a shame that Mawai had had no close kin to avenge him, since everyone knew where the culprits were presently located.

This was the only recorded case of homicide in the memory of living informants which it was possible to ferret out in 14 months of fieldwork in 1970–71 and 1975. While in matters of violence one can never be sure that one has gotten "all the facts," it does seem to me that the frequency of homicide in the Uonken population, at least, had to have been extremely low. In the course of genealogical inquiry, only these two murders (of Mawai and his son, and the vengeance wreaked on Eugenio's father) came up, and the inquiry went as far back as 1900.

The retribution wreaked on Eugenio's father by Moises Garcia is noteworthy. Mawai was Moises's FZDHB, a classificatory cross-cousin, but the two men were of different generations. Moises's retaliation may well have been related to prior conflicts with Takisha, since both he and Takisha lived at Karinakon. It was extremely difficult to obtain information about Takisha, even from his own offspring resident in Maikanden in 1970–71.

The rather startling fact about the homicide was its lack of any following violence other than the fatal beating of Takisha. Both of the reported murderers are known individuals, living in known locations on the western fringes of Pemon territory. Needless to say, they do not circulate in the Uonken region. The inconclusive outcome of the matter greatly grieved the informant, who was not related to Mawai. Clearly here was a case in which vengeance should have been exacted but was not, given the failure of any of Mawai's kin to take action. Mawai had a brother's son resident in Uonken, but the man was young at the time of the murder and made no move against either of the culprits. The culprits fled into an area where one of them, at least, had the support of his close kin, including his father who was a capitan in that area. The inconclusive nature of the retaliation for Mawai's murder testifies once again to the sporadic and ineffectual nature of redress in a situation where no members of the victim's sibling set can be mobilized in his support or in retaliation for a wrong, even in a matter as serious as homicide.

We shall see, in the account which follows, that it requires special circumstances for concerted action to be taken against a specific individual by a group of people of the order of a neighborhood or set of settlements, and that even then such action may be blocked or rendered only partially effective. The above homicide incident shows how even the most grievous offense in the society may ultimately go unavenged, if the offenders can find asylum with their own close kin and if the victim has no siblings available to take up his cause.

Sorcery

In January and February of 1971 the entire southern portion of Pemon territory was hit by a measles epidemic. In the Uonken region, and particularly among the people of the Makarupai River area which includes Maikanden, the epidemic was very severe. It resulted in over 30 deaths, all of them children or youths under 15, during those two months. On a Sunday afternoon in early February an assembly met in

Maikanden to level sorcery accusations at Flavio Mateos (see Chapter
IV), a shaman from the Aripichi Falls area. The assembly was addressed
to Flavio's mother-in-law, who had been summoned from the far northwest of the region, where she lived, to bear the messages to Flavio. She
spoke little, disavowing any knowledge of sorcery, and was addressed
for nearly two hours as capitan Jaime Portales, Paulo Castelar, Jorge
Castelar, Anibal Montano, Marco Garcia, Rigoberto Portales, and
Javier Castelar reiterated their assertion that the shaman Flavio had
something to do with the fact that children at Maikanden were dying.
Children in other parts were sick but were not dying.

Rigoberto Portales, a man who lived far down the Caroni from Maikanden, asked why strange cries were heard in the night when his young
daughter died at their downriver settlement. Why were strange-looking
tracks, similar to those of the jaguar, found around the settlement during the child's illness? What was the shaman sending in their direction
to make the children die? His brother, capitan Jaime Portales, reiterated several times his position that some shamans helped while others
did evil. Why was Flavio sending evil this way?

Flavio's mother-in-law was instructed to transmit the message concerning the signs, the tracks, and the numbers of children dying to
Flavio. The woman again disclaimed knowledge of anything, but said
she would transmit the message.

About five days later word came to Maikanden that the capitan's
summons to shaman Abel Portela had been received and that Abel had
come as far as Rigoberto's settlement downstream on the Caroni. However, word came that when Abel and his son-in-law arrived at Rigoberto's settlement, they found anteater tracks all over, and two bodies,
which had been buried inside the house, disinterred and the flesh partially eaten, apparently by the dogs of the place. The same thing was
found at a settlement farther upriver, where one body had been disinterred and the flesh partially eaten. Abel then sent word that he was not
coming to Maikanden and was returning home immediately. Talk with
several informants revealed that nobody believed that it was either dogs
or an anteater which dug up the bodies and ate them, but that these
happenings were the result of sorcery against the people there. About a
week after these reports Abel Portela arrived in Maikanden to consult
with capitan Jaime Portales about the epidemic, the shaman Flavio
Mateos, and countermeasures against Flavio's presumed doings.

A few days after Portales's consultation with Abel, Anton Bandino, a
man from the Old Mission settlement and a parallel cousin of Flavio
Mateos, went to Maikanden and got into an argument with capitan Portales over Flavio and the accusations. Anton told me later that Flavio
was a brother and that the capitan was wrong in his reasoning; people
had been sick all over and it was only due to faulty care of their children

that there were so many dead in Maikanden and in the downriver settlements.

In early March the accusation had been extended to Flavio's relatives by marriage, including Quincio Serrano and Jorge Belen, two men from the north end of the valley of the Karuai who were relatives of Flavio's mother-in-law. Portales had called for these men from the Mauruk area, to the north of the Old Mission settlement, to come and discuss the matter at Maikanden. They had done so but maintained, like Anton, that if the children had died, their parents were at fault for not looking after them properly, since everyone's children had been sick. In a conversation with me both Quincio and Jorge Belen discussed *muran*, things which have the power to kill people. It was maintained by Anton, Quincio, and Jorge Belen that *muran* had been found all over the valley since the start of the epidemic, and not just in the area around Maikanden. Anton went on to recount a conversation that he had had with a man from the northwest part of the region the week before. The man asked, "Had they been praying? Had they been dancing (Hallelujah and Chochiman)? No." Hence the deaths were merely punishment for past neglect of praying and dancing on the part of those whose children had died.

Sometime before March the door of Quincio's brother's temporary house some distance from Maikanden had been broken in. Quincio's relationship to Flavio's mother-in-law, who had been accused at the assembly in February, led him to suppose that the capitan or another of the people from Maikanden was responsible for breaking in the door.

The capitan himself gave the following account of Flavio's guilt in an interview in July, 1975. In 1969 Flavio wanted to take as wife a daughter of Marco Garcia but was refused because the girl was unwilling. Marco lost two children during the epidemic in early 1971, killed by Flavio, in order to take revenge. At that time the capitan sent for one of Flavio's mothers-in-law, who admitted nothing. Subsequently she moved to the Aripichi Falls area of the Caroni, where Flavio lives. Capitan Portales then called for Abel Portela to come from the Avikara area (not far from where Flavio resided) to aid the people in Maikanden. Abel came but, on his return to Avikara, was taken ill. Later, in 1974, when Flavio and his relatives had all fled to the Aripichi Falls area of the Caroni, Abel became extremely sick in Remotota, Rigoberto's settlement, and was taken to Maikanden. Capitan Raimundo Losada then called a gathering in Uriman (mid-1974) to which he summoned Abel, Flavio, and Agnes, and accused Flavio of trying to do away with Abel. Neither Agnes nor Flavio, according to Portales, admitted anything. Portales stated that, as of mid-1975, people in Kamarata wished to do away with Agnes, but were advised by a capitan in Kamarata that the consequences would be grave if they did.

While the series of events related by the capitan is long and compli-
cated, it can only be seen in the light of a major upheaval which threatened many members of the Makarupai River area population simultaneously, and provided the opportunity to air long-standing grievances
against the shaman Flavio. Remembering the alignment of leaders,
both capitanes and shamans, which was outlined at the end of Chapter
IV, we can see that the epidemic precipitated a further cleavage in the
break between those who were aligned with capitan Landaeta on the
one hand and capitan Losada on the other. The shaman Abel Portela's
alliance with Losada was firmed up by the conflicts between Losada's
chosen representative in Uonken (Portales) and the shaman Flavio,
which were long-standing. In 1968 Portales had accused Flavio of causing the death of his wife's sister's husband in an accident in the forest (a
tree fell on the man and he was killed, a happening which was universally thought to be Kanaima), as well as causing the death of his younger daughter on a trip downstream on the Caroni, not too far from
Flavio's home settlement. Marco Garcia's accusations of Flavio's supposed retaliation in the matter of a proposed marriage to Marco's
daughter have already been mentioned. The accusations leveled at
Flavio's mother-in-law in Maikanden in February, 1971, by many of
Jaime Portales's brothers-in-law and sons-in-law stemmed from the
death of their sister's husband in 1968 and from the loss of his only two
surviving children by Jaime's wife's half-brother during the epidemic.
The only accusers who were not directly related to Jaime's or his wife's
sibling sets were Marco Garcia, who had lost two children himself, and
Anibal Montano, whose three daughters had been very ill during the
epidemic.

Flavio's parallel cousins in the Old Mission settlement experienced
difficulty in countering the accusations leveled by those to the south in
Maikanden. First, they were split on the question of Flavio's guilt. One
of them, a younger brother of Anton (the man who had argued so vehe-
mently against Jaime Portales's blaming Flavio) named Roberto
Medina, said that he had warned Flavio on a past visit to the Old Mission settlement that if anything happened to his (Roberto's) children, he
would literally "put a bullet through him." Roberto thus stayed out of
any support efforts by Anton and those farther north, such as Quincio
Serrano and other relatives of Flavio's mother-in-law. The mother-in-
law was also suspect, since she was reported to have made a trip to the
mouth of the Karuai to gather *muran* for some unknown purpose just
prior to the onset of the epidemic.

In March, 1971, Justo Fabregas was called to a meeting in Apoipo
with several leaders from the Icabaru area (including Ruben Monagas,
a leading capitan and trader from the Icabaru area who had long-standing grievances against Flavio) to discuss the assassination of Flavio by

means of ambush on the Caroni. There were rumors that despite Justo's opposition to such an attempt, Marco Garcia, Jaime Portales, and several others actually carried out the attempt but failed. It was known, however, that Flavio kept close to home in the Aripichi Falls area and did not attempt any trips to the Uonken region. The Aripichi Falls area was at that time an asylum for several refugees from conflicts in the Uonken region—the son of capitan Landaeta, reported to have murdered Mawai in Uonken in 1961, was there, as were Flavio and his mother-in-law from the northwest part of the Uonken region.

The leaders and their allies were further separated into two opposing camps throughout the central portion of the tribal territory by the events of 1968–71. Losada's opposition to Flavio and to the (former) capitan of the Uriman area, Landaeta, was hardened by the happenings in Uonken during the epidemic. Flavio's near relatives in the Uonken area were split, as described above. One part of the Old Mission settlement, led by Anton, claimed that all the accusations put forth by those in Maikanden were untrue, and that the deaths in the Makarupai and downriver areas were the result of lack of ritual observances by the parents of the deceased children and simple negligence. Another part, more or less of the opinion of Roberto Medina, said this was none of their affair because their children had not died and they were unsure of the extent of Flavio's involvement. They preferred to stand to one side. Here we see the difficulties in mobilizing both vengeance (on the part of Portales and the Makarupai River people) and countervengeance or support for the accused. Jaime had to seek aid from capitanes as far away as Icabaru, and was only able to mount an assassination attempt (according to reports) with those men whose children had died as a result of Flalvio's actions. At least one such attempt was slowed down by the refusal of the capitan segundo, Justo Fabregas, to participate; we see the attitude, manifested on both sides of the argument, that unless a direct threat was felt against the nuclear family or the sibling set of a given individual, he was reluctant to participate in any concerted action with regard to the accused, either for or against.

The case of the accusations against Flavio is a rather neat demonstration of what can be called the inability of Pemon society to mobilize opposition in internal conflict situations. This can be called the "fragmentation in the feud." E. Colson (1953: 210) stated of the Rhodesian Tonga: "In a society of this type, it is impossible to have the development of the feud and the institutionalization of repeated acts of vengeance, for each act of vengeance, like each original incident, mobilizes different groups whose interests are concerned in the particular case and that alone. It would also lead to a general community disruption, affecting those who must live in the midst of the turmoil and yet are not directly concerned with it."

The Pemon illustrate not just this principle in operation but a further principle which extends to all facets of Pemon life: the tendency for any conflict to be unable to build up past the autonomy, and de facto isolability, of the minimal units of the society, the nuclear family and sibling set. Any concerted action above these levels — as for example, Jaime's assassination attempt against Flavio — requires that each participant feel himself, his sibling set, or his nuclear family directly injured and able to sustain whatever counterretaliation might be brought about as a consequence of the act of vengeance. This does not mean that vengeance will not be wreaked — consider the attack on Takisha after the murder of Mawai — but it means that such action will not always hit directly at the offenders per se, and that it often takes a tremendous effort to convince people to mount such vengeance. This is not simply a matter of the so-called "cross-cutting ties" of which anthropologists are fond. It runs much deeper than that, and can be considered to be a fundamental characteristic of Pemon society, one that was manifested in their "melting away" resistance to the Capuchins of the eighteenth century as well as since, in their "permeability" as a social system. This is the tendency for conflict to melt away or be moderated simply by the difficulty of mobilizing anyone to do anything about it, particularly if there is difficulty in showing a direct threat to a given individual or family unit.

The arguments surrounding Flavio's guilt or innocence reflect another crucial aspect of the difficulty of mobilizing people — alternate explanations of the kind of powers or forces involved in the conflict are always offered by opposing viewpoints. The man who supported Anton by noting that the deaths of the children in the Makarupai area were due to lack of piety and ritual observances on the part of the people there was expressing a common theme in Pemon life, that misfortune is the result of a personal disequilibrium which in turn results from failures to observe the proper ritual acts, thus incurring a personal imbalance with the spirit world. A spiritual disequilibrium may, of course, be caused either by personal failures or by outside malevolence, and that is what the arguments as to causation are about. If the individual in question is known as *sakorope*, or is out of tune with others in his immediate settlement or household, the imbalance will often be seen as a personal failing, provided that the injury is illness rather than an accident or insult, which can be construed as the result of outside forces. Even on a larger scale, where many individuals have been affected, we can see from the nature of Anton's and his backers' arguments regarding Flavio and the Makarupai River people that personal failings provide a ready explanation for misfortune.

Flavio can be said to have breached several levels of norms in the long series of conflicts with the people of the Makarupai River area. His attempt to secure a third wife against the wishes of the girl herself, and by

means of intimations of supernatural threats if his wishes were not adhered to, was seen by many as an abuse of the powers of the shaman in
an all-too-familiar vein — the disruption of the marriage system. Not
only did Flavio already have two wives, but he invoked the threat of supernatural powers in a negotiation where such invocation was improper.

The arguments and counterarguments over Flavio's guilt, and the
splits which the Old Mission people found in their ranks as a result of
sentiments like those expressed by Roberto Medina, point up a north
versus south split in the valley of the Karuai which has structural as well
as situational significance. Not only were all the deaths concentrated in
the south portion of the valley and adjoining areas, but the sibling sets of
the northern part of the valley were ranged against those of the southern
part in the course of the arguments over Flavio's guilt. Capitan
Portales's choice to transmit the accusations through Flavio's mother-in-
law, who had connections to the sibling sets of Quincio Serrano and
Jorge Belen in the north part of the valley, made this inevitable. Only
the split in the sentiments of the Old Mission people prevented their alliance with Jorge Belen's and Quincio's sibling sets from farther north.
The whole dispute can be seen as one among three cognatic kin groups,
that of the Makarupai River people, led by capitan Portales, and consisting mostly of his sibling set and that of his wife, and those of the Old
Mission (split by Medina's arguments) and the northern part of the
valley (related to Flavio's mother-in-law).

The arguments can be seen as expressing the structural opposition referred to among cognatic kin assemblages, and as arguments about the
nature of power involved in the epidemic. Both sides argued for imbal-
ances in the relation of the Makarupai River people to the spiritual
world. Those who wished to head off accusations against Flavio
couched their version of spiritual imbalance in terms of personal infractions, individual neglect of observance of proper food restrictions (one
must abstain from *cachiri* and "hot" foods like peppers at the very least,
when one's children are sick), and failure to observe properly Hallelujah
and Chochiman rituals. Flavio's accusers couched their argument in
terms of direct outside intervention (Flavio was a Kanaima) causing the
manifested spiritual imbalance. Capitan Portales's contention was that
the attack on their children constituted an application of particularized
shamanic power in a negative sense. Those who saw their children die
could not all have been personally negligent, and the concentration of
deaths in one area was too severe to be accounted for in any other way.
Flavio's past infractions against people of the area (attempt to take an
undue number of women, cause of the death of the capitan's daughter
and wife's sister's husband) were evidence aplenty of his animus against
them.

The inconclusive outcome of the accusations resulted only from Flavio's success in assuring himself of asylum by means of his continued co-residence and alliance with the out-of-favor (and out of circulation) capitan Landaeta in a remote area of the western portion of Pemon territory; along with this was Portales's inability to mount a successful assassination attempt in this remote area, far from the Uonken region with which he was familiar. Old disputes — the conflicts between Flavio and Jaime went back well over five years at the time of the epidemic — even though they are not defused, simply flare and then fade. Just as old capitanes never die, old disputes don't either. They remain simmering in the background, gradually bringing about new alignments of leaders and testing the effectiveness of leaders in the process.

The two "sides" or alignments of leaders outlined in Chapter IV were both cause and consequence of the events of 1970–71 and the accusations against Flavio. Losada, an influential figure throughout the western portion of Pemon territory, had, in addition to his long-standing but muted differences with Landaeta, committed himself to Portales's fortunes by instigating Portales's installation as capitan in the Uonken region in 1969. Over the course of 1970–75 Losada attempted to bolster his situation and sought Valerio Ojeda as capitan segundo, indirectly seeking to neutralize the supernatural power represented by Ojeda's "brother" Gaspar and Gaspar's daughter-in-law, Agnes. The epidemic of 1971 in Uonken evidenced the weakness of Losada's contingent in the spiritual domain, since the "good" (or curing) shaman Abel Portela was unable to combat what was felt to be a supernatural attack on Portales's neighborhood. The fact that Losada rapidly became a follower of the San Miguel prophet (see Thomas, 1976) upon the advent of the San Miguel religious movement in 1974 is perhaps an indication of the felt deficit of supernatural strength in Losada's alignment of leaders. The two roles of capitan and shaman always operate in tandem, and Abel's failure (Abel himself became ill, rather than successfully combatting Flavio), coupled with Jaime's failure to do away with Flavio, indicated a serious vacuum in leadership in the Uonken area, as well as reflecting badly on Losada. The leader-as-resource is looked to for a response, and if he cannot produce one, failing to mobilize the injured, he not only suffers himself but changes the relative strength of the alignment with which he is associated.

The outcome of epidemic and the resulting accusations should not be thought of as any kind of "victory" for Flavio and Landaeta. Flavio bore the brunt of extreme restrictions on his free movement, and Landaeta, though he ventured downstream to Uriman as the occasion warranted, remained in eclipse as a leader. In a sense, both alignments of leaders in the central portion of the territory were weakened by the accusations. Landaeta's contingent successfully fended off a real assault on their standing (and on Flavio's life) but remained under a cloud, with Flavio himself losing virtually all contact with his relatives in the Uonken region. Losada's contingent was shown to be unable to press its point of view, its version of events, successfully, and was shown to be woefully lacking in spiritual power as well as organizational acumen. Remember that Justo Fabregas successfully opposed at least one attempt by Portales to organize Flavio's demise, even though another attempt was later organized without Fabregas's knowledge.

The competing explanations of what happened and the competing notions of the origin of forces responsible for the deaths manifest a clear internal/external dichotomy which pervades Pemon thinking in many realms, though it is often stretched into a continuous range of near versus far. Just as we have seen (Chapter III) that Pemon kinship terminology can be manipulated to invoke either a restricted genealogical model which defines relatedness very narrowly or a wide model which brings outsiders closer into the center of the kindred, so also spiritual power can be ranged on a continuum of close to distant as regards its origin.

Conflict Fade-Out

The above illustrative material serves to demonstrate certain broad patterns in the Pemon handling of conflict. The invocation of moral rules or characterizations by and of themselves is never sufficient to move an accused or accuser or to bring about mobilization for redress in Pemon society. While people are all familiar with and support the general norms which decry that which is lying, angry, or stingy, or that which brings about injury through abuse of spiritual or secular powers, the pattern of seeking redress is more than this. The initial withdrawal of the injured party is always followed by an attempt at mobilization of support, either by seeking mediation (as when Franco's father sought the aid of capitan Jaime Portales against the *peleador* Pancho) or by moving a group of kinsmen and associates to take action (as in Jaime's attempts against Flavio). The degree of success in mobilizing support can be thought of as a function of those available who are members of the victim's sibling set or nuclear family or who are settlement mates, and of the extent to which potential supporters can think of the threat as one which affects them or their own nuclear families.

The fading away of conflict can best be thought of as the influences toward fragmentation which prevent the buildup of support groups for either accused or accusers. There is first the problem of direct internal opposition — e.g. a member of a sibling group may consider that the threat to his family is not great enough to warrant action, and defer action until he feels threatened more directly. This is illustrated by Roberto Medina's actions running counter to Anton's attempt to mobilize support for Flavio. Next is the difficulty of agreement on just what type of power is at stake in the conflict or just what type of power has caused the supposed infraction. If the matter can be construed as a situation which has come about as the result of personal failure to maintain proper balance with the spirit world or in close personal relationships within the nuclear family or settlement (as in the case of wife-beating), then most often there will be little possibility of mobilizing a suprasettlement group of individuals to effect redress. This means that almost all Pemon conflicts, even very severe ones (e.g. the homicide case described above) have a tendency to defuse themselves as a result of structural fragmentation and ideological disagreement on the exact type of power involved. When death results from illness or unexplained accident, Kanaima is always responsible, but there then remains the problem of attribution of the specific Kanaima involved (whether the Kanaima is a malevolent shaman, a tribesman from a distant location, or those outsiders who are not even Pemon).

This agreement on the power forces at issue may be the hardest to achieve and, in the case of serious illness or accident, the most crucial part of the process of mobilization of support for redress. As Roberts (1979: 183) has noted, it is crucial to find "the relationship of rules to power within a particular process." In Pemon society there are moral rules which dictate the normal state of affairs (summed up in the concepts of not being *kamaiyek*, *sakorope*, or *amunek*), but these moral rules are subject to a set of tactical or pragmatic responses which determine how they will be acted upon. These meta-rules define the tactics and strategy of moving people in concert and the achievement of an ideological consensus on the forces and power types involved in the conflict. The difficulty of defining conflict is a major brake on its spread. As long as conflict can be defined as only interpersonal (individual versus individual, family versus family, or sibling set versus sibling set), the conflict situation is seldom able to agglomerate forces at a higher level of integration.

I ascribe this not simply to the "overlapping" or "flexible" qualities of cognatic organization but to the Pemon tendency to shift boundaries inward when the need arises. Such a shift was discussed in the context of kinship disputes and the contests between father-in-law and son-in-law in Chapter III. In that instance, a very narrow definition of kinship relatedness was invoked by a son-in-law in order to justify a break with his father-in-law and to distance himself, in both physical and social space, from the father-in-law. Responses to the sorcery accusations described above can be thought of in the same fashion. Roberto Medina made clear in his response to Flavio that the crucial unit for him was his own nuclear family, his own (no one else's, not even his siblings') children and their welfare. If that welfare was threatened, and only then, he would move directly into action against Flavio. Likewise, even though Flavio was a parallel cousin (brother in Pemon classification), Roberto would not move into action on Flavio's behalf. This type of response represents a decompositional tendency which can only be overcome by referring the conflict to an overarching type of power which has become manifest in the infraction at issue. This means, for example, that Jaime Portales had to point to a long series of injuries supposedly emanating from Flavio which showed a direct use of spiritual and secular power against Jaime and by extension the others whose children had died in the epidemic.

This overarching type of power — by reference to which a large support group can be mobilized — represents a form of what we shall call "generalized" power in Pemon life. By generalized power I mean power which has potential effects above and beyond a particular instance, infraction, or illness. The power normally brought to bear by shamans or *taren esak* is particularized power — it is focused on a specific situation or a specific malady and has no implications beyond that situation. Generalized power, on the other hand, is that which can simultaneously effect transformation on a broad front — it is community-wide, above and beyond particular interests. The most prominent forms of generalized power in Pemon life are Kanaima, whose pervasiveness is taken for granted by all Pemon, and the redemptive power represented by prophets and embodied in religious movements such as Hallelujah, Chochiman, and San Miguel (see Thomas, 1976). Ultimately, sorcery is concerned with the elevation of a problem thought of in terms of particularized power (e.g. specific actions of a shaman) to a problem of generalized power (the shaman or other person as Kanaima) which must be handled by a river area as a whole.

The principal forces which can overcome the structural fragmentation pervading Pemon life are ideological notions. Both the notion of Kanaima and the notion of redemption inherent in the various prophetic movements are such forces. These are *cultural* forces par excellence. In any situation of conflict, illness, or injury, it is the very definition of power involved in the situation, as well as which parties are involved, which is at stake.

This brings us back to our theme, the "fragmentation in the feud." The normal state of affairs is seen to be one of particular, individualized conflicts, two- or three-party hassles which don't extend beyond the individuals or nuclear families involved. As long as alternative interpretations of abuses can be presented which keep the conflicts particularized, it will be hard to convince potential adherents to the side of either party that it is their concern, or worth their while, to take retributive action. A specific delict can only be propelled into the realm of involvement of a larger number of people if it can be shown that a generalized threat exists. Pemon peaceableness can most fruitfully be seen as a result of the difficulty of moving people to this view. In effect, peacefulness in Pemon life exists because power itself is seen as particularized in the normal course of things, and because this separation and specificity of power itself is reflected in organizational fragmentation made possible by restricted definitions of relatedness. The feud is not so much constrained by cross-cutting ties (though these do exist) as it is by ideological definitions of power types and social structural restrictions on mobilization, both of which act in concert.

This atomism can only work if it is universal; that is, if one group within the society were enabled to develop wider cohesion by any means (ideological, structural, or technical), then the system as a whole would end in chaos. Thus proceedings in which one capitan is edged out (Chapter IV) or in which sorcery accusations are leveled (see above) center as much around differing definitions of what kind of power is involved as around the specific infractions of the offenders. Thus also the importance of knowledge and expertise on the part of Pemon leaders: it is at once a restrictive expertise, one which limits their sphere of operations and at the same time dictates that the one realm affecting everyone — the realm of the spirit — is the last to be broached. It is only invoked in the last analysis.

CHAPTER VI

Themes in Pemon Life:
Three Tales

Myth, as one author has remarked (Burridge, 1967: 91), has been "anybody's plaything." A wide variety of approaches to myth, by a wide variety of scholars, testifies to this. Perhaps the most comprehensive recent evaluation of ways of looking at myth is that of Kirk (1970), whose preliminary typology of functions includes three basic rubrics (Kirk, 1970: 252ff.): (1) narrative and entertaining; (2) operative, iterative, and validatory; and (3) speculative and explanatory. Above, we have spoken of myth as warning, injunction, and rationalization. Levi-Strauss has concentrated on the third of Kirk's rubrics, and has been primarily concerned with myth as a mechanism for the resolution of contradictions via a series of logical "codes" (sociological code, culinary code, etc.). Whatever one thinks of Levi-Strauss's *Mythologiques*, the anthropological study of myth will never again be quite the same. However, the problems faced by the interpreter of a given social reality are somewhat different from those of the comparative mythologist. Both, to be sure, face the problem of bounding a corpus (Levi-Strauss has not, in fact, done this) and of stating just what they are after in the stories.

Burridge (1967) has rather convincingly shown, to me at any rate, that Levi-Strauss focuses on content as well as form in his treatment of myths, despite Levi-Strauss's programmatic statements to the contrary. Pemon tales, if they are to tell us anything meaningful about Pemon life, must be examined from a point of view which takes content into account. Our interest here is *not* to examine the whole body of Pemon tales with an eye to analyzing it as a group of texts (this is a task for another work). The body of recorded Pemon tales is extensive (Koch-Grunberg, 1916–28, vol. II, translated in Koch-Grunberg, 1953; Armellada, 1964, 1973; Simpson, 1944), and a complete analysis would require a volume in itself. Some selection is necessary, for the tales cover a wide variety of topics, differ widely in length and scope, and were collected at varying times and places. Koch-Grunberg collected a series of tales in 1911–12 near Roraima, Armellada began collecting tales in the 1930s and has continued up to the present, and Simpson collected one version of an important tale during his stay in Kamarata in 1939. Armellada's 1973 work gives transcriptions of the originals in the Pemon language, but his work contains mostly less important tales.

On a preliminary basis, we can identify six separate areas of Pemon statements about ideology and cosmology:

1) Explicitly expressed norms: references by informants to the way things should be done — e.g. the *wa?ni mure* marriage rule.

2) Tales told in small gatherings, usually around bedtime, with the overt objective of entertainment and, to some extent, education in the broad sense.

3) *Taren*: magical invocations (see Chapter IV), both curative and preventive, held or "owned" by individuals.

4) Statements about Kanaima, the spirit of evil in all its forms and manifestations, and about plant and animal spirits, particularly those plant spirit helpers used by shamans (e.g. *ayuk*); also statements about the spirits known as *mawari* (see Chapter IV), who appear in human form, live in the tops of mountains, and are often responsible for stealing souls.

5) Statements in and about syncretistic religious observances — the ceremonies, prayers, and chants of Hallelujah (see Butt, 1960), Chochiman, and most recently San Miguel (Thomas, 1976).

6) Contemporary Catholic and Adventist precepts.

Our purpose here is not to present a complete treatment of Pemon thought or even, as mentioned above, to treat the complete corpus of recorded tales. We must be conscious that only a small portion of Pemon thinking will be visible through the lens of the tales. This raises problems of the representativeness and importance of the material selected to be treated. Also, material in the tales relates not only to our principal object of study, Pemon social relations, but also to *taren*, the spirit beliefs, the geography and place names of Pemon territory, the symbolic interpretation of the cultural and natural world, and much more. Here I wish only to examine the tales as symbolic statements about the form and content of social relations, including affective elements. The tales can, if properly integrated, in some sense bridge the gap between the level of our diagram (see Chapter III) on which are found affective, normative, and cognitive inputs into Pemon classification of others, and the symbolic level. The question of the relationship between ideas and social relations (or ideology and social structure, to put it in more abstract terms) has always preoccupied anthropologists. The tales can reflect social reality, contradict it, or simply, in some cases, be tangential to it, and all this within the confines of a single narrative. Since our purpose here is to cast some additional light on Pemon feelings about social relationships, three tales have been selected that deal extensively with the commonly occurring relationships previously discussed. These are:

1) The Makunaima sequence, or creation tales. These relate the adventures of two culture heroes (brothers) in the creation of Pemon land, crops, techniques, and, to a certain extent, social practices. They constitute an extended commentary on the nature of Pemon male siblingship.

2) The story of Wewe and his brothers-in-law, which focuses on own-generation affinal relations.

3) The Maichak tale, which recounts the trials of a son-in-law with his father-in-law, a king vulture.

In each case I have selected one recorded version of the tale for presentation here. The Makunaima sequence is taken from Armellada (1964: 27–69), the Wewe story from Koch-Grunberg (1953: 104–9), and the Maichak tale from Simpson (1944), with some changes in wording for the sake of clarity. Alternate versions of the Maichak tale are found in Koch-Grunberg (1953: 88–98) and Armellada (1964: 87–100). The rendering of the Makunaima tale was done by Anna V. Thomas.

THE MAKUNAIMA

A long time ago the sun was a person. He spent his time clearing brush and burning it to make fields for planting ocumo. He ate only ocumo; his face shone.

One day after working, he went to a stream to drink and bathe. As he approached, he noticed an eddy in a deep spot in the stream, as if a person had just gone under water there.

He was puzzled by this, and so when he returned on another day he approached more cautiously. He was able to see a small woman, with long hair that went all the way down to her feet, bathing and playing in the water, splashing the water with her hair. She became aware of him and plunged, but the sun managed to grasp her hair. "Not me, not me!" cried the being, whose name was Tuenkaron. "I will send you a woman to be your companion and wife." So he let go of her hair and released her.

The next day, as the sun was clearing and stacking up trunks and branches to make his field, he saw a white woman, whom Tuenkaron had sent him, approaching. "Have you cleared the field?" she asked. "Not yet," the sun replied. "I have only cleared this small area that you see here and have put together these few piles."

Later the sun said to the woman, "Take these ocumos I've baked out of the embers and we'll eat them." She did, and said to the sun, "Here they are." They ate.

Then the sun said to the woman, "Burn these brush piles," and she lit them with a split stick and some dry kindling. When she said, "The fire's going now," he said, "Go and get some water." She went to the stream with her gourd and bent down to get the water, but as she was filling the gourd, her fingers softened and lost their shape, and then her arms, and then her whole body. She collapsed into a little heap of clay. The woman had been made of white earth.

When the woman didn't return, the sun went to look for her. But all he found at the stream was some turbid water, where the woman had dissolved, clouding the water. He was disgusted. "So this is what Tuenkaron sent me," he said. "A woman who isn't even any good for getting water!" He went further upstream so he could at least drink some clear water. Then, as it was getting late, he went home to sleep.

The next morning he was back at work on his field, and at midday, just as he was about to go and eat, another woman appeared. This time Tuenkaron had sent him a black woman, black as the people of that race.

"Have you cleared the field?" she asked. "Well, yes and no," the sun replied. "I have cleared this little bit here." Then he said, "Go bring some water and we'll eat together." She went to the stream and brought some water, and they ate ocumo together. After their meal the sun went back to work and said to the woman, "While I continue stacking, you burn those piles over there." She took a split stick and went to set the fire. But as she knelt by the fire, blowing on it, her face melted and then her arms and then her whole body. She collapsed into a heap of wax. That woman had been made of wax.

The sun had turned around several times to check on the fire, but since he didn't see any smoke he went to see what was happening. "But I told her to burn those piles," he said to himself as he went. Quite a surprise greeted him when he got there; the woman had melted and was now just a heap of wax.

Then the sun marched down to the stream saying, "All right; that Tuenkaron is a wicked and deceitful creature. Now I'm going to dry up all the water in this stream." But Tuenkaron heard him and answered, without letting herself be seen. "No, wait," she said, "Don't do it. Wait. I'll send you another woman."

The sun was not placated, and that night he lay down angry. But the next day he went to his field as usual, as soon as it was light. As he stooped over his work, a reddish, rock-colored woman appeared, holding a bowl in her hand.

"Have you cleared the field?" she asked. But the sun was suspicious and pretended not to hear. "Why don't you answer me?" the woman asked. "Because you are all frauds!" the sun replied. "You all collapse or melt!" "Very well, then," said the woman. "I'll return to Tuenkaron."

"Wait a minute," the sun said. "I'll test you." He told her to light a fire, and she lit it and didn't melt. He sent her for water, and she brought it and didn't dissolve. He told her to cook ocumo in her bowl, and saw how she placed it on some rocks and kindled a fire underneath. He carefully observed all of her ways and abilities.

Late in the afternoon the woman said, "I have to go back now." "All right," said the sun, "Prepare my meal for me so that you can go back." After she had done so, she said, "I'm going, but I'll be back early tomorrow morning." "Yes, come early," said the sun.

The next morning the sun went to work earlier than usual. The woman showed up very early too. The sun tested her again: he had her bring water and start a fire and cook. He saw that she didn't dissolve or melt or break apart, and she became pleasing to him. She filled his eye.

That afternoon they went together to bathe in the stream, and the sun saw clearly that the woman was reddish, like the bits of firestone found in riverbeds. She was neither black nor white. "Let's go to my house," said the sun. But she replied, "I haven't spoken to Tuenkaron about that." "What does that have to do with it?" said the sun. "I couldn't possibly," she said, and so the sun said, "Well, then, at least come very early to prepare my food." "All right," she said, "and I'll talk to Tuenkaron about staying with you."

The next morning the woman came very early and prepared food. She baked ocumo, and she dug up manioc and grated it and made manioc bread. And that night she stayed to sleep with the sun and from then on they lived together always.

They had several children, and these were the Makunaima. Some people say that the name of the mother was Aromadapuen, and that the names of their children were as follows: Meriwarek, the first-born, then Chiwadapuen, a girl, then Arawadapuen, the second daughter, and then Arukadari, the youngest, often called Chikɨ.

II

When the youngest was still in his mother's belly, the sun went on a journey to Iken to buy cloth, salt, and other things for them all. Before he left, he marked off the months he would be gone. But he did not return when he had said he would. The months passed and many more; the sun did not appear.

They worried a great deal about what might have happened to him. "Our father said, 'If I don't come back at the expected time, go out along the path I took and look for me,' but we haven't gone." "Maybe the *mawari* saw him coming back with all the things he bought and became envious and locked him up." "Let's go find Father." They went on talking like this.

One day at this time the youngest of the Makunaima came up to the eldest as he was making a bow for his arrows and sharpening his fishhooks. The little one asked for a bow of his own. So his brother picked up a small stick and tied some cotton cord to it and gave it to the little one. But the little fellow wouldn't take it. "Not this," he said. "Well, what was it you wanted?" asked his brother. "I've made you a bow and you're not paying any attention to it." He shaped a stick like a shotgun for him, but the little one didn't want that either. "Not this," he said again.

So the elder brother went back to sharpening fishhooks with the little one sitting by his side. "Watch out," he said, "don't let the filings fall in your eyes." But the little one kept on sitting beside him, gathering the filings from the hooks and the wood shavings from the bows. And little by little he made his shotgun: the butt, the barrel, the hammer, the breech, and all the rest of it. He made a complete shotgun with nothing left out. His brother saw him doing all this but he thought it was just a toy.

He made the powder and shot too, and when everything was ready, still sitting right beside his brother, he made a tremendous blast. "Caramba!" yelled his frightened brother. "What are you doing? Give me that — let me see it!" "No, no," said the little one. "I asked you to make a shotgun like this, but you weren't paying attention to me. This shotgun is just for me and I won't give it to anyone."

At that point, the brothers decided it was time to hurry up and go look for their father.

Their mother, seeing that all of her children were going, went along too. They walked and walked and arrived at a fork in the road, and had to stop and think about which path to take. "This one is more worn," they said. "He probably took this one." But then they also thought, "But who knows? He might have taken the overgrown one." They decided to take the overgrown one. And when they encountered some human droppings, they remembered their father's having said, "Where the path forks, so that you won't take the jaguar's path by mistake, I'll

defecate at the side of the path and leave some feathers of birds I've killed too."
Since they found these things, they continued, reassured.

What they didn't know was that the jaguar had overheard their father's conversation and had moved the droppings and feathers to trick them.

They kept on walking, and just as it was getting dark they came upon a house. It was the house of the jaguar's old wife. "Where are you going?" she asked. The mother of the Makunaima replied, "I'm going with them. They're looking for their father." "You haven't chosen your path well," said the jaguar's old wife. "But since it's getting late, why don't you stay here overnight and resume your journey tomorrow?" "All right," they said, and they spent the night there.

III

The next day the women deloused each other while the Makunaima went out on the savanna to shoot birds with their blowgun. There were a lot of little birds nearby, but they didn't hit any. One *kachipiu* bird seemed to be playing with them; their darts kept missing the little bird and sticking in the *mateurai* grass. They pursued the little bird until they had used up all their darts, which couldn't be recovered because they had changed into little flowers in the grass.

"Kachipiu, kachipiu," said the little bird when all the darts were gone. "Brother, listen to what this little bird is saying," said the youngest. "It isn't saying anything, it's just singing," said his brother. But the little brother insisted, "It is saying something. Wait, I'll startle it so you can hear it again. It's saying, 'Kachipiu, don't go far, the jaguar's old wife is poisoning your mother.'"

They ran back to the house, but it was too late. Their mother had already been poisoned by the jaguar's wife's lice. "Why have you poisoned our mother?" they cried. "I didn't do anything, she did it herself!" the jaguar's wife replied. "I told her not to eat the ones around the ears because they're poisonous. But she paid no attention and ate them anyway. I didn't want her to poison herself!"

While this was going on, they heard the jaguar coming. "What will become of us now?" they said. Very quickly they chewed their *kumi* and cast a spell and changed into chiggers, and hid in their mother's belly.

The jaguar came in and said, "Who killed this old woman, caramba? Well, all we can do with her now is open her up and gut her and eat her." When he slit open her belly he said, "Look at that, there are some little eggs in here! We'll have these eggs to begin with." So his old wife started to cook them in her bowl.

But they cast another spell, and while the bowl boiled and said, "Bubble, bubble," they said, "The cold of the sea, the cold of the sea." And at that, the bowl didn't boil. It didn't even heat up.

Then the old woman tried to break the eggs on the drinking trough. But as she was striking her hand against the trough while saying, "Pow! Pow!" they said, "*Saprai, saprai,*" and sprang out of the trough unbroken. She tried to roast them on the coals too, but they sprang away the same way.

Then she put them in the basket in which she kept bits of meat and roasted fish and ocumo and sweet potatoes, but the next day she found that they had eaten the food. After this happened several times, she very carefully set about trying to find out who had eaten what she had put in the basket. And one day as she watched, hidden, she saw the eggs crack open and saw them emerge as two little frogs and eat her food. When she tried to catch them, they popped back into hiding in the eggs.

"Caramba!" she said. "Stop doing this! Show yourselves as you are! Instead of stealing my food, you really ought to appear as people to clear a field for me." Then they did appear as people, and quickly grew big enough to be people who could clear a field. But the jaguar's wife didn't realize that they were the Makunaima, the sons of the woman whom she had poisoned with her lice.

IV

In a very short time the Makunaima, unrecognized, cut a large field for the jaguar's old wife. When the branches had dried out well, they told the old woman, "We'll burn the field now. While we're starting the fire around the outside, you start it in the middle." They split some sticks of *araira*, which is a wood that burns very well, for themselves, but for her they split some of *kricho*, a wood that burns poorly and won't produce a flame.

The old woman spent some time crouched down, blowing on her kindling, but couldn't get a flame. But they, on the other hand, went to opposite sides of the field and in a moment had a fire going all the way around it.

The old woman heard the crackling of the flames and stood up to look. The poor thing realized that she was surrounded on all sides. "So this is why you sent me into the middle, to surround me with flames!" she cried. "You fiends!" she shrieked desperately. "Now I'll cut you off wherever you may flee! I'll fall upon you wherever you may be, on the savanna or under water!"

They took off at a run while the old woman cursed them. When they got to a river and saw a cayman on the bank, they chewed their *kumi* and changed into flies and placed themselves near the cayman to be swallowed. They were already in the cayman's belly when they heard the explosion of the old toad wife of the jaguar. When the flames got to her, she spattered in pieces in all directions, and these are the firestones that are found all over.

When the firestones began to rain down, the cayman submerged himself but the stones fell over the top of him, and these are his scales. The water heated up so much that it boiled, but the cayman resisted the rain of fire.

This is why firestones give off sparks, and this is why caymans have scales. This is also why toads can swallow fire without being burned; they are children of the old toad wife of the jaguar, who poisoned the mother of the Makunaima.

After the rain of firestones was over, the Makunaima came back out of the belly of the cayman, who had swallowed them without chewing when he opened his mouth to breathe. And they continued their journey.

V

After the Makunaima had avenged themselves on that crafty toad, the jaguar's wife, who had poisoned their mother, they had a good laugh at the old woman's curses and continued their journey. They went upriver in their canoe and arrived at Mt. Roraima. The little one, Chikɨ, tied the canoe to one of its peaks, the one that appears split off from Roraima.

Then they continued overland and arrived at the mountain we call Wei-tepui, Mountain of the Sun. And there Chikɨ saw what looked like a door and wanted to see who it was who lived there. Someone at the door asked, "What do you want here?" Chikɨ answered, "I'm looking for my father." "You can't see him," came the reply. "He's been injured and he's being kept hidden here."

Quite a lot of *mawari* came and went. A young girl among them felt sorry for Chikɨ and took him by the hand, and the one at the door said to them, "You could slip in next time there's a crowd, so they won't notice you. But you won't be able to see him; I've already told you that."

The girl showed Chikɨ a huge pot under which they had his father shut up. The pot was upside down but its rim was a tiny bit uneven, so that on one side the light of the sun could be seen shining out from inside. Chikɨ quickly fired his shotgun at the pot and shattered it.

The explosion was terrible and the *mawari* were very frightened. "What's going on here?" they said. "Who did this?" "There he goes, stop him!" they said. But Chikɨ fired again and dazed them all and they felt blinded. The sun, Chikɨ, and the girl seized the moment to escape.

The sun was very weak from being locked up so long. He went up to the sky, taking Chikɨ's shotgun with him, and that's where he is now, as the sun; sometimes, even when there are no clouds, there are lightening flashes from his shotgun. And the girl went up to the sky as a star.

But Chikɨ and his brother continued journeying near Roraima.

VI

In those days the Makunaima didn't have much food. One day Chikɨ saw a very large lizard, called a *maimaima*, probably the mother of all these reptiles. He said to his brother, "Look at that lizard sprawled out asleep at the opening to its burrow. Wait here, I'm going to take off its tail and we'll eat it." "Don't do that, little brother," his elder brother said. "Be careful or it might eat you." But Chikɨ didn't listen. He threw himself at the lizard, grabbed his tail, and yanked at it till he pulled it off.

They roasted the tail and tasted it, and saw that it tasted like fish. "This is delicious," said Chikɨ. He was so taken with it that the next time he saw a *maimaima* lizard he wanted its tail too. His brother cautioned him again to be very careful because he could get eaten, but he didn't pay any attention. He threw himself at the lizard and grabbed it by the tail, but this lizard wheeled around and swallowed Chikɨ. Then it went back to its burrow.

Wondering what to do to rescue him, his brother lit a fire at the opening of the burrow and burned some peppers over the fire and began to sing, "You swallowed my little brother, *Maimaima*, now come and eat me too." At this, the lizard emerged. There was the elder of the Makunaima burning peppers, and as soon as the lizard stuck its head out he whacked it hard with a stick and cut open its belly.

There he found Chikɨ, who got up laughing as if nothing had happened. But his elder brother had been frightened and saddened at finding himself alone, and said, "Don't do that again, my little brother! You see what happens when you don't pay attention to me."

VII

In those days the Makunaima didn't have fishhooks or axes or knives. But Chikɨ noticed that the heron had a fishhook. He said to his brother, "Let's go to the heron and buy the hook so we can catch some good fish." At that time they had been catching only small fish which they partially cooked on rocks heated by the sun.

So they went and found the heron on a big rock from which he was casting his hook into a deep pool. "Brother, sell us your fishhook," they said. But he replied, "No, I can't do that. I have only one hook and I need it to catch food for myself and my wife and children. The most I could do for you would be to make you a hook like it." So he did, but it was made of wax and it bent and didn't catch any fish.

When they approached the heron, he had just caught an *aimara*. They asked for it and the heron gave it to them, and they saw that it was very tasty. This made them want the hook even more, and they started thinking about how they might steal it.

Chiki went downstream a little, dived into the river unseen, and changed into an *aimara*. Little by little he got closer to the heron's hook and gave it a few tugs. The heron pulled out the hook, but got nothing. The heron cast again and this time Chiki was on the hook. But when the heron pulled out the *aimara*, the elder of the Makunaima realized that it was his little brother and asked the heron to give it to him. The elder brother went off, and when they were where the heron couldn't see them, his little brother changed back into a person.

For a third time Chiki approached the hook, and this time he took along a ray's tooth. He gave the hook a good tug and cut the line. The heron pulled fast, but pulled out nothing; he found that a very large *aimara* had gotten away with his hook. Chiki got out of the water out of sight of the heron, very happy with the hook he had stolen. And the heron went home and told his wife a very large *aimara* had gotten away, taking the hook with it.

The Makunaima followed the heron home to see what he would say to his wife. They overheard him say, "I'm coming home without anything because a very large *aimara* took my hook. I guess now I'll have to go to Iken to look for some more material to make another one."

The Makunaima decided to go along too. When the heron took wing, they did too, the elder as a swallow and the younger as a hummingbird. The heron flew and flew and arrived at the mine of fishhook material, with the hummingbird right there behind him. The swallow got there a little later.

They watched the heron extracting the material, just like clay for making bowls, but it was iron. They waited till the heron had left and then they took out plenty of the material for themselves. As they were returning they said, "Now we'll make axes and machetes and knives." Chiki said, "I'm going to make a shotgun." His elder brother said, "No, little brother, don't get involved in dangerous things. You might get hurt." But the little one kept to his purpose and made a shotgun. His brother made only axes and machetes.

VIII

In those days the Makunaima had no fire and endured a lot of cold. They had tried to make fire in various ways but hadn't succeeded. They realized that rubbing one's hands heated them up, and this gave them the idea that one could start a fire with one's hands. So they stuck some splinters of wood into their skin, but their hands became infected and they still didn't have any fire.

But Chiki saw that the curassow was an owner of fire and always had fire in his house. So he thought he might arrange to steal the fire and become an owner of it himself. "Look, I'm going to change into a cricket and get into the curassow's house and steal fire from him," he said. But his brother said, "Be careful, little brother. The curassow's children might kill you playing with you, or they might eat you." But Chiki paid no attention.

Chiki entered the curassow's house as a cricket and jumped over to the fire. The curassow's children grabbed him and played with him in various ways. Chiki watched the curassow start a new fire. He stacked up a pile of split wood and breathed hoarsely onto it, and a spark lept from his throat to the wood and the fire caught.

When there were coals, one of the boys playing with the cricket put some little pieces of coal on its back. Then the cricket sprang up very high, escaping from the boy's hands and out of the curassow's house. He got to where his brother was waiting for him and said, "Now we have fire and can cook our fish!" Before that, they had eaten them raw or heated them up a little on rocks in the sun.

And this is how the cricket came to have those little white spots on its back.

IX

In those days the Makunaima had no fields. They followed the animals and ate what they ate.

One day they went to the agouti's house and said, "Well, here we are." They were ravenously hungry, but the agouti didn't have anything to eat. They lay down to sleep and noticed that the agouti was so stuffed that he was belching. "I'm going to sleep with my mouth open, as was recommended by some people from far away," said Chikɨ. "Me too," said his brother. "Me too," said the agouti. Chikɨ stayed awake, and when the agouti was fast asleep he could see some *pupu* seeds between his teeth.

In the morning when they woke up, Chikɨ asked the agouti, "Where did you find the *pupu* fruit?" "Over there on the ground," the agouti replied. "Tell us where so we can gather and eat some too," said Chikɨ. The agouti told them to follow him and they came to a tree under which there was a lot of fallen fruit. The Makunaima ate until they were full.

Soon Chikɨ said, "Brother, let's cut down the tree and we'll get plenty of fruit." His brother said, "It's better just to gather the fruit that falls and leave the tree standing." But Chikɨ didn't pay any attention and cut down the tree. After this they suffered a lot of hunger again.

They went to the paca's house, as they had to the agouti's, and repeated the story about sleeping with one's mouth open. They found that he ate sweet potatoes. They went to the peccary's house and found manioc, and they went to the parrot's house and found corn. They went to the houses of the other animals too. But each time Chikɨ tore out or cut down the plants and they fell back into hunger.

So they went back to the agouti's house. He was a great food-finder, and after they had cut down the *pupu* tree he had gone and found the Wadaka Tree and had done very well eating the fruit that fell from it. They slept with their mouths open again, and when the agouti was fast asleep Chikɨ looked in his mouth and saw bits of banana between his teeth. "Where did he find this fruit?" Chikɨ said to his brother. "When he leaves, let's go and follow him."

But the agouti ran too fast for them. So the next day they sent a squirrel, who could leap from tree to tree, to follow him, and soon the squirrel returned to tell them.

When they arrived at the Wadaka Tree they saw a lot of bananas under it, and they ate till they were so full they belched. Then they looked up and saw that each branch bore a different kind of banana. All of the varieties were there.

Chikɨ said, "Let's cut down this tree so we'll have plenty of fruit." But his brother said, "No, it's best just to eat the fruit that falls. Let's not cut it. Let's leave this marvel for our children to see." "Why should we?" said Chikɨ. "As long as we leave the trunk, they'll believe it." They argued a lot about this, but Chikɨ never paid any attention and always won out over his brother.

X

They began cutting down the Wadaka Tree, Chikɨ on one side, his brother on the other. It took them a long time, and they weren't cutting at the same level. The elder of the Makunaima, since he didn't want to cut the tree down, said "Thud, *waina* tree." This is the name of a tree of very hard wood, and he wanted them to tire and stop cutting. But Chikɨ said, "Banana tree," which is very soft, so that they would finish quickly.

From time to time, while they rested, they made baskets in which to carry the fruit when the Wadaka Tree fell. They made a very small basket for the agouti, and then when the tapir came and asked for one too they made him a big, loosely woven basket. And that's how they came to make all different kinds of baskets, large and small.

The Wadaka Tree had vines of different colors and thicknesses all over it. As the brothers were cutting it, these vines changed into the various kinds of snakes.

The cuts weren't even on the two sides of the tree, and when it was half cut it keeled over so that it came to rest on top of Mt. Iru-tepui. The Makunaima tried to get one of the animals to go up and free it. They asked the monkey, but he said no. Others refused too. They were afraid because there were all kinds of wasps up there.

Then the squirrel showed up and they asked her. "You're so good at getting around in the trees, little sister," they said. "Won't you go and free the Wadaka Tree?" She said she would, although she was afraid that it wouldn't be easy. "I'll see what I can do," she said, and she scurried up the tree.

And even though she was getting stung by the wasps, she cut here and there as fast as she could and managed to free the Wadaka Tree, and it came crashing down. The tree fell towards Inkareta, but some branches fell over here on this side. There are places here where bananas, pawpaws, and other plants grow by themselves, and we call pawpaws, which grow by themselves in many places, "Makunaima fruit."

When the trunk of the tree was cut open, a river could be seen inside with *aimara* and other big fish in it. So the Makunaima made a plug of tightly woven matting and wax to seal it off. When the tree fell, water started to gush out of the cut trunk and they hurried to seal it. But while they were busy filling their basket with fruit to take with them, the monkey came poking around and unplugged the hole, and a huge flood of water came gushing out, with all kinds of fish in it, and washed away the plug and everything else. The water carried bananas, pineapples, sugar cane, pawpaws, manioc, ocumo, sweet potatoes, and all the things the Wadaka Tree produced, to all parts of the world.

When the agouti saw that the land was being flooded, he quickly filled his basket with everything he could and ran off to hide in a hole in a tree, which he sealed off with wax from the inside.

The Makunaima, too, looked around for a place to climb up out of the flood. Chikɨ went up a *maripa* palm and his brother went up a *waruma* palm, and they spent one rainy season in the crowns of these trees living on their fruit. One day Chikɨ said to his brother, "Try some of my fruit." Before tossing it up to him, he put it in his prepuce to warm it up. His brother did the same with some of his fruit before sending it over as a return for the gift. And that's why these fruits are so greasy.

The Makunaima could tell when the waters were going down by the sounds made by the seeds they dropped. And when they could hear that fruit was no longer falling in water, they carefully descended and slowly came down out of the mountain.

The agouti, trying to find out if all that water was still there, made little holes in his wax plug from time to time, and if any water came in he sealed it up again right away. He was sitting down all this time keeping a fire between his paws, which is why he has a curved-up tail with reddish hair near it.

When the Makunaima came down from the palms and the mountains, the earth and even the rocks had become softened. During this time they amused themselves by making rocks and rapids just for fun. There are rocks in which you can still see their footprints. And the baton marks on the flat stones where they danced holding their batons are from this period too. The Makunaima went to many places and painted rocks and other things, so people are still often reminded of them today.

XI

The Makunaima lived in many places and traveled to many places, but one of the places people still point out today is Mt. Aruadan, one of the crests over the Karauetka Valley, the valley of the Kukenan. Aruadan served as a house for the Makunaima. There is a large rock there that is flattened like a big baking slab. There are lots of chiggers and fleas there, and the Makunaima are said to have lived there a long time. The elder brother and his wife and one of the sisters of the Makunaima and Chiki and the elder brother's mother-in-law lived there.

One time while they were living there, the elder brother went on a trip to Iken to buy powder, shot, firing pins, cloth, and other things they had run out of. Chiki cried a lot after he left. The mother-in-law asked him, "What's the matter? Why are you crying?" She told his sister to take him to bathe to quiet him down. "Let's go, little brother," she said. But he didn't want to go with her. Then the old woman pointed to his sister-in-law and asked him, "Do you want her to take you?" "Yes," said Chiki.

His sister-in-law took him by the hand and said, "Let's go," but Chiki said, "No. Take me piggy-back." So his brother's wife carried him to the river on her back, and when they got there she said, "Take your bath, little fellow." A little later she said, "Come over here so I can get you washed properly." While she was washing him, Chiki changed himself into a grownup and began to look at her genitals and to play with them. She saw him as so handsome that she responded to him and they ended up copulating. When they came out of the water, Chiki changed himself back into a little child. He got back up on his sister-in-law's back and she took him home without saying anything about what they had done.

The same thing happened again many times. Chiki got used to having his sister-in-law take him to bathe or to go out with the excuse that he had to relieve himself, in which case he always told her to take him behind a hill where they wouldn't be seen. But one day the dog followed them and saw everything.

After several months had gone by, the elder of the Makunaima signaled his return by setting fire to some savanna grass, and the women made *cachiri* for a party to welcome him. When he was near home he fired his shotgun a few times and Chiki came out to meet him dancing. They drank and danced till they were drunk, and Chiki, in his drunkenness, sang, among other things, "Just like the hole of a beehive is the one my brother's wife has." The elder brother heard the song. He didn't make too much of it because of his brother's condition, but still, it left him feeling suspicious.

Chiki and his sister-in-law continued as before. One day the elder Makunaima sent his dog after them, and the dog came back and told him everything he had seen. But Chiki realized this and took the power of speech away from dogs, and since then they have not been able to speak.

Another day Chiki was crying and his brother slapped him. But he didn't bring himself to speak out. Then Chiki, realizing that his brother was disgusted and hostile toward him, started thinking about getting away and living alone with the old woman.

XII

At the time of their falling out, Chiki thought a lot.

One day he said to the old woman, whom he called Mother, "Mama, close your eyes and say, 'I'd like to be on top of the mountain to see the view from there.'" She said it with her eyes closed and, to her surprise, found herself on top of the mountain.

Then he said to her, "Mama, close your eyes and say, 'This is where my house should be.'" She did, and the house she wanted immediately appeared.

Then he said to her, "Mama, close your eyes and say, 'This is where a field should be.'" She did, and instantly a field appeared full of bananas, ocumo, sweet potatoes, manioc, sugar cane, etc.

While Chikɨ had everything in his field and also managed to hunt, his brother down below was often hungry. The old woman felt sorry for her son-in-law and so would throw down some bananas along with the peels she was discarding. Chikɨ noticed this and asked her, "Why are you throwing away bananas along with peels?" "Oh, your poor brother," she replied. "Some brother," Chikɨ retorted. "He slapped me!"

But gradually Chikɨ calmed down and said to the old woman, "Why don't you make some *cachiri* for them and I'll invite them to come and dance." When the *cachiri* was made, he said to her, "Now close your eyes and say that there's a path down the mountain." She did, and a path down the mountain immediately appeared.

Chikɨ went down to his brother's house and stood outside the door and said, "Are you here?" "Yes," they replied from inside in a vexed tone of voice. "We're here." "My brother," Chikɨ asked, "Do you have any rope?" His brother replied from inside in the same vexed tone, "We don't have anything here."

But Chikɨ found some fibers lying around and twisted them into a rope, and made a noose and set it up along a tapir's track. In the morning he said to the old woman, "I'm going to check my trap," and he went and found that the tapir had gotten hung. "Here's the tapir," he shouted loudly so that his brother would hear him and come. But his brother and the others said, "Now, what would that racket be about?" and paid no attention.

He went back to his brother's house and started chatting. He said he'd already eaten the tapir he had caught in his trap. His brother and his people said to each other, "Could this be what all the shouting was about?" Then Chikɨ said, "I'm going to go and check the trap now. If you hear me call, bring the pack, axe, and machete and we'll cut up the tapir." After he left, they said, "Could this be true? Let's sharpen our machetes well, and if this turns out to be some kind of a hoax, we'll try them out on him."

Very shortly they heard him call, "Here's the tapir, bring the pack!" They went and found out that in fact Chikɨ really had devised a way to catch tapirs in a snare.

XIII

When the elder brother finally decided to go up to his brother's for the *cachiri*, he got together a lot of other people to go with him because he was afraid of his brother. But Chikɨ had had the old woman prepare all kinds of drinks—*paiwa* beer, pineapple juice, *cachiri*, *auyama* juice, manioc juice, and more—in order to extend a warm welcome to his brother.

On the appointed day Chikɨ went to the edge of the summit to see him coming with his family. When he saw a lot of other people coming along too, he decided to change them into *moriche* palms. He let the one in front, who was ahead of all the rest like a dance leader or a fast runner, get halfway up the mountain and there he stopped him cold. "Stay right there as a *moriche* palm!" he said, and he stayed there and has been there ever since. He changed all the other people his brother had brought along into *moriche* palms too, some at the foot of the mountain and some further up, according to where they were at the time.

He let only his brother and his family come up to him, and they danced and drank till they were drunk. Then the two brothers lived together once more, in the house high on the mountain with the field Chiki̇ had there.

One day while they were living there, the elder brother went toward the mouth of the Apanguao River to hunt deer. As he was walking on the savanna, he saw a beast he had never seen before. He had been bent over, and as he straightened up to get a better look, it put him to sleep. After that, all he could do was go back home.

He told his wife, "I ran into a beast that filled me with sleepiness and I don't know what it could have been." Chiki̇ wasn't there, but he knew what his brother had said. When he got home, he asked, "What are you saying, my brother?" and his brother replied, "You tell me." "You were saying that you had run into a beast that made you sleepy, my brother," said Chiki̇. "Right," said his elder brother. "Then we ought to go take a look at it," said Chiki̇.

They went and found it in the same place. The elder of the Makunaima cautioned his brother, "When you straighten up, that's when it makes you sleepy." But despite being forewarned, they opened their eyes wide and stared right at the beast to get a good look at it, and it dazed them and made them drowsy. It was Torpor, the father of sleep.

After that happened, Chiki̇ said, "Let's go kill it." "Fine," said his brother. They went after it again, walking hunched over. But when they got near it they straightened up, and once again it made them so sleepy that it left them groggy.

So they abandoned their bows and arrows and went after it with sticks. This time they stayed hunched over till they reached it, and then, without straightening up or trying to look at it, they beat it to death and chopped it up into pieces.

And this is why sleep hasn't been able to take possession of people and keep them asleep all the time. All of it was divided up, with something for everybody, because they chopped it up in pieces. So we sleep, and then we awaken.

XIV

The story of the Makunaima ends with their leaving the valley of the Kukenan and going off in the direction of Remonota to the land of the Brazilians. Some say they went to Iken, just as their father had at first when they wanted to buy things from the clothed people.

If you take the path that goes down out of these mountains where we live toward Boa Vista through Warai, you'll come across a little stream called Merok. The place where that stream joins the river is definitely known to have been one of the sites of the Makunaima. It's a place through which the fish always go upstream to dance in the season of the rising waters, and they ate great quantities of these fish. You can see whole mounds of fish scales changed into rocks there.

One day as they were starting to walk around these new lands, Chiki̇ tested his brother. He tore off a few *muku-muku* leaves and turned them into ray fish. His brother didn't know about this and stepped on one and got stung. He cried out a lot from the pain, but he healed himself.

The elder of the Makunaima retaliated by stripping an *uru* plant of its leaves and changing them into piranhas. He put them in the river crossing and Chiki̇ got bitten. But he too healed himself, speaking his own name like this: "Forefather Makunai, Forefather Chiki̇, Forefather Anike."

Chiki̇ was tireless in his inventions. Walking around there, he created the animals' rocks, the birds' rocks, and so forth. Then he told his brother, "Look, you shouldn't just go wandering around anyplace at all to go and relieve yourself. I've designated special rocks for the animals and for the birds and for the rest of them."

"Why is my little brother keeping me from going wherever I want with these animals' rocks and birds' rocks and all?" said the elder brother. Then he had to think up spells for all these things so that his children wouldn't have to suffer the consequences of his brother's whims. And he said, "When my descendants get sick on account of the animals' rocks and the birds' rocks and the rest of them, I'll cut short the harm, I'll put a stop to it and reduce it to nothing, I, Forefather Makunai, I, Forefather Anike."

Analysis of the Makunaima Tales

The Makunaima sequence, as recorded by Armellada, can be considered as a "charter" myth along several dimensions. In the section on the creation of a wife for the first Pemon (the sun) by a water nymph, the basic sexual division of labor and the ideas of proficiency in subsistence tasks as a prerequisite to a successful marriage are laid out. Sun and water are initially opposed, and the sequence goes:

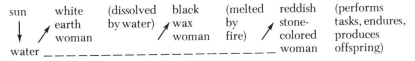

The opposites sun and water are mediated by a progression which results in an equilibrium between two poles. The white earth woman is dissolved by river water, a low element as well as being the element which created her. The black wax woman is higher (wax is found in bees' nests, in trees, off the ground) but absorbs heat (drains the sun?) and disappears. Finally, the reddish stone-colored woman is intermediate in color and durable, like stone. Stone or rock ($t\dot{i}k$) can be either on the ground or extending upward toward the sky ($w\dot{i}k$ is the word for a sizable hill of rock). Likewise, there is explicit reference in the story to the sun watching the third woman placing ocumo on the rocks and making the fire. Stone griddles ($pta:ri$) were formerly a necessity for baking manioc cakes. One could see this initial passage of the creation tale as Levi-Strauss would have it, a passage from nature to culture via successively mediated oppositions. So far, so good. More can be got from it, however, by looking at the charter aspects of this portion of the tale in a more generalized way.

First, the sun is in a high position but sustains a lack (has no wife). The sun versus water opposition is a hierarchy in several senses: (1) spatial position (though not entirely — rain clouds block the sun), and (2) sun evaporates water (overarching power, witness the sun's threat to dry up Tuenkaron's stream). The creation of successive candidates for the sun's wife (which he obtains, in the last analysis, by threatening the water nymph) is accompanied by a series of challenges — "Have you cleared the field yet?" — and tests — cooking, drawing water, etc. — from both parties. At the "charter" level, these challenges and tests parallel the successive mediation of the spatial and power oppositions and at the same time mirror the customary protestations regarding fitness for subsistence tasks which formerly characterized the process of arranging marriages.

At the most general level, what is happening is the transformation of a hierarchy which is incomplete and distant, and ultimately sterile because of lack of connection between polar elements, into a modified hierarchy which is less distant, completed (links formerly separate end points), and fertile. This hierarchy is transformed in two ways, one which moves a natural opposition (sun versus water) into a cultural union, and the other which changes one kind of hierarchy into another, via a process of challenge and counterchallenge referring to the norms of marriage arrangement and to the sexual division of labor. The division of labor transforms a culturally sterile hierarchy into a fertile complementarity which is less hierarchical and less distant. Hierarchy must be attenuated in order to produce fertility. This fertility is maintained by proper fulfillment of obligations.

The subsequent sections of the Makunaima tales can also be viewed through this double lens of "charter" and "explanation" (at the level of general logical oppositions). The sections are:

A. The Sun and Tuenkaron (I)
B. Search for and Rescue of the Sun Father
   1) Death of Mother (II, III) and Vengeance (IV)
   2) Release of Sun Father (V)
C. Food Creation and the Tree of Life
   1) The Lizard's Tail (VI)
   2) Heron and Fishhook (VII)
   3) Curassow and Fire Theft (VIII)
   4) Agouti and the Tree of Life (IX, X)
D. Disputes between the Brothers and Their Resolution (XI, XII, XIII).
E. Coda (XIV).

The family of the sun father, as it appears in this version of the tale, was as follows:

The two sisters do not appear in the tales except for mention of their names. The section on the search for the sun father begins the adventures of two culture heroes, the brother Meriwarek (referred to as elder brother) and Chikɨ (sometimes referred to by this name, which is a nickname, and sometimes as younger brother or "little one"). In Koch-Grunberg's rendition (1953: 45–61) of the Makunaima tales, the younger brother is called Makunaima and the elder brother Jique (= Chikɨ). The nickname is significant, and the Armellada version seems more logical, since the Pemon word *chikɨ* means chigger, an irritating flea which burrows under the skin, particularly on the feet and ankles, lays eggs, and can cause considerable discomfort though not major harm. In section II the first portrayal of interaction between the two brothers can be set out as follows:

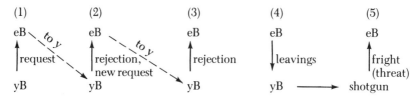

(1)   (2)   (3)   (4)   (5)

The pattern here is important, for it will be repeated, with varying outcomes, throughout the Makunaima story. Chikɨ rejects something (advice, an object given to him, invocation of a verbal norm, etc.) coming from his elder brother, who is responsible but who gets exasperated. In the course of disobeying or circumventing his elder brother, Chikɨ (who has the same irritating, ubiquitous qualities as the chigger and who, in effect, lays eggs, i.e. creates) usually brings something into being. This creation is either out of nature into culture, as in the tree-of-life incident, or within nature itself, as in the "father of sleep" incident. Chikɨ also brings about disasters like the flood in the course of creating. Chikɨ thus combines creativity, rambunctiousness, and, to some extent, outright disregard for his elder brother's admonitions. On the other hand, the elder brother is responsible (often cautious), and pulls Chikɨ out of scrapes time after time. This is the overt content of the elder brother/younger brother hierarchy as expressed throughout the tale.

We have moved, in the short space of sections I and II, through three separate notions of hierarchy:

H₁ ⟶ H₂ ⟶ H₃

H_1		H_2		H_3	
sun versus water	(distant, separate, infertile; nature)	sun and red-stone-colored wife	(partly separate, complementary, fertile; natural and cultural)	eB versus Chikɨ	(two poles within single unit; common substance and cultural creation)

The unity of the two brothers is stressed in the events following the poisoning of their mother. They change into chiggers (effectively becoming twins) to escape the jaguar. Later they change into flies to hide in the belly of the cayman (a second twin identity).

The various contests which form the latter part of the tale can be schematized as shown in Table 9.

Table 9. Contests in the Makunaima Tales.

	(1)	(2)	(3)	(4)	(5)
Chikɨ versus Lizard	yB disregards eB advice, eats lizard's tail	yB repeats, eaten by lizard	eB tricks lizard, rescues yB	yB laughs it off	
Chikɨ versus Heron	eB and yB request hook, refused, heron gives wax hook	yB becomes *aimara* fish, gets caught	eB rescues yB	yB, as *aimara*, steals hook	Coda: eB makes axes, machetes; yB makes shotgun
Chikɨ versus Curassow	yB disregards eB advice, becomes cricket, enters house	Curassow's children play roughly with cricket	yB = cricket, steals fire		
Chikɨ versus Agouti	yB tricks agouti, learns of food	yB cuts down tree, brothers end hungry	Repeat (1), (2) with paca, peccary, parrot		
	(4)	(5)	(6)	(7)	
	yB enlists squirrel to follow agouti	squirrel locates tree of many fruits	eB against cutting down tree, both use spells, yB wins, tree is cut	squirrel untangles vines, tree falls, flood ensues, fruits spread everywhere	

Table 9 (continued)

	(8)	(9)	(10)
	Coda: agouti seals self in tree, saves self from flood	yB, eB take refuge in trees, exchange fruits after putting them in prepuce	yB, eB come down after flood subsides

	(1)	(2)	(3)	
Chikɨ versus Elder Brother	eB journeys to Iken (as sun father had done)	yB seduces eBW, repeatedly	eB returns, learns of deception, slaps yB, mutual hostility	
	(4)	(5)	(6)	(7)
	yB magically transports eBWM and self to mountaintop, creates house and fields there	eB often hungry, eBWM throws down food to him.	yB descends, invents tapir snare	yB directs eBWM to make *cachiri* for party
	(8)	(9)	(10)	
	yB allows only eB and family to ascend to party	eB and family live with yB on mountaintop	Coda: brothers leave for Brazil, still testing one another, eB invents *taren* (spells) against "whims" of yB	

These contests can be looked at as a series showing the progression toward the intermediate (between two separated poles) type of hierarchy which was necessary for creation in the first part of the tale:

	(1)	(2)	(3)	(4)
Locus	ground	water, air	ground, air	ground, trees
Type	Chikɨ versus lizard	*aimara* (fish) versus heron	cricket versus curassow	Chikɨ versus agouti
Outcome	failure, yB rescued by eB	success, yB gets fishhook, still has to be rescued by eB	success, yB steals fire, does not need to be rescued	initial failure, success, disaster, safety

Chikɨ begins on the ground, goes underwater and into the air, comes back to the ground but leaps into the air as a cricket, and lastly is on the ground but seeks safety in the trees (and cuts down the Wadaka Tree, the tree of many fruits). Again we have a series of spatial hierarchies which lead to an intermediate and productive outcome (this time in the trees). These could be labeled as follows:

$$H_1 \longrightarrow H_2 \longrightarrow H_3 \longrightarrow H_4$$

no separation   maximum separation   separation lessened   intermediate degree of separation

In section I of the tale there was a progression from maximum spatial separation (infertile) to intermediate spatial separation (fertile, produces culture heroes), and finally to a hierarchy within the bounds of a single unit (eB/yB). In Chikɨ's contests it is the lack of spatial separation (H_1) that is infertile, unsuccessful, and uncreative, while the intermediate degree of separation (H_4) is successful, fertile, and creative, though with difficulties.

In Chikɨ's contest with his elder brother the following sequence occurs: separation (eB leaves), seduction (yB takes eBW), hostile separation (yB and eBWM to mountain), reconciliation, and prophylaxis (eB produces *taren* against "whims" of yB). A necessary separation, the journey to Iken, leads to a hostile separation, which is mediated by an affine whom Chikɨ transforms into a near relation (a mother). The text says "He called her Mother," but in effect she fills the position of wife while she and Chikɨ are up on the mountaintop. Thus Chikɨ's seduction of his elder brother's wife is followed by a transformation of his eBWM into a wife; i.e. the mother replaces her daughter. The mediating role of the eBWM is based on the possibility of her being simultaneously "mother" and, via the mother-daughter identity, a surrogate wife. Thus we have the transformation from the most distant social category (opposite sex, first ascending generation affine) to the "mother" category, and then back to affinal status, but in Chikɨ's own generation (surrogate wife). Her mediating role between Chikɨ and his elder brother rests upon her partaking of both affinal and consanguineal qualities.

The creation tale comes to an end when the elder brother creates *taren* to counter the negative effects of the younger brother's activities.

The elder brother maintains his responsible role (including his family and in-laws), but creation is not finally inhibited. In the conflicts between the brothers the role of affinal relationships is present but not stressed. In the following tale affinal relationships play the central part, and we can see how conflicts generated by them can result in unbridgeable (and ultimately fatal) separation and hostility.

WEWE AND HIS BROTHERS-IN-LAW

A shaman, Wewe by name, was brother-in-law of three hunters who killed much game, deer, peccaries, curassows, and other animals. He also went hunting daily, but found nothing. One day he came upon a tree that was fallen and dead. All the little birds cried for the tree, because it had been their uncle.

The shaman wanted to shoot down the little birds that were crying for the tree with his blowgun. They changed into people and shouted, "Don't shoot at us." Beside the dead tree was a small gourd, which the shaman wanted to get from the little birds. They said, "You don't know how to work with it." Previously he had complained to the little birds and had told them that he never succeeded in bringing down any game. The little birds gave him the gourd and taught him to use it. They told him that the owner of the gourd had always filled it half-full with water. They also said, "Don't speak about the gourd to your brothers-in-law. You told us that you can't hunt anything successfully." They told him not to appear with the gourd in the house of his brothers-in-law.

The shaman filled the gourd with as much water as the little birds had taught him to. He filled it halfway and set it down by the side of the stream. The stream dried up and he caught many fish. Afterward he poured the water from the gourd into the stream, which became newly filled with water.

He hid the gourd in the hold of a tree trunk and went home with the fish. He ate many fish with his brothers-in-law, but the brothers-in-law were suspicious, because he had never brought anything home before. They ate fish for two days. He had brought them in a basket which he had made of bacaba palm leaves.

The next day his brothers-in-law sent his son with him to see how he caught the fish. He did as before and caught many fish. His son saw everything, including where his father had hidden the gourd. After they returned home, the brother-in-law who had sent the boy with his father asked many questions, but the boy revealed nothing. His father had told him to keep quiet.

Then the boy's uncle said, "What are we going to do now with our brother-in-law? Let's prepare *cachiri*." They made *cachiri* for the shaman. The *cachiri* was very strong, but he accepted it. (It was a mistake for the shaman to accept the *cachiri*. He should have known that they only gave it to him so that he would reveal everything.) His brothers-in-law asked him to go fishing, so that they would have something to eat (as is the custom even today). The shaman said, "I will go fishing for two days." (Now they had the opportunity to find out how he caught the fish.)

The shaman returned with a basket full of fish. His brothers-in-law sent his wife and her three sisters to meet him, to offer him *cachiri* (as is the custom even today). The women met him and gave him much *cachiri* and became very enthusiastic about him. They returned home, and the brothers-in-law joined in and had a good time with Wewe. This had never happened before. Previously they had ridiculed him and hit him, because he had brought nothing (as is still the custom today), but they drank much *cachiri* and danced in the house.

Wewe had brought the gourd with him. The women had encountered him at the stream (which was close by) and he had not had time to hide the gourd in the hole in the tree. Afterward he did not remember to do so. The gourd was in his hunting pouch. He drank much *cachiri*, danced, and gave the pouch to his wife for her to put away. While he was dancing, the brothers-in-law were looking through his things and asked his son (whom they threatened with death if he did not tell) where his father kept his things. They grabbed the boy outside the house. When he cried, his mother came outside to see what they were doing with him. She asked her brothers, "Why do you want to kill your nephew?" They replied, "We want to know where his father's gourd is." (They knew nothing yet for sure in this respect, but wanted to discover how he caught the fish.)

The woman said, "Why do you want the gourd? You are drunk and cannot catch fish now." They let the boy go and the woman told them were the gourd was. Taking the gourd they went to fish. They also took the son of the shaman, and all of them were drunk. They wanted him to show them how to catch fish. The boy's father was drunk and sleeping; he knew nothing.

They arrived at the stream and put a little water into the gourd. The boy said, "My father said that the gourd should be half-full." Then they filled the gourd half-full. The stream dried up and they caught many fish. When they had gathered up the fish, one of the brothers-in-law said, "Now we will fill the gourd completely." But the boy said, "No. My father only filled it half-full." His uncle said, "No, we are going to fill it up all the way, so that the stream will be completely dry and we can grab more fish."

They filled the gourd and it broke open. So much water gushed forth from the gourd that everything was inundated and the three men, along with the boy, were carried away by the torrent. The three men saved themselves, but the boy was carried away with the gourd and drowned. The gourd was lost. When the three men returned, their brother-in-law was already awake. They said to their sister, "We lost the child. The water carried him away." The sister fought them, and said that they were wicked and shameless because they had lost the child.

The father went looking for his son every day. He met Dzalo, the water opossum. Dzalo had a long paddle in his hand, so long that it reached from one side of the river to the other. When he struck the water with it, the shallow part of the river stopped moving and dried up. Wewe had hidden himself stealthily to grab the water opossum's paddle. When he stretched out his hand, the water opossum saw his intention and asked, "Why do you want the paddle, brother-in-law?" Wewe asked the water opossum to give him the paddle. He was asking a lot. The water opossum gave him the paddle and taught him how to use it. He said, "Do not strike much in the center of the river, but always close to the bank. If you strike in the middle, the river will flood everything." He should always strike close to the bank, so that the water would stop.

The water opossum gave him the paddle and Wewe took it with him. He went to another river and did as the water opossum had taught him. He struck the water with the paddle, close to the bank, whereupon the river dried up along the shallows and he caught many fish. Every day he brought fish home.

The brothers-in-law realized that he always brought many fish, but they thought that he had again found a gourd. They became suspicious. The next day the shaman went fishing and the brothers-in-law went along behind him, watching everything. They hid themselves and saw where he hid the paddle. When Wewe left, they stole the paddle and did as their brother-in-law had done. They got fish every day, without his knowing about it.

Then they said, "Let's strike the paddle more in the middle of the river, so that it will become drier and so that we can catch even more fish." One of them said, "Let's not do that. We already lost the gourd and now we are going to lose our brother-in-law's paddle too." But the others did it anyway. They struck the paddle in the middle of the river. A lot of water came, flooding everything, and they lost the paddle. They returned to the house and told the shaman that they had lost the paddle. He did not reply to them, but became angry and silent.

Afterward Wewe went out every day looking for the paddle. He met Dzalo, the owner of the paddle, to whom he complained that the brothers-in-law had lost the paddle. The water opossum said, "The crab has the paddle. He plays with the paddle and dries up the river." The crab had the paddle under his arm. Dzalo grabbed the crab. The crab said to the water opossum, "If you want to eat me, eat only my body and leave the arms, because a lot of water will come out of them." He said this only to frighten the water opossum. Dzalo ate only the body of the crab and left the arms, because he was afraid that a lot of water could come out. (The water opossum even today does this.) The paddle has stayed in the arms of the crab ever since. The water opossum said to the shaman, "The crab hid the paddle, but I don't know where. Look for the paddle, perhaps you'll find it." Wewe went out every day looking for the paddle, but never found it again.

He met the howler-monkey, who was grooming himself with a comb. He positioned himself behind the howler, who did not see him, to steal the comb from him. He hit him in the hand with the blowgun and the comb fell. Wewe grabbed the comb, and asked the howler to give it to him. The howler taught him how the comb worked. He said, "When you pass the comb along the back of your head twice, all the game animals will come: tapir, deer, peccary, paca, curassow, and others. But you must be up in a tree when you comb yourself." Wewe climbed a tree and did as the howler had taught him. All the animals came and he killed many with the blowgun. The comb for this reason is called Comb-of-the-Game-Animals. Afterward Wewe hid the comb in the forest, in a hole in a tree, and returned home.

The brothers-in-law went after him to discover what new thing he had arranged. They saw how he used the comb. He killed many peccaries and took them home. The brothers-in-law did as he had done, killing many animals and afterward putting the comb back in its place. They asked the shaman for the comb. He gave them the comb, because he was already tired of it, telling them that they must climb a tree before combing themselves and not remain on the ground, in which case they would be eaten by the peccaries. And if they passed the comb through their hair more than twice, jaguars would also come.

They did as Wewe had taught them and every day brought home much game. One time they climbed a tree and rested on a badly tied hunting platform. One of the brothers-in-law said, "Let's comb our hair more times, so that more peccaries will come." They combed themselves more times. Many peccaries came. The brothers-in-law had placed the comb on a cross-tie of the platform. The peccaries banged into the platform, which was not secure. The comb fell and the peccaries took it away. Afterward the vine holding the platform together broke. Two of the brothers-in-law fell and were torn to pieces by the peccaries. The third, who was the youngest, held on tight and saved himself. He returned home.

Wewe felt the loss of his son deeply and wanted revenge on the brother-in-law. The brother-in-law told the shaman that the other two brothers-in-law had been torn to pieces by the peccaries and that the comb was lost. The shaman responded, "Didn't I tell you? But you are headstrong. The comb was my tool to call game animals, but not to cause you grief." His mother-in-law, who had lost her sons, told him she did not believe him and that she would not recognize him any more as a shaman.

Wewe went out looking for the comb. He found the tracks of the peccaries and followed them. He found an armadillo seated in front of his burrow with the rattle of the peccaries in his hand. The armadillo shook the rattle and sang, "I play the rattle of the game animals." Then all the animals came. When the animals had gone, Wewe struck the hand of the armadillo with the blowgun and the rattle fell. The shaman took the rattle with him, killing many animals with the aid of the rattle and afterward hiding it in the hole of a tree. His brother-in-law knew that he had the rattle. Afterward Wewe always took his brother-in-law with him and they brought home much game.

One day he sent his brother-in-law out to shoot peccaries, but he strongly cautioned him not to loose the rattle. The brother-in-law climbed the tree with the platform, shook the rattle and sang, "I play the rattle of the game animals." Many peccaries came; he shot at them with the blowgun but did not kill them. He had placed the rattle behind a vine which held the platform together. The vine broke and the rattle fell. The peccaries took away the rattle. The platform crumbled. The brother-in-law fell and the peccaries tore him apart. Then the shaman told his wife that the peccaries had killed her brother and that they had also taken away the rattle.

Afterward Wewe followed the tracks of the peccaries to seek the rattle. He did not return home that day, but slept in the forest. On the following day he went out after the peccaries again and slept in the forest another night. Thus he did for three days. On the third day he found the peccaries eating lunch and drinking much *cachiri*.

The peccaries said, "What do you want here?" He replied, "I am looking for the rattle." The peccaries told him that they could not give him the rattle now. They gave him food and a lot of *cachiri*, because he was very hungry, since he had not eaten for three days.

They said that they would give him the rattle if he became the same as they were and transformed himself into the "Father of Peccaries." There came many peccary-girls and gave him the rattle so that he could direct them every day in their dances. He went with them to the house of the peccaries and is still there today as the "Father of Peccaries."

Analysis of the Wewe Tale

Wewe's transition from a position of inferiority to one of power is a progressive resolution of the conflict between brothers-in-law (see Table 10). The resolution does not take place in the human world, however, and Wewe's ascendancy over his human brothers-in-law occurs as a consequence of his progressive substitution of helpers from the animal world for his human affines. The use of the "brother-in-law" term between the animals and Wewe is as a greeting term between unrelated males, but it implies the potential for a reciprocal brother-in-law relationship to form. For the human brothers-in-law the combination of greed, lack of knowledge, and failure to exercise proper caution brings about disaster. A proper balance between Wewe and his human brothers-in-law is not achieved, despite a temporary equilibrium, when

Wewe and his single remaining brother-in-law go hunting together. Wewe's contest with his human brothers-in-law is an essay on a shamanic battle in which Wewe, by means of threats and cajoling, obtains the means to be successful and thereby allows his brothers-in-law to undo themselves.

Table 10. Schematization of the Wewe Tale.

A. Initial disparities

Wewe	versus	brothers-in-law
shaman	versus	laymen
one	versus	three
unsuccessful	versus	good hunters

B. Gourd

(1)	(2)	(3)
birds give magic gourd, teach proper use	Wewe uses gourd, gets many fish	WBs steal gourd (by threats), misuse it (greed), lose gourd, Wewe's son killed

C. Paddle

(1)	(2)	(3)	(4)
water opossum is "bro-in-law" of Wewe, gives him paddle, teaches him proper use	Wewe gets many fish with paddle	WBs steal paddle, misuse it, lose it	Coda: crab versus water opossum; paddle lost

D. Comb

(1)	(2)	(3)
Wewe takes comb from howler-monkey, howler teaches him proper use	Wewe uses comb, gets much game (peccaries)	Wewe gives comb to WBs, they misuse it, lose comb to peccaries, two WBs killed

E. Rattle

(1)	(2)	(3)
Wewe steals rattle from armadillo	Wewe gets much game, goes hunting together with WB	WB goes hunting alone, killed in accident, rattle lost to peccaries

F. Coda

(1)	(2)
Wewe trails peccaries for three days, goes hungry	Wewe accepts rattle and becomes "Father of Peccaries"

A compressed schematization reveals the progression of magical power which accrues to Wewe:

Section	B	C	D	E	F
Magical aid	gourd	paddle	comb	rattle	rattle
Donor	birds	water possum	howler-monkey	armadillo	peccaries
Catch	fish	fish	peccaries	peccaries	
Results	son dies, gourd lost	paddle lost	comb lost, two WBs dead	rattle lost, one WB dead	Wewe leaves human world

The rattle is Wewe's last and most powerful magical aid, and is used in the final section of the story as an accompaniment to the dance of the peccary-women whom Wewe leads after becoming the "Father of Peccaries." Pemon shamans do not use rattles in their curing séances, but they do use a leafy branch of a certain plant (*wopa*) which they rustle. Wewe has left the human world and taken on a new set of affines — his animal helpers the birds, water opossum, and so on — and then becomes the leader and "father" of some of the most dangerous of game animals. Peccaries travel in groups and can be fierce if aroused. When Wewe says, "The comb was my tool to call game animals, but not to cause you grief," the mother-in-law, "who had lost her sons, told him she did not believe him and that she would not recognize him any more as a shaman." This passage can be taken to mean Wewe's mother-in-law no longer believed that Wewe was a good, or curing, shaman, but that he had turned toward the malevolent use of shamanic power. From the perspective of his human affines, Wewe's shamanic power (not their own greed and malfeasance) had produced evil results. For them, Wewe had become a peccary which attacked the human brothers-in-law and killed them. The story resolves the conflict between brothers-in-law with a transition from culture to nature, and the acquisition of a new set of brothers-in-law and the annihilation of the old set.

The spatial associations of various elements of the story and the course of Wewe's relations with animals show that the lack of resolution of conflict in the human realm can be contrasted with Wewe's progressive incorporation into the animal world. There is no marked change of spatial associations in the story; all the events take place rather close to the ground and things are on a more or less horizontal plane (equality, reciprocity):

Section	B	C	D	E	F
Magical aid	ground	water	tree	bushes	bushes
Donor	trees	water	tree	ground	ground
Catch	water	water	ground	ground	

Wewe's treatment by his animal helpers parallels his own behavior toward his human brothers-in-law. Wewe shows restraint toward his human brothers-in-law (despite their threats and tricks and the death of his son), and the various animals show restraint toward Wewe even though he threatens them, takes their magical aids, and hunts game animals. Wewe ultimately joins the peccaries, who not only are his avengers but who also belong to the realm of the beings who have shown restraint toward him. The quality of restraint in this moral tale is a precondition for "negotiated kinship." The relationship between Wewe and his human brothers-in-law is a comment on the open-ended quality of these relationships as well as on their potential hostility. Balanced reciprocity must be continually renegotiated, and is subject to potential disturbances at almost any point in the sequence of interaction. The warning in the tale indicates that if things get too far out of balance, they cannot be brought back to any lasting equilibrium in the realm of culture.

The story becomes even more clearly an essay on the substitution of relationships based on mutual restraint for those in which mutual aggression is present if we consider the triangular set of mutual relationships between Wewe, his human brothers-in-law, and the animal world (see Figure 17).

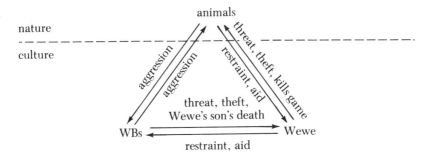

Redrawing this and letting h stand for hostility and aggression, and r for restraint and aid, we can see the following configuration of relationships:

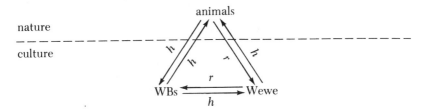

Figure 17. Relationships between Wewe, his brothers-in-law, and the animal world.

The animals are thus out of balance with the human protagonists (taken as a unit), and Wewe redresses this imbalance by joining the peccaries. The initial disparities between Wewe and his brothers-in-law can be redressed only by both restoring the imbalance in the original circuit and leaving the cultural world in order to do so. Wewe's brothers-in-law are out of balance with Wewe and with Wewe and the animals taken as a unit, and the result is that the circle of relationships ceases to exist (the human brothers-in-law are eliminated). Disharmony in the cultural realm leads to leaving it altogether, and to the substitution of another realm for it.

MAICHAK

Maichak did not know how to make manioc presses and sieves but his brothers-in-law did. One day his brothers-in-law asked him to come with them to a place two days away. When they got there, they said, "Who will stay here, and make a press and other things so that we can have manioc bread?"

"I will," said Maichak, although he did not know how to make a press and other things used to make manioc bread.

"All right," said his brothers-in-law. "But do it just as fast as you can. We are going out hunting, and this afternoon we will come back with peccaries, and the women must have some manioc bread ready for us when we get here."

The brothers-in-law went out to hunt. Maichak went to get the fibers to make the press and other things. He went away after breakfast and came back about noon. He got the fibers all ready, but he did not know how to make a press. So of course he could not do anything. The women had the grated manioc paste all ready and were waiting to squeeze the poison out of it and make manioc bread. The brothers-in-law came with peccary meat.

"Where is Maichak?" they asked the women.

"He is out making a press," said the women.

They sent a boy to call Maichak. They were very hungry.

"Did you make a press?" they asked Maichak.

"No, I do not know how," said Maichak.

"Well then, why did you try?" they asked him. And they got very angry and abused Maichak.

The brothers-in-law made a press in about two hours.

"All right," they said. "Now we will teach you how to behave."

So they tied Maichak's hands together and his feet together, and they hung him up alongside the press, and they impaled him on a sharp stick and killed him. But Maichak got up again from death and was alive again.

The brothers-in-law and Maichak started home with the peccaries. Maichak said for them to go ahead and he would follow, and they said all right. Maichak went with his wife to hunt for peccaries, and the brothers-in-law went to Maichak's house. Maichak got some peccaries. Then he said to his wife, "Your family was abusive to me, and I am going to take my revenge on you."

He killed his wife, and he salted her body, and put it on the platform where he had his salted peccaries. Then he made an enormous carrying frame. He put the salted wife and salted peccaries in the carrying frame and took them to the house of the parents of his wife. His mother-in-law gave him some manioc bread and some peppers. She gave him three or four of these peppers. Then she asked him, "Do you want to eat now?"

Maichak said, "No, first I will go and bathe."

Maichak went to bathe, and his mother-in-law took the carrying frame and took out the meat and saw that some of the meat was her daughter. She shrieked and cried and the brothers-in-law ran after Maichak to kill him. Maichak ran away into the forest.

Maichak broke off a piece of the manioc bread and cut one of the peppers in two and put them in the fork of a tree, saying to them, "Let me know if my brothers-in-law come this way."

Farther along, he took another piece of manioc bread and cut another pepper and did the same thing with them. When he had gone about half a league into the forest and had come to a river, he heard loud cries from the manioc bread, which was really being taken away by a bird.

"Men are coming," said Maichak.

He got into a canoe on the river but he did not know how to paddle. As he was being carried down the river, a bird sang to him, saying to him, "Dip in the paddle, dip in the paddle."

Another bird warned him that his brothers-in-law were still following him. He paddled down the river for two days, until he came to a big tributary. He paddled up the tributary for ten days, until he came to its headwaters. He had with him manioc and bananas and all kinds of plants, done up in a small package, in a carrying frame. He stopped and built himself a house, and planted a garden and lived there all by himself.

Piaima, an animal-man who lives in the mountains and in the forests and who can be seen only by a shaman, not by common Pemon, came to Maichak and taught him to make presses and all kinds of fiber weaving. Thus Maichak learned to weave fiber and to do all kinds of men's work, and he lived happily.

While he was making his fields, he lived on wild fruit. Later he had manioc to eat. He got tired of nothing but manioc so he went out hunting and killed a deer. As he was eating venison on another day, he thought about how lonely he was. He said, "I am going to get a king vulture to keep house for me."

Maichak went out and killed a tapir. Then Maichak smeared rancid grease all over himself and when the tapir was putrid, he lay down alongside it and pretended to be dead.

The vultures came to eat the tapir and the man, and Maichak grabbed a king vulture and went home with it. He used to bring the vulture meat and they lived together for some days. Maichak would go out to hunt about an hour after sunrise, and when he came back at sunset he would find manioc bread and *cachiri* and other things to eat and drink all made, but only the vulture would be there. The truth was that during the day the vulture became a human and made all these things, and then at night turned back into a vulture.

Maichak asked, "Who made the manioc bread and the *cachiri?*"

One day Maichak said that he was going to hunt and that he would not be back until after dark, but he sneaked back to the house about noon, and there he saw a beautiful woman, making manioc bread and *cachiri* and other things. Maichak asked, "Where did you come from?"

The woman replied, "I am the king vulture woman and I live here with you."

They lived there together for a long time, and the king vulture woman remained a woman. One day she said, "If you would like to see my father, we will go to my house."

She took Maichak to see her father. When they arrived outside the house of the king vulture father, whose name was Atito, she said to Maichak, "You stay here and I will go ask if Papa will receive you."

Whenever any visitors came to see the king vulture father, he used to kill them and eat them. The daughter said to him, "I have brought you a son-in-law whose name is Maichak."

The king vulture father said, "All right, daughter, let us see what sort of character he has."

The daughter went and got Maichak and came back in the house and presented him to her father. The king vulture father said, "All right, if Maichak is a good worker, he can live here. But if he is not, I am going to eat him."

To test Maichak the king vulture father sent him out to drain a big lake. It was an enormous lake, the biggest in the whole world, and Maichak had to drain it in one day to get fish for the king to eat. He had to do this all in one afternoon or die.

Maichak was sitting pensively when a dragonfly came flying up and said, "Why are you so sad, Maichak?"

Maichak said, "I am sad because I have to drain this enormous lake in one day, or the king vulture father will kill me."

The dragonfly said, "All right, then, I will help you."

Multitudes and multitudes of dragonflies came to help drain the lake. Then a bird came flying up and asked Maichak, "What is wrong?"

Maichak said, "I have to drain this enormous lake in one day or the king vulture father will kill me."

The bird said, "I will sing to let you know when the daughter is coming, so that she will not see that the dragonflies are doing your work."

The bird went and mounted guard a little distance away. Every half-hour the daughter came to see the work but the bird always warned Maichak. The dragonflies and Maichak drained the whole lake and finished it about the middle of the afternoon. The daughter came and found that the work was all done, and they got great quantities of fish for the king vulture father.

Next day the king vulture father said, "Very well daughter, he seems to be a good worker. But we shall see. We will give him a three-day test. If he passes this test, you can marry him, and if he does not, we will eat him. He must build me a house. Here is an enormous stone, and he must build me a house right here."

The daughter said to Maichak. "Tomorrow in one day you must make a house on that stone."

Maichak went to see the place. There was nothing but a big stone. There was no dirt or anything. Maichak was very sad.

(Remember that at this time, it was years since he had left his brothers-in-law, his mother, his father, and the rest. They all thought he was dead.)

Maichak said, "I cannot build a house on this rock. Anywhere else would be all right but not here."

But shortly after sunrise he went to cut wood. He got together all kinds of animals and birds. They all worked together and they gathered all the materials for a house, but they could not make any holes in the rock to set up the posts.

Then a worm appeared and said to Maichak, "You have to build this house in one day. How are you going to do it?"

Maichak said, "I do not know because I cannot make holes in this rock."

The worm said, "Very well, Maichak, I will burrow into the rock and you can set up the four poles in the holes that I make."

They did so. So Maichak finished the house and the animals thatched the roof. Everybody went to see the house. The king vulture father asked, "Is it done?" and the daughter told him that it was all done.

The king vulture father said, "All right, now tomorrow, Maichak must make a shaman's stool. It must be made out of stone. It must be enormous. It must be able to walk by itself, and it must look like me."

Nobody but the daughter knew what the king vulture father looked like. He had two heads, and he wore earrings on both. Next day Maichak tried to make the stool. A termite came and said, "What are you doing?"

Maichak said, "I have to make a stool that looks like the king vulture father and I cannot."

Maichak did not know the king vulture father had two heads. Then a hummingbird came and he asked, "What are you doing, Maichak?"

Maichak said, "I have to make a stool that looks like the king vulture father and I don't know what he looks like."

The hummingbird went to look at the king vulture father. The king vulture father never paid any attention to visitors. He would not turn his heads, so they could not see what he looked like. The hummingbird sang and sang, but he could not see the king vulture.

Then another small bird came and asked Maichak what he was doing, and Maichak told him. This bird went into the king vulture father's house and he sang and sang. The king vulture father finally turned his heads to see the bird. The bird saw that the king vulture father had two heads and he went and told Maichak about the heads and the earrings on each of them. Maichak told the termite how to make the stool, and the termite made it, and finished it before noon. Maichak had finished his three-day test in two and a half days. Maichak put the finished stool in the king vulture father's house and called him and the daughter.

The king vulture father said, "Can it be like me?"

The stool said, "I am just like the king vulture father," and it came running up like a dog.

The king vulture father was terrified and ran away. The king vulture father said, "Maichak has frightened me, so I am going to kill him."

The daughter went and warned Maichak of her father's intentions. Maichak ran away again. Now he was running away from his brothers-in-law and also from the king vulture father.

He came to a big mountain. The king vulture father's men were still chasing him and Maichak did not know how to get down the mountain. Then a lizard appeared and asked, "What is the matter?"

Maichak told the lizard about the king vulture father.

The lizard said, "All right. Jump on my back and I will take you down."

Maichak got on the lizard and rode him. Down they went. There was a big tree which fell down. While they were still coming down, the lizard stopped about a hundred yards from the bottom and told Maichak to jump. But Maichak said it was too far. Finally they came to the ground.

Maichak did not know where he was. He wandered about at random until he came to a big river, and then he walked upstream along the bank. He came to a stream and he walked up it. This was in Kamarata and he found his family's house there, but he was afraid to let them know that he was there because of having killed his wife. He stayed hidden for three days.

Maichak had two sisters and a brother. One of his sisters had been a girl when he left home and was now a woman. The other sister was just a baby when he went away and she did not remember Maichak. She used to ask, "How many of us are there, three?" and they would reply, "No, there are four of us, counting Maichak who is dead."

The girls used to go down to the river to bathe. Maichak had turned himself into a little fish in the river in order to hide. When the girls bathed, Maichak touched the older girl intimately.

The girl said, "I will go get a sieve and see what fish is touching me."

She went and got the sieve and went into the water. She gave the sieve to the smaller girl and told her to catch the fish when she shouted. Maichak touched the girl again and she shouted to the smaller girl to catch him. She caught Maichak, who was a little fish.

The girl said, "You touched my sister so I will roast and eat you."

Maichak turned back into a man and said, "I am your brother."

Everybody was happy.

The little sister ran to the house shouting, "Here is my brother."

Now Maichak had learned everything in the course of his travels. He stayed for some time at home and everybody wanted to see him.

He knew everything, he could do everything. He preached and taught, showing the other Pemon what to do and how to make everything that they needed. His fame extended far and wide and many other Pemon came to him to learn.

(There follows a coda, recounting Maichak becoming fearful, causing an earthquake with his trembling, and his departure to no one knows where.)

Analysis of the Maichak Tale

The version of the Maichak tale given above is only one of three recorded Pemon versions of this story, and the central portion of the tale appears much more widely distributed in northern South America (see A. Colson, 1976: 1). The other two Pemon versions differ substantially from the one set forth by Simpson, and must be taken into account. The initial portion of Simpson's version (1944: 264–66) is omitted above, since it is quite clearly the Wewe tale in attenuated form. The story really starts when Maichak is unable to make a manioc press and conflict with his brothers-in-law becomes acute on that score. This occurs both in the Simpson version of the tale and in Armellada's version (1964: 87–100). In Koch-Grunberg's version (1953: 88–98), however, the initial portion of the tale relates the story of a war in which Maichak's settlement is wiped out and he is the sole survivor. After the massacre Maichak goes to nearby settlements looking for people, but everyone has fled. From this point on, Koch-Grunberg's version is virtually the same as those of Simpson and Armellada. Armellada's final portion of the tale differs substantially from those of Simpson and Koch-Grunberg. A general schematization takes these alternate versions into account:

Part	I	II	III	IV
Happening	conflict, disruption, death	Maichak lives alone	marriage to vulture woman and visit to sky	return to own relatives on earth, without vulture wife
Armellada	affinal conflict		(same in all three versions)	Maichak makes new wife with own blood and semen

Part	I	II	III	IV
Simpson	affinal conflict	Piaima instructs Maichak		Maichak is bachelor, teacher
Koch-Grunberg	warfare			Maichak is bachelor, brings corn from sky

A. Colson (1976) has interpreted Armellada's version of the Maichak tale as a mythical resolution of the conflict between "blood kin and affines" and has used data from the Yekuana (Arvelo-Jimenez, 1971), Pemon (Thomas, 1973), and Maroni River Carib (Kloos, 1971) to analyze the "affinal triangle" of father-in-law, in-married son-in-law, and wife's brother among Carib-speakers of northern South America. Her interpretation squares with our discussion of the continuum of affinal obligation and the phenomenon of a sister's daughter marriage in Pemon society (see Chapter III above and Thomas, 1979). Armellada's version of the Maichak tale can be seen as follows:

Part	I	II	III	IV
	failure of first marriage because of lack of skills and failure of balanced reciprocity with brothers-in-law	alone, self-sufficient through magical aid (birds make *cachiri* for Maichak)	second marriage, outside of human world; failure of marriage because of conflict between father-in-law and son-in-law	third, incestuous or quasi-licit marriage; Maichak creates a wife from own semen + own blood + gourd

We can see the Armellada version (following A. Colson, 1976) as a commentary on the desirability of marrying as close as possible in genealogical terms, to the point of the quasi-licit sister's daughter union or even closer. Pemon marriage statistics (Thomas, 1973: 287–91; 1979: 66) fall rather nicely into three categories of relatedness: "ZD," cross-cousin, and genealogically unrelated spouses. These can be seen as corresponding to Maichak's third, first, and second marriages respectively. On a very abstract level we can show the following progression in the Armellada version of the Maichak story:

Part	I	II	III	IV
Marriage type	cross-cousin	none	unrelated spouse	incest (or ZD?)
Characteristic	balanced reciprocity (WB/ZH)	aloneness	f-i-l/s-i-l hierarchy, but *not* MB/ZS relationship	F/D or MB/ZD relationships

The sequence shows a failure of the first marriage and a series of incidents which lead to a resolution by some kind of involution, a return to Maichak's own natal family or creation of a wife from his own semen and blood. All of the final incidents after Maichak's return to earth carry implications of abnormality, violation of custom, or simple anomaly. In the Armellada version the incest prohibition is violated, and the generative power of *mu* (semen) and *mɨn* (blood) becomes completely turned in on itself. In both other versions Maichak remains a bachelor (which is not unheard of in Pemon society but is definitely out of the ordinary); Simpson's version has Maichak as a teacher, and in a quasi-prophetic role ("He preached and taught, showing the other Pemon what to do and how to make everything that they needed. His fame extended far and wide and many other Pemon came to him to learn"). Maichak's prophetic role is associated with remaining a bachelor and with his prior incestuous incident with his sister at the time of his return to his own natal family ("Maichak touched the older girl intimately").

The sequence of the unions is important, since the main portion of the tale concerns Maichak's relationship with his king-vulture-woman wife and her father. They are maximally distant from Maichak, since they eat carrion and are sky beings. The king vulture is referred to in Pemon as *kasanak*, and in the Maichak story the father-in-law is *kasanak-potorɨ*, the father of the king vultures. The sky associations of these beings mean that their house is found beyond the clouds, beyond the mountaintops. The Pemon word *kak*, meaning sky, is the same as the initial morph in *kasanak*. Thus Maichak's second marriage is maximally distant in its associations with physical space, and the social relationships portrayed parallel this. This is an unsanctioned union in which Maichak captures the king vulture woman and entreats her to become his wife (in the Koch-Grunberg version, for example, Maichak grabs the king vulture woman and says, "I am alone, with no one to help me; change into a woman"). In the Koch-Grunberg version of the story Maichak's helpers, in accomplishing the impossible tasks set him by his father-in-law, are all addressed as "brother-in-law." Shamanic power enters into the story, since Maichak is a shaman and the contest (for such it is) with the father-in-law must be seen in this light.

A brief examination of the various animal protagonists and helpers in the central portion of the Maichak tale shows quite clearly that the entire series of tests which set Maichak against the impossible demands of his father-in-law is a kind of contest between the low (in alliance with Maichak) and the high (the king vulture affines) (see Table 11). All of the helper birds are small, relatively innocuous types, and Maichak's other helpers are insects and worms. The use of the "brother-in-law" term is, as in the Wewe tale, basically a courtesy usage (the Simpson version of the tale does not record this usage, but it is explicit in the

Table 11. Schematization of the Maichak Tale.

(1)	(2)	(3)	(4)
Maichak and king vulture woman live together after he captures her	wife wishes him to meet WF	Maichak goes to sky with wife and is presented to WF	WF threatens: "If not a good worker, I'll eat him"

Tests (brideservice)

(5)	(6)	(7)
lake to be drained	house for WF to be built on stone	stone shaman's stool to be made in image of WF

Helpers

a) dragonflies	a) many birds and animals	a) hummingbird (fails)
b) bird as guard	b) worm	b) other small bird (succeeds)
		c) termites (note: the name Maichak means "termite")

Result

success, much fish for WF	success, house done in one day	stool completed, WF terrified, WF says will kill Maichak, Maichak flees after king vulture wife warns him

Koch-Grunberg version), but one which implies the potential for substituting the helping affines for the demanding ones. Maichak's identity with the termites who work the stone into a shaman's stool (*murei*) is intriguing, since the Pemon work stone (in this century at least) mainly in conjunction with the *pta:ri*, or stone griddles for baking manioc bread (some of which were still in use in 1970). Quite clearly, the difficulty of stone working and of learning of his father-in-law's two heads represents the most impossible of tasks, and Maichak, fulfilling the demands to the letter, unleashes the stool and terrifies his father-in-law. The two-headed representation of the father-in-law is explicit, and the Armellada version of the tale notes that one head gives Maichak a rotten drink, which Maichak gives to his king-vulture-woman wife, and the other head gives him a sweet drink, which he takes.

Maichak routs his father-in-law and flees for his life, abandoning his spouse and returning to his own natal family. By so doing, he in effect gives up marriage in favor of either bachelorhood or incest, depending on which version of the tale you consult. The bachelorhood status is worth some attention, since it points to a parallel between Maichak's visit to the sky and the voyage of the souls of both prophets and shamans to the heavens in their dreams or trances. Sexual abstinence is a requisite (at least for an initial period) of both shamanic training and the accession to the status of prophet. Butt (1960, 1971) has described the appropriation of the methods of the shaman by the Hallelujah prophets of the late nineteenth and early twentieth centuries among the Akawaio and Patamona, eastern neighbors of the Pemon (there were Pemon Hallelujah prophets, as well). Seen in this light, Maichak's journey to the sky becomes simultaneously three things: (1) a marriage to an unrelated spouse; (2) a shamanic soul flight to the sky in which Maichak does battle with an enemy, his father-in-law, with the aid of various helper spirits (there are no explicit correspondences between the animal protagonists of the story and the usual plant spirits which aid the shaman, however); and (3) a journey to the sky in search of redemption and sacred knowledge. Both supernatural power and the authority of the father-in-law can be portrayed as coercive, potentially arbitrary, external forces.

The portrayal of the contest between Maichak and his father-in-law starts off with the conventional tasks of brideservice (providing fish and game for the father-in-law and the wife's family, house building). The demands of the father-in-law are impossible ones, however. The warning aspect of the Maichak tale is clear and overt — the debt to one's father-in-law can never be fully paid off, and the son-in-law is always subject to potential demands because of this unpayable debt. Ultimately Maichak must flee after besting his father-in-law, and the gap created in the sequence of capture, impossible demands, and magical retribution is unbridgeable. In the initial portion of the Makunaima tale, an initial cross-sex hierarchy which was maximally distant and infertile was transformed into a fertile complementarity between the sun and his wife through a series of threats, false promises, challenges, and eventual achievement of an intermediate hierarchy. In the Maichak tale, we have a different kind of maximally distant hierarchy, what may be called the hierarchy of demands without reciprocity. The father-in-law/son-in-law relationship is a transaction in which an initial grant from one side (the daughter) is followed by an open-ended, one-way potential flow of services and gifts in the other direction. In the case of a father-in-law to whom one is not related by prior genealogical ties, there is no mitigating connection to attenuate the one-way aspect of the relationship. Thus the kind of hierarchy represented in the Maichak tale is negatively valued and extremely dangerous.

Power and Social Relationships in the Tales

In the three tales considered, social relationships were inseparable from ideas of supernatural power, whether it was the transformative power of the culture heroes or the shamanic power represented in the Wewe and Maichak tales. At the end of the Makunaima story the Makunaima leave for Brazil. Once the creation is accomplished, the Makunaima and their transformative power, a kind of generalized power, recede into the background, to be replaced in other tales by supernatural power which is much more specific in nature. In the Wewe story we can see the particularization of supernatural power very clearly, since each magical object which Wewe receives is good for a given task and must be used in a precise way, according to a set of instructions given him by the donor. The generalized power of the Makunaima does not represent a continuing force in Pemon life. In the myths shamans are taught by Piaima (the forest demon), but it is knowledge represented by specific techniques, specific helper spirits. Piaima is visible only to shamans, while the Makunaima are no longer in evidence (note that Kanaima, a generalized power if ever there was one, does not appear in the tales).

The prophetic element in the Maichak story must be interpreted in the light of the otiose character of the Makunaima. There is no way of placing the Makunaima and Maichak tales in any order in terms of their time of origin, but the creation sequence is logically prior to the Maichak tale. Maichak's trip to the sky and return as a teacher and prophet can thus be seen as an attempt to recoup the generalized transformative power (now redemptive) of the culture heroes. It is clear from our account of Pemon leadership that prophetic power in some sense subsumes or encompasses shamanic power, and that the prophet uses many of the techniques of the shaman (see Thomas, 1976; Butt, 1960). With the transition from nature to culture in the creation tale, generalized power is lost, and people are left with specific remedies for specific ills (*taren*, created by the elder of the Makunaima). The advent of the Christian God and the Hallelujah religion in the late nineteenth century once again opened the way to a kind of supernatural power that Pemon society knew in the beginning, but which was represented only by Kanaima after the departure of the culture heroes. The Maichak tale, as recorded in 1939, incorporates (tangentially) the possibility of attaining this generalized power. Maichak's status of bachelor represents an unusually strong emphasis on the ritual purity which is necessary to open up the new source of supernatural power (that of the Christian God, who of course does not appear in the tale).

Pemon tales, to my knowledge, are not embodied in rites. The old dances and songs (*tukui* and *parishara*) were related mainly to hunting magic and the like, not to the tales. The shamanic powers represented in the tales are visible in everyday life only in curing, sickness and death, and misfortune. But shamanic power can be accumulated, built up over time, added on to by increments of knowledge about the spirit world. In a spiritual combat between shamans, the one who *knows* more will ultimately win, since he or she is able to command more spirit helpers in the battle. In the contest between prophets and shamans, however, the contest is one of ritual purity versus knowledge. The prophet knows the ceremonies, prayers, and chants whose objective is to produce a pure individual who will, by main force as it were, stand against the knowledge of the malevolent shaman.

I wish to connect three conceptual domains, those of kinds of hierarchy, kinds of power, and kinds of potential or actual conflict in social relationships. The kinds of hierarchy we have characterized (from the analysis of the Makunaima tale) as (1) maximally distant and infertile; (2) intermediate distance, complementary, fertile; and (3) hierarchy within a single unit, culturally creative. To these we can add (4) maximally distant, potentially fertile (Maichak and the king vulture woman), and (5) middle distance, continually negotiable, potentially either productive or disruptive (Wewe tale), no hierarchy in effect. In the Wewe tale continual renegotiation of the relationships is accompanied by running conflict which progressively worsens until Wewe moves into the new set of relationships (in the animal world). The H/W and eB/yB asymmetries which are emphasized in the Makunaima tale both represent embodiments of a type of hierarchical relationship in which the upper pole is that of responsibility and nurturance (note that the eZ/yB and eZ/yZ relationships also represent modes of this type of hierarchy). It may be charcterized as the hierarchy of responsibility and of responsiveness, which does not admit the possibility of one-way imperatives from the upper pole of the relationship to the lower one. Remember, of course, that all sibling relationships are *relative* (never absolute) hierarchies (when seen from outside, the sibling set is an undifferentiated unit). With this basic type of hierarchy are associated the generalized power concepts discussed above — the generative power of *mu* and *min*, the creative power of the culture hero brothers, the redemptive power of the prophet. All of these power concepts have the aspect of givenness, if not of immutability (prophetic power is both achieved, by attaining the requisite degree of purity, and simply given, in the sense that there is no guarantee of a proper vision or the insight to interpret it). Also, all of these power concepts are forever; they are inherent parts of the world, even though they may not be tapped at all times.

Contrasted with this is the hierarchy of demands, exemplified in the Maichak tale, a hierarchy in which there can be no responsiveness, no negotiation, leading to the need to fulfill the demands to the letter, and to a consequent explosion which ends the relationship altogether. This is to be thought of not just in terms of hostility (there is certainly enough hostility in the nonhierarchical situation of the Wewe tale) but also in terms of the unfulfillable nature of the demands. This negative type of hierarchy represents directly coercive power, arbitrariness, and nonnegotiability. In between these two forms is the realm of specific, particularized power, which may be retributive, curative, or preventative, and which is most clearly represented in the Wewe tale. This is the widest domain of Pemon social life, and there are various means for trying to convert other types of power into this type. While the particularized power, associated with the balanced reciprocity and middle-range social distance of the brother-in-law relationship (from the male point of view), can result in grave outcomes, it always carries with it the potential for re-establishment of a relationship of the same type, though in a different mode or with different people. Particularized power can be additive, cumulative, and it can, as in the Wewe tale, also be lost (shamans can, of course, lose their effectiveness over time, as well as "go bad" as Gaspar was alleged to have done; see above, Chapter IV). It does not have the firmness or the givenness of the two modes of generalized power.

These three power types relate directly to the possibilities for conflict portrayed in the tales. Within the realm of generalized but not directly coercive power, conflicts exist but are in theory reparable, even in instances where they are drastic and much hostility is aroused. Conflicts in the realm of particularized power are ongoing, can break out at any time, but allow for changing partners or renegotiating the terms of an existing relationship. Thus relationships falling within this power type have a maximum of potential variability — they can range from very solidary to relatively hostile in tenor — and a maximum of potential volatility. In this realm additions of knowledge, specific skills (everyday or supernatural), and interpersonal adeptness weigh very heavily in determining the course of the relationship. You can set your own terms if you can get the other party to go along.

These lessons from the tales can be represented as follows:

Power Type	Characteristics	Social Relationships	Type of Hierarchy
(1) generalized	transformative, generative	natal family	positive hierarchy of responsibility
(2) particularized	curative, preventative, retributive	all middle-distance relationships	none
(3) generalized	arbitrary, top-down, imperative	f-i-l/s-i-l (G + 1 affines)	negative hierarchy of demands, unfulfillable obligation

Conflicts in the tales occur more or less within each power type. Of course, as we have seen in previous chapters, conflicts also occur in which a person or aggregate of persons attempts to appropriate one type of power to use in a situation in which normative convention would dictate that power relations are of another type. For example, in father-in-law/son-in-law conflicts the son-in-law may assert that type (2) holds and try to alter the grounds of the relationship. Or an individual may use type (3) in an attempt to win benefits that should be allocated within the purvey of type (2) power relations (e.g. capitanes or shamans trying to obtain inordinate numbers of wives by what, in Pemon eyes, constitutes fraud — a disallowed manipulation of power types as well as social relationships). We shall see, in our conclusions, that these ideal types of qualities of power are played out in strategies for assimilating the socially distant and for maintaining personal autonomy.

CHAPTER VII

Conclusion:
Separation, Equality,
and Autonomy

We have shown the operation of basic principles of hierarchy, reciprocity, and of types of power in the various domains of Pemon life. A unity in these principles, and in the conditions for their operation, can be seen by comparing the patterns already described. I have summed up central themes in Pemon life as separation, equality, and autonomy because these are consonant with the primacy of balanced reciprocity and the subordination, as principles, of the two hierarchy types (the hierarchy of demands, the hierarchy of responsibility) to it. The field that constitutes Pemon social life is both open and continuous. People may be incorporated, or moved closer into a given individual's range of associates, by a variety of techniques and for a variety of reasons. But there is no sharp delineation of the Pemon social world into "us" and "them." There are, in the social as well as the physical world, no sharp, bipolar distinctions but, rather, continua of distance and relatedness along which individuals, as well as appropriate social practices associated with individuals and even underlying principles themselves, may be ranged. These continua do have end points, but it would not be correct to imply that the Pemon operate in the world with these end points uppermost in thought or action. Before making explicit the relationships among the continua which underpin the social field, a short digression into Pemon spatial concepts is necessary.

Near and Far

When Pemon discuss or use concepts of distance, there are, in ordinary conversation, few absolute referents in space other than specific place names. There is no metric applied to space, and the only metric applied to journeys is occasionally that of time, a one-, two-, or three-day walk, for example. Distance reckoning begins more or less where one is standing, but the words for "here" or "just here" (*tarɨrɨ, setɨ*) are infrequently heard. Most things are *mɨrɨtɨ* ("there") or *mɨrɨtɨrɨ* ("a little farther over there"). *Chintɨ* is "way over there," *kaiwinɨ* is "beyond, far past," and *amwiicha* is far. The term "near" in most common use is simply *amwiichabra* or *amwiichaneke* ("far not"). We can range these terms on a continuum outward from a given point, but no strict measure could be applied to it. Each term is fluid, and only expresses its meaning in relation to all the other terms in the continuum. This is reminiscent of Lorna Marshall's discussion of the !Kung referring to band territories with references like "beyond the such-and-such baobab." Such apparent vagueness is also found in Pemon reckoning, but Pemon know and have named the physical landscape in such a detailed manner that the relational continuum of distance reckoning is more than sufficient to communicate what needs to be known.

The continuum is relational, not absolute, and in this parallels the continua of kinship relatedness, marriage types, and principles of hierarchy and reciprocity to be detailed below. More significantly, the continuum of spatial distance moves outward from a central point (the speaker), but the end points partake of different qualities. "Here" *(tarɨrɨ)* is part of a continuum which includes "far," and "near" is referred to by negating the category for distant. That which is right on the spot is not only the opposite of "there" but also part of the continuum which includes all the other terms. Each term then assumes the value of some proportional part of the continuum, but that part is not an absolute, fixed proportion — it stretches and bends with the actual, named physical landscape. Likewise social relatedness, and the range of application of different principles of social interaction, stretch and bend with application to the actual, named social field of persons.

Strategies for Assimilating the Distant

We have seen that Pemon matrilocality and marriage practices often involve receiving an outsider into the household or the settlement, that trade partnerships are established in which the partners treat each other as respectful brothers-in-law (see Thomas, 1972), that quid pro quo interaction may be codified and systematized by the wide use of the brother-in-law (*yese*) term, and that ritual specialists such as the big trader are welcome far from their natal areas. All of these incorporations of socially distant individuals revolve around ex post facto terminological usages which paper over unrelatedness in the name of de facto cooperation and reciprocity.

The distant person who abides and acts like a brother-in-law in fact is one. What this means is that small groups — households and settlements — are continually trying to select, out of a wide range of persons in the social field, individuals who will fill the bill of reciprocity among individuals and households in close proximity. To do this, households must not only attract those who are proficient providers but also those who can defer when necessary to the needs of the household for abstinence (as in the sickness of a household member, when food restrictions are enjoined), forbearance (as with aged memebers), and cohererence (as in concerted fending off of inordinate demands from others in the settlement or river area). But the strategy for attracting and holding such individuals is itself ultimately founded on the idea of quid pro quo. It is not sought to bind the individual totally, to exploit or sap his ritual knowledge, or to make inordinate demands upon him (remember the warning contained in the story of Wewe!). The strategy means that small exchanges, of hospitality, gift items, cooperative work, participation in ritual food restrictions, must accrue gradually over time so that the erstwhile outsider is a full participant in the household or settlement but does not become subordinate or sacrifice his autonomy in so doing. Over the long run, the services rendered by the outsider must balance out with the services rendered to him — otherwise the refuge of his natal kinsmen is open to him, and it is assumed that he might be driven back to them. For the strategy for building a household and settlement, as we have shown, involves keeping as many as possible of your close kin around you, but it also involves attracting and keeping outsiders. This must be carried on in such a way as to make them full *and* autonomous participants. That a selection process of personal mutuality and equality of proficiency between residents and outsiders is involved is evident. There are, of course, certain individuals who are particularly desirable, and in Pemon society these are most often ritual and trading specialists. Because of the security which these individuals can bring to a household or settlement, they are particularly welcome. They complete the settlement in a way that ordinary individuals cannot.

Pemon processes for converting the socially distant into full membership in a given household or settlement cannot move the individual inward by reference to real or putative genealogical attachments in the past, since genealogies are extremely truncated. This means that the middle-distance social categories (e.g. *yese, yeruk*) are singularly loose in application and singularly a function of immediate behavioral cues and interaction.

Fending People Off

Outside of all the standard practices for restricting interaction—scheduled avoidances, absences at the residences of distant relatives, or simply wrapping the edges of the hammock around one's face and retiring—Pemon life manifests a singular ease of justifying nongiving, nonaid, or nonsupport. In a classic pattern, if a Pemon individual wishes to fend off requests for aid, interaction, or whatever, the only requirement is to cite the necessity of a nuclear family member or sibling for one's time, effort, and support. To this competing obligation there can be no reply, since the household and sibling set have not just the right but also the *obligation* to demonstrate antonomy and have first, and pre-emptive, call on their members. We have seen the invocation of restricted definitions of relatedness in denials of support in conflict situations. The counterpart of these restricted definitions (which are ultimately based on the minimal, or narrow, definition of kinship relatedness as absolutely common substance) is the invocation of obligations to primary relatives as a dodge which cannot be countered. There are always competing obligations in any individual's social world, but there are not always "ways out" which are irrefutable, as this one is in Pemon life.

This should not be thought of as a merely "I have to tend to my own affairs" or "mind my own business" mentality. It represents the recognition that the minimal units of Pemon social life are both nominally and actually autonomous, separate, and discrete entities. Within these units there is no fending people off, except by some kind of actual physical separation (the separation of hearths at either end of a house containing the nuclear families of father-in-law and son-in-law is such a mechanism). Outside them, things are negotiable, and a part of negotiations is the possibility of invoking competing obligations to primary relatives.

In addition, individuals can be fended off by assigning them to the category of the distant—those from outside one's river area or region. This is usually done indirectly, through a third party, but the message is clear—those people are from over there, they are not from here, and I'm not obliged to them. This kind of distancing most often occurs among same-generation males, who may be linked to a common father-in-law or brother-in-law but who wish to avoid interaction or cooperation. The transmission of the message is usually left to the linking father- or brother-in-law.

Ultimately Pemon means of fending people off relate more to the absence of initiating interaction than to anything else. In a system of spatially dispersed settlements, the paths one chooses to follow over the land and the times one travels dictate who will be met.

A crucial aspect of the ease and possibility of fending people off is the minimal use of sociocentric categories for people in everyday life. There are a few sociocentric categories (e.g. those for age — *mure, aeketon, nosanton,* etc.) which carry universal imperatives for interaction, but these are little used for the most part. The use of the relativistic, egocentric terminology prevails in daily life, and this means that the negotiability inherent in these categories is available when needed. The differences in age which are so prominent in Pemon sibling terms are all dyadic, relative differences — one is elder brother or elder sister in one context and younger brother or younger sister in another. The combination of this egocentric terminology with place-specific references for individuals gives a wide range of possibilities for locating a given individual, either in direct interaction or in reference, at a desired remove from the speaker. Both the linguistic possibilities and the behavioral reality reflect an optative, egocentric social universe — a society made up of points in a social field which are mostly grouped from the perspective of a single point within the field.

Allowable and Disallowable Hierarchies and the Extension of the Realm of Balanced Reciprocity

We have identified modes of hierarchy and reciprocity as basic principles whose operation is most graphically embodied in Pemon tales. These principles permeate Pemon life in general, and can be seen to underpin thoughts and action in all of the four dimensions — kinship, leadership, disharmony, and myth — discussed above.

The two types of hierarchy, which I have called the hierarchy of responsibility and the hierarchy of demands, can be further analyzed in conjunction with the concept of balanced reciprocity as principles which underpin both structure and process in Pemon life. Both types of hierarchy are open-ended and involve asymmetrical flows of affect, support, and commitment from some individuals to others. Balanced reciprocity, on the other hand, can be both open-ended and closed off at a specific point.

The hierarchy of demands is most clearly represented in the relationship of father-in-law and son-in-law and involves, at the lower pole of the relationship, dependency and responsibility to accede to virtually any demands made by the father-in-law. This type of hierarchy represents a one-way extractive process (debts to the father-in-law can never be finally paid off). It can be seen also in the declining days of certain capitanes, when they abuse their followers, coercively take too many wives, and in general provide little hospitality or aid for their adherents in the local area (e.g. the case of Landaeta). The "abuses" of leadership stem from a change in which the leader-followers relationship passes from balanced reciprocity between the two poles of the relationship to the hierarchy of demands, in which mode the leader is seen as an extractor after the manner of the father-in-law. The hierarchy of demands represents a negative relationship between leader and adherents, since the imbalance of benefits is not readily tolerated by the followers.

This situation quickly brings about a response, and the process may go in two directions — toward the immediate restoration of balanced reciprocity, with the installation of a new leader or possibly the elimination of a shaman considered to have "gone bad," or toward the rise of an essentially transformative type of leader in the person of a prophet. This can be seen as the assertion of the hierarchy of responsibility, a true "father" role in the leadership domain. In one of the possible paths back from the imbalance created by marriage system abuses or other abuses on the part of leaders, the transition from balanced reciprocity to the hierarchy of demands is followed and countered by the rise of a leader who embodies the hierarchy of responsibility. The prophet is such a leader, who through his own sacrifice and self-purification takes responsibility for his followers and their immanent redemption. The prophet's role thus resembles, on a higher plane, the parent/elder sibling role within the nuclear family and sibling set.

The cycling of religious movements in time (Hallelujah, Chochiman, San Miguel; see Thomas, 1976) testifies to the oscillatory characteristics of the dominant leadership forms. These oscillations can be seen as a process in which conflicts arising out of the disruption of balanced, transactional relationships between leaders and adherents represent a transition into the form of a negatively valued type of hieararchy. This form of hierarchy is maximally distant in social terms and engenders a community-wide response which may take the form of the assertion of the redemptive and solidary qualities of the positively valued hierarchy of responsibility, in the person of the prophet.

This entire process can be thought of as a cycle which reflects broad correspondences with the social structural characteristics of Pemon society. These correspondences can most readily be seen in tabular form (Table 12).

The processural aspects of the above correspondences go beyond the leadership domain. While all three modes of hierarchy and reciprocity are in play at most times in the life cycle of a given individual, it can easily be seen that the relative importance of the various modes varies through the life of the individual. A male goes from A to C to B (as shown in Table 12), from the primary importance of nuclear family to that of G + 1 affines to that of his own generational cohort as a mature

Table 12. Social Structural Characteristics of Pemon Society.

Principles and Domains	Characteristics and Examples		
	A	B	C
Power types	generalized, transformative, redemptive	particularized	generalized, extractive, punitive
Hierarchy and reciprocity	responsibility, affect, nurturance	quid pro quo	demands, negative affect, fear
Leadership	prophets	transactional: shaman and capitan in normal times	abusive shaman or capitan
Myth	culture heroes: sun and Makunaima	Wewe	king vulture (versus Maichak); Kanaima
Kinship	Nuclear family and sibling set	G 0 affines; G 0 unrelated persons	G + 1 affines
Marriage types	ZD	cross-cousin marriage	unrelated spouses

adult. Though there is some asymmetry between males and females in this progression since females are less likely to be under the thumbs of their parents-in-law, the women will also experience a broadly similar cycle, given the frequent deviations from matrilocal residence. To be sure, this broad representation is at a very general level of abstraction and doesn't express the fine-grain differences among male and female life-cycle trajectories discussed in Chapter III.

It is clear, from Pemon myths as well as the evidence of daily life, that the hierarchy of demands represents a minimally allowable type of relationship (at any level) for the Pemon. Likewise, the most potent leadership form embodies a maximally allowable form of hierarchy which is identified not only with the parent/child relationship but also with the internally ranked ordering of the sibling set. Of course, all prophetic movements die down at some point, and normalcy returns in the ordinary transactional leadership and particularized power embodied by the capitan and shaman. The transitions of power types and hierarchy types from one mode to another follow a predictable sequence: balanced reciprocity is transformed into the hierarchy of demands which in turn gives way to the hierarchy of responsibility which in turn dissipates into balanced reciprocity again.

Balanced reciprocity is the predominant type, just as particularized power is the predominant power type in Pemon life as a whole. In this triadic structure and process, the mean and the middle ground of balanced reciprocity is the normal state of affairs in adult social life. That the correspondences in Table 12 exist has been shown in our examination of the various domains of Pemon life. Their import is crucial in that the Pemon social system cannot be encompassed by any strict dualism which splits the world into "us" and "them." Just as the continuously rolling savanna spreads far and wide, so the continuous Pemon social field spreads over it. What we have labeled A, B, and C are merely three rather more stable interactions in this fluid social field.

There is a further implication of the relative importance of balanced reciprocity as a principle of Pemon social life. The chaos of negotiation and negotiated relationships is dominant over the order of relatively fixed hierarchical relationships. The balance point, the equilibrium condition, of Pemon social life is a midpoint which is helter-skelter, open-ended, and indeterminate by comparison with the two hierarchical conditions. Hierarchy in Pemon life is less enduring than the free-for-all of negotiated, balanced reciprocity. That this should be so both across time and through time represents a major characteristic of Pemon egalitarianism. Ultimately that which is most disordered from our vantage point is most orderly, most equilibrated from the Pemon point of view, and that which seems most orderly for us quickly destabilizes in their social world. While the relations between primary relatives are by and large hierarchical, this gives way to the sibling set as a unit, conjoined or disjoined with other like units in a series of exchanges of personnel as siblings move through time. Again, in the overall ordering of Pemon life, it is the balanced reciprocity characteristic of exchanges between sibling sets which dominates the rank ordering within the sets and within the nuclear family.

Pemon society is one in which there can be only temporary apices. Through time, the interacting cohorts of siblings and nuclear families exchange personnel; through time, leaders rise and fall, providing varying degrees of integration of their followers up to the point of a maximum in the case of prophets, only to return to the normal, transactional mode of mediation with humans and spirits by the capitan and the shaman. Through time, conflicts flare and then defuse themselves in a chronic failure to mobilize people to enforce sanctions or vengeance — even temporary apices of groups focused on a single instance of retribution are, as we have seen, difficult to build.

This prevalence of balanced reciprocity can only occur because power itself is not seen as a readily generalized commodity. Kanaima, the one all-pervasive and truly generalized power in Pemon life, ultimately comes from outside of wherever one is. Kanaima is a generalized force which injects disequilibrium into a world which is normally equilibrated and in balance. Harmony is the normal state of things, just as power is normally particularized.

Love, Fear, and Autonomy

Autonomy is a balance point, midway between love and fear, and Pemon life is an attempt to maintain that balance point intact. The lack of enforcement of sanctions for delicts shown above (Chapter V) is something which is more or less difficult for us to comprehend. That Pemon society has functioned in this manner with a low level of violence for at least 150 years is a matter of historical record. How, from our perspective, are we fully to understand this?

The usual response is to discuss "strongly internalized norms" and socialization practices which produce individuals capable of a high degree of self-control. To be sure, the conditions of constant interaction and solidarity within the Pemon household and settlement are conducive to a heightened awareness of others' moods and needs and of the necessity of adapting oneself to them. Particularly since such units are small (remember that the maximum number of people in a settlement is usually less than 50), they must exact a fair amount of deference and cooperation from their members in order to function. Nevertheless, since a study of Pemon socialization is beyond our scope here, and our focus is in another direction, we can examine structural and processual factors which tend to support the autonomy of the individual to a degree not found in our own way of life.

First, being Pemon involves life-long membership in a nuclear family and sibling set, both of which units operate in all aspects of life. The Pemon nuclear family is not a "launching pad" from which offspring are shot off into social space after the fashion of our own society, but a solidary unit which produces, consumes, travels, and participates in rituals as a unit. It is a floor, a baseline which almost no Pemon is without. Though there are losses by attrition and the nuclear family gives way to the adult group of siblings, the implications of such membership for the individual are far-reaching. We have already discussed (Chapter V) several aspects of the inviolability of nuclear family solidarity. This inviolability is extended to all such units in the society.

Fear, in Pemon life, is always produced by that which is most distant. The idea that one could be victimized by a Kanaima from one's own family or sibling set is quite alien to Pemon. One can have disagreements with those who are close, but they do not sorcerize one. Likewise, the first response of Pemon to insult, injury, or personal friction is *to move*, to put distance between oneself and the problem. Ths response, which renders the fear-distance equation a tautology, testifies to the extent to which response to friction is felt to be *in one's own hands*. Asylum is not only a right but also a fairly common occurrence, asylum for victims or victimizers as the case may be.

Pemon autonomy is not being alone. It is a balance point wherein the individual seeks to remain at one with the primary units of the society while putting maximum possible distance between himself and harmful individuals or situations. In Pemon life there are outs, options to move on, to protect oneself by removing to a distant area — there is always a back door. There are no final judgments made as to the rightness of individual action by societywide institutions. Such judgments can only be made by at most areal groupings of cognatic kin, and leveled against an outsider. Pemon peaceableness is a function of always having an available out as well as being able to narrow relatedness when so desired. What this means is that, beyond the minimal level of nuclear family and sibling set, each individual defines a unique social field, established in great measure at his own option.

Near Is "Not Far"; the Social Structure of "Gentle People"

In a brief digression into Pemon spatial concepts we mentioned that the most common means of expressing "near" was as "not far" — the opposite of distant. I feel that this usage, understood in combination with the Pemon adage "When we get too close together, there are fights," provides crucial insight into the "why" of Pemon life. In our own thinking, and in line with the Durkheimian thrust of thinking in social anthropology, *the* problem of society is solidarity, what kind of social "glue" holds people together. Indeed, the paeans to "togetherness" are ubiquitous in our own society. This has rendered our understanding of societies like the Pemon somewhat myopic, at best. We *assume* that order and solidarity go hand in hand or, rather, that solidarity is necessary for order. We are hard put to see order and solidarity in the rather random scatter of dots representing Pemon settlements on a map, because we have difficulty conceiving of a social system which exists *to keep people at a reasonable distance* rather than bringing them "together." The continuous aspect of the Pemon social field means that individuals choose where to range others in the set of categories and where to put them in intensity of interaction.

The lesson of Pemon society for our own thinking about social life would seem to be in part that mechanical solidarity in the sense of Durkheim's usage may not be solidarity at all; for Pemon the normal state of things is that people are separate and autonomous, that they are as much concerned with maintaining a reasonable space, both social and physical, between themselves and others as they are with interacting with others. It is no accident that Simpson (1940: 527) referred to the "democratic and individualistic" society of the Kamarakoto in 1939. We might go some way toward a better understanding of societies like the

Pemon if we examined more closely our own presuppositions about "individualism." If my understanding of Pemon society is correct, then a crucial aspect of their way of life is the quality of autonomy evidenced by individuals. Pemon social life can be seen as much from the perspective of an *enabling device* for this autonomy as it can from the perspective of society as a constraint upon the individual. The Durkheimian perspective of social anthropology has emphasized structural constraints on individual action in the effort to understand such egalitarian societies. The flip side has seldom been mentioned—Pemon society compels us to ask how things work in the virtual absence of the possibility of externally imposed sanctions. A reasonable answer is that our biases in seeking control mechanisms have shielded us from considering the open-ended, apparently chaotic, and continually renegotiated social relations in such societies as viable because they produce what might be called "reciprocal autonomy." Autonomy works in Pemon society because the possibilities of economic coercion are so extremely limited (see K. Adams, 1976) and because it is universal throughout the society. That is, it is the uniformity of the practice of extending autonomy as a prerogative *of the other* which enables it to work. Pemon action with regard to the negative hierarchy of demands can be seen as a refusal to accept a perpetual breach of personal autonomy. Reciprocal interaction is not just mutual restraint, it is also *enabling* in the sense that it leaves open and expandable the dimensions of a relationship. The relationship can wax and wane, and reliability within it becomes a function of the history of interaction rather than a simple dictate of the relationship itself.

Pemon society recreates itself in every generation as old sibling sets disappear and give way to new ones. Likewise, within and between generations individuals are involved in continually recreating their own social field. Using the maximum of possibilities created by a minimum of kinship rules, and counting on a world in which power is limited and partitioned into context-specific bits, the individual maneuvers by extending to others the same space he grants himself. This mutuality has limits and cannot be overtaxed. After all, "When we get too close together, there are fights."

Comparative Aspects

Pemon society exists in a geographical redoubt, a headwaters region which effectively protected them from outside incursions by Europeans and South American nationals until the extended missionary efforts of the 1930s. Such geographic protection was certainly a major factor in enabling Pemon society to continue in its egalitarian and peaceable ways. A near parallel may be found in Stauder's (1972) assessment of "anarchy and ecology" among the Ethiopian Majangir. The Majangir exhibit many parallels with the Pemon, not the least of which is their amorphous social structure similar in operation, if not in detail, to that of the Pemon. A Pemon would easily recognize the small, mobile households, the neighborhood beer parties, and the lack of formality which Stauder describes.

It is notable that Pemon society in many ways resembles the social arrangements found in foraging societies more than it does many horticultural adaptations. It is not our purpose here to treat correspondences between ecology and social structure or to speculate on the ecological determinants of Pemon life. It is evident that it would be hard to conceive of Pemon society outside of the demographic constraints associated with a low-density population (see Thomas, 1973). The dispersion of power and far-flung individual ties found among Pemon which make them reminiscent of foraging societies are, however, part of the moral order that constitutes Pemon life. With its disappearance (Chapter VIII) will pass a singular, if loosely defined and variable, experience of human mutuality and recognition.

Epilogue:
The Coming of Hierarchy and
the End of the System

Change has been a continual process in Pemon society over the last 300 years. Continuity has been the object of study in this book, though there has been no effort to leave out the effects of other cultures on the Pemon. It is my feeling that the social system described in this book was coming to an end even in 1970 when I first visited the Pemon. It is difficult to say what we mean when speaking of the end of a social system, since societies many times are transformed rather than wholly disappearing. While, as we said in the Introduction, the egalitarian forces in Pemon society will influence events for some time to come, the egalitarian social system described here is probably, for all practical purposes, gone.

One decries the outright murder, thefts of land, depopulation from new diseases, and the interethnic stratification which result when the "criollo" meets the "indio." All of these and more are well-documented effects of Western societies on aboriginal peoples (see Bodley, 1975). Those who think that the rapacious quest for land, minerals, and timber can be stayed are seriously deluding themselves, unless Western society itself, and its agents, can be slowed down. Some advocate the "selective" taking of elements from Western culture—"medicine," "education"—in the often vain hope that aboriginal societies will survive, though in an altered state.

The Pemon have shown tremendous resilience in having survived the various and continuing incursions (briefly described in Chapter II) on their society during the past several centuries. Their population is now growing rapidly and they are exporting people to locations outside the tribal territory (see Thomas, 1973: 74–78). Some will undoubtedly argue that the social system described here ended with the coming of the Capuchins in the 1930s, and a good case could perhaps be made for

that. I first came to Uonken some 11 years after the establishment of a
mission in the area, and was privileged to find several older persons who
had lived the pre-mission life, and to get a glimpse of things before the
settlement pattern had been totally and irrevocably altered in the direction of larger agglomerations.

Several Venezuelan anthropologists (e.g. Mosonyi, 1972, 1975) have
discussed the concept of "ethnocide," by which I take them to mean the
destruction of a people's culture, while leaving the population
biologically intact. Whether or not what is happening, and will continue to happen, to the Pemon falls under that rubric I leave to others to
decide. The greatest tragedy of the Pemon experience will not only be
that the Pemon will end up on the bottom rung of the Venezuelan class
ladder, or only that they will feel, collectively and individually, the
sting of prejudice and exploitation at the hands of the criollo population. These are, to be sure, bad enough. Interethnic and class stratification cannot but produce tremendous havoc for the Pemon. But even
worse will be the internal stratification of the Pemon themselves, the exploitation of some Pemon by others.

Let me give a few examples of what I mean. In 1970 a Pemon from
the Santa Elena area (the area of the tribal territory most affected by
criollo culture) hired some of his wife's relatives from the Uonken area
to work on his claims in the Guaniamo mines on the upper Cuchivero
(outside the Pemon territory, in another part of Estado Bolivar). The
men were hired as wage workers, given supplies for their maintenance,
and dealt with like any wage laborers anywhere else, for the most part.
(There was no question of the traditional quid pro quo *yese* relationship
coming into play in these dealings.) Upon my return to Uonken in July,
1975, after a four-year absence, I was rather surprised to find that a
former out-migrant had returned to the area and, since she worked at
the local mission, had hired a local person at a daily wage to construct
and finish a house for her. The man who was hired had a large family to
support and needed the cash. That the relationships of these two people
would ever again function along traditional lines seemed doubtful to me
at the time. Internal stratification extends beyond the straightforwardly
economic, into the realm of attitudes. It is rather sad to hear young men
and women with criollo educations speak of a fellow Pemon as *indio
sucio* (dirty Indian) or *indio malo* (bad Indian). They say it in Spanish,
not in Pemon.

These examples may seem minor, even trivial. They are not. Formerly, there were a whole series of limits on hierarchy and the potential
for control of others, and the accumulation of power, even in the supernatural realm, could ultimately be checked. There was no single measure of a human being, and hierarchy was limited by the separation of
scales of evaluation, the incommensurability of different skills and dif-

ferent ways of knowing. Pemon society was not all of a piece, some kind of seamless web. There were many points of disarticulation, many disparities of degrees and kinds of knowledge. But these disparities were not allowed to impinge on personal autonomy.

It is only with the advent and complete penetration of that single measure of human beings, Western currency, that the system will disintegrate. As Burridge (1969b: 42), among others, has pointed out, money (multipurpose Western currency, not things limited to functioning as rationing devices) does provide a unitary measure of human beings. Money, as we know it, is inseparable from a hierarchy of persons measured by it. I have previously argued (Thomas, 1972; 1973: 166–248) that the Pemon trade system to a certain extent allows the internalization of money value accrued in transactions with the Venezuelan national economy, and the translation of some of that value into Pemon terms of exchange. Even so, the ability of the trade system to accomplish this is limited, and ever-increasing numbers of items are becoming absorbed in strictly purchase dealings.

There are some Pemon who welcome the flood of goods from the outside, and demand services from the Venezuelan national government—medicines and schools, mainly. But the sense of relief at the coming of an external power which E. Colson (1974: 62ff.) describes for the Tonga of Rhodesia does not seem to characterize the Pemon. Colson's (1974: 113) statement—"Like most of us, they do not want Utopia. They want good government and the honoring of the Social Contract"—seems to me to be a rather poor apology for colonialism, though her argument that anthropologists romanticize these peaceful peoples must be taken into account. I can do no better than to quote a Pemon from the middle reaches of the Caroni:

> We ask for land so that we may live. To live according to our ways, as we lived at first, to use fish poison, be free, but if we go to work, if a company comes, we cannot be free. Someone will come here to direct as chief of the work, who will direct us to cut all that down, then plant this: rice, corn; paying, and then we cannot live freely. We cannot use fish poison, we cannot go fishing, we can't do anything, and so we don't like this. Since right now I have no work to do, since no one tells me what to do, I am here right now, on my own account. I like to be free, when I go to the other side (of the river) to fish, I catch a fish, I have a shotgun, I go to the bush to shoot a curassow, a guan, for me to eat. Even though I make, say, 20 bolivars a day, I cannot be free.

Some Pemon do want goods and services, I see little evidence that they want outside control in any real sense of the word.

A complete discussion or evaluation of the multitude of effects of Western culture and its agents on the Pemon is beyond our scope here. Anthropologists are often accused of wishing to create "human zoos" where they can go to study things in some kind of "original" state, and of being unrealistic about the actual situation of the peoples they live among. This accusation is a red herring, for any sensible anthropologist, whatever his theoretical predilections, recognizes that there is no such thing as a pristine situation — indeed the very possibility of his presence precludes this. What talk about "pluralism" and "selective" contact fails to confront is that there has been one basic outcome of the contact of the aboriginal peoples of lowland South America with any form of Western culture — these peoples have either been destroyed outright or forced to become what the dominant society requires: a reserve labor army that can be easily administered under conventional jurisdictions. Even where indigenous communities have been able to organize themselves (e.g. the Shuar Federation, Ecuador; see Salazar, 1977) against the outside, they have to do so on terms set by the dominant culture.

The attitudes of that dominant culture are reflected in its statements about indigenous peoples, in its legal codes, and in the actual behavior of criollos toward indigenous peoples and their leaders, both on the frontier and in the criollo centers of power. An example of these attitudes is to be found in the following statement from the work of an eminent Venezuelan historian (Moron, 1964: 19-20):

> Experience has shown that it is impossible to maintain aboriginal cultures in co-existence with creole culture, but that on the contrary the former must be incorporated into the latter. This may appear unjust if regarded from an emotional point of view, but not so if one follows the lesson of history, of human progress. Only through miscegenation has the aborigine joined civilisation, for one cannot call civilised those inaccessible groups which still live their primitive life, not even those groups which practise a way of life like that of the creole peasant. This truth must be respected for its historical weight, with no attempt to produce reasons of an exclusively sentimental nature. The fact that there exist as isolated examples particular individuals capable of living within the framework of a superior intellectual culture — there is no other suitable expression — shows that the race is capable of becoming civilised when it finds appropriate conditions. But these conditions are precisely those offered by the homogeneous group, the creole group. It does not, therefore, appear to be possible for us to advance the Indian, to civilise him, while at the same time conserving his political community structure nor his economic and social position. The intense pressure of the proximity of the creole, the progressive degeneration of the Indians' own way of life, the obliteration of their native customs and language owing to their adoption of Castilian and to the practices of society as ordinary Venezuelans understand it, will decide the fate of those Indians who still remain.

> The war of extermination was cruel, and the treatment on an inferior plane offered by their protectors to the Indians until a short time ago turned out to be unworkable. If the war perfidiously destroyed, the protection merely debased. Neither method has anything to recommend it and therefore scholars and politicians today are seeking a new approach to the prob-

lem, even though in Venezuela it has lost its former importance. One first, very general conclusion has been reached: the Indian, the minority, must be incorporated into the life of the nation. But how? This is the real question today, and so far it remains without answer.

Should the Indian communities be preserved? No one can seriously desire this. The communities must gradually disappear, their demise helped on by well-planned and organized political action, such as seems to be emerging today. It must be hoped that in the near future — when the forest has been conquered and the land filled with towns and cities — not one group will remain which still speaks Carib or any other aboriginal language, and the problem of the Indian will be a purely ethnological one. To aim at the opposite is to seek to turn back the process of culture to stages already left behind by Venezuela.

One can only assume that Moron's ode to progress and the obliteration of the aboriginal peoples is to be taken seriously, that it represents what he considers hard-headed realism. There is little evidence to suggest that the long-term future of people like the Pemon in Venezuela will be ultimately different from that of other lowland indigenous peoples on the continent, though the process may be slower and less drastic than in other places. It is clear to me that the majority of Venezuelans still maintain, in their minds, not just the overwhelming distinction of "civilized" versus "primitive" but also the distinction which the Iberian conquerors made when they described their ventures into the interior with phrases like "We were five men *(hombres)* and ten indians *(indios)*." That is, aborigines are to be distinguished from human beings. This is not the place to attempt any kind of recapitulation of the disputes among historians as to the intentions of the Spanish crown regarding the aboriginal peoples, the so-called Black Legend, and the dispute over whether aborigines had souls. We are here speaking of contemporary Venezuela.

The attitudes of the Venezuelan government and the Capuchin missionaries are well summed up in the phraseology of their agreement of 1967 regarding the duties and administration of the missions of the Caroni and Tucupita. The agreement divides the Apostolic Vicarate into two parts: "the Civilized, which encompasses all of the cities, towns, and settlements incorporated into the civil regime of the Republic," and the "Indigenous or Missionary, which encompasses the rest of the cited territories, inhabited exclusively by indigenas not incorporated into the national life." (Armellada, 1977: 399). The Capuchin order, by the agreement, promises to "progressively civilize and evangelize those aborigines found inside the Mission zone." (ibid.: 400). It is the stated objective of the Capuchin order to bring about population concentration, put Pemon children in mission boarding schools, and "encourage among the indigenas agriculture, keeping of domestic animals, and traditional crafts, introducing more advanced methods and techniques and a more adequate division of labor" (ibid.: 401). While it is not always clear what is meant by "civilize and evangelize" (a slight change from the old "reduce and civilize," which meant to gather the indigenous peoples into population concentrations and make Spaniards out of them), the continued vestment of all civil and religious authority in the hands of the Capuchin order represents the clearest testament to the actual situation of the Pemon.

There is a countervailing perspective to the one taken here, which has found increasing attention among anthropologists in recent years, and that is a perspective which sees Amazonian indigenous peoples in a continuous process of "ethnogenesis" in their interaction with the national cultures of which they come to form a part (see Whitten, 1976: 265–85; 1978; and Goldman, 1979: 299–303, for a slightly different perspective which discusses cultural revival). Several Venezuelan anthropologists of varying persuasions (Mosonyi, 1975; Arvelo-Jimenez, 1972) have called for government action which would aid, not impede, the organization and self-organization of the indigenous peoples of Venezuela. There has been, since the early 1970s, an Indigenous Federation of the State of Bolivar (Federacion Indigena del Estado Bolivar), of which a Pemon leader was president for a time. The internal opposition to this man's leadership, and attempts to intervene in his actions by members of governmental and sacerdotal hierarchies, were extensive according to the man himself. (I discussed these matters with him in Caracas in 1975.) The perspective of those who discuss "ethnogenesis" is certainly a valid one, and calls attention to the re-creation of cultural forms in new guises, as part of an ongoing process of adaptation. In expressing my disagreement with their perspective, I do not mean to imply that cultural forms are static or that one should idealize some pristine (and nonexistent) past. Nor do I wish to minimize the obligations of anthropologists to state clearly and forthrightly the actual situations of power, control, and exploitation in which those they study find themselves. The Pemon have clearly been in a process of adaptation to continuing incursions for a long time. There are now several organizations (the International Work Group for Indigenous Affairs, Cultural Survival, Survival International, OXFAM) working actively to support authentic self-determination on the part of Amazonian peoples, and one cannot but laud and support their efforts (see Ramos and Taylor, 1979; Cultural Survival, 1979). In my own thinking, a central question which anthropologists must face is the degree of fluidity they wish to allow in their set of concepts, particularly in the concept of "ethnicity." Whether people are or are not representative of a certain cultural form or ethnic unit many times rests upon what they themselves claim to be. What I am pointing out here is that, though the Pemon may call themselves Pemon in some future situation in which they have become integral parts of rural Venezuela, in effect *campesinos*, they may well not be members of the egalitarian social system described in this book.

I do not wish to minimize the resilience, sagacity, and adaptiveness of the Pemon or of their leaders (see Arvelo-Jimenez, 1976–77). However, in order to respond to the pressures of all the incursions, they will in my opinion increasingly have to become other than what they are and have been. The Pemon will someday tell their own story, and my feeling is that they may well have little use for much of the record that Western society has compiled about them. (Either way, the part of their story that I know is here.) Statements like those above are usually met with the preachment that some anthropologists are hopelessly unrealistic and outmoded and only wish to preserve "ways of life" as "objects of study." There is only one alternative defensible in human terms, the one thing that the juggernaut of Western civilization cannot and will not do: "Leave them alone, let them be."

Appendix:
Fieldwork among the Pemon

Anthropological accounts of fieldwork experiences are numerous, though it is my own conviction that the real fine grain of these experiences only comes out when groups of anthropologists get together in the wee hours of the morning to swap fieldwork stories, as old soldiers swap war stories. Here I merely attempt to describe the outline of what I did in the field and how it was accomplished. My original objectives in going to the Pemon were centered on the desire to study nonmonetary trade. Upon my arrival in Venezuela, and after some discussion with Walter Coppens in Caracas, the Pemon seemed the most suitable group to work among, since they are central participants in an extended inter-tribal trade network (see Thomas, 1972). Since I was sponsored by a combined U.S.-Venezuelan project on the human genetics of the peoples of southern Venezuela, part of my job was to gather genea-logical information which would be useful to geneticists.

Entrance into the field was facilitated by the aid of personnel at the Instituto Venezolano de Investigaciones Cientificas (IVIC), and through them I contacted personnel of the Malaria Control Division of the Ministry of Health and Social Assistance (MSAS). The Malariologia personnel in Cd. Bolivar, on the Orinoco, were most helpful in orient-ing me regarding conditions in the Gran Sabana and neighboring areas such as the Paragua drainage, and I was able to "tag along" with malaria control crews in both the Paragua drainage and the middle Caroni drainage during the first few months of my field reconnaissance. As will be apparent from the accompanying list of fieldwork dates, loca-tions, and topics, I had to move around considerably during the course of fieldwork in order to accomplish the study of a far-flung people in-volved in long-distance trading relationships. Likewise, I elected to set-tle down (October, 1970–May, 1971) for intensive study of the central region of the tribal territory in order to gain the necessary in-depth understanding of Pemon life which would illuminate the relationships between demographic and settlement patterns, kinship, and the Pemon trade among themselves and with other groups. The principal geographical focus of my studies was the most remote and least ac-culturated portion of the tribal territory, in the areas of Uriman and Uonken. This selection was purposeful on my part, for I wished to learn as much as possible about what Pemon life was like aside from the ex-igencies of interaction with the dominant national culture.

Life among the Pemon is life on the move, and I used every available means of transport in the course of my time in the Gran Sabana, in-cluding DC-3, canoe, jeep, and a lot of time spent on foot, walking be-tween settlements. During the period October, 1970, through May, 1971, I probably logged an average of two to three hours every two days on the move, with my pack and field books and equipment on my back. Pemon are much too independent to wish to settle in as aide-de-camp for some outsider, and when I was not a guest in their houses (which was quite often), I cooked and kept house on my own in a field house lent to me by a Pemon friend from the Old Mission settlement in Uonken. In Pemon society, hospitality is the rule, and they themselves often go for extended stays in distant settlements, becoming participants in the daily life of the settlement, going to the fields with their hosts, participating in food preparation, and generally becoming just another settlement member, albeit a temporary one. My own need to gather information altered this pattern somewhat, though I attempted to maintain direct reciprocity with my hosts by providing additions to the food supply in those settlements I visited (some rice and tinned sardines or tuna are most welcome when the visitor is helping consume the head of settle-ment's manioc supply).

My contacts with my hosts were facilitated by gaining familiarity with the Pemon language, something which I had begun with bilingual informants soon after entering the field in May, 1970. I was able to gain enough fluency in Pemon to conduct all interviews and discussions in the Pemon language after about December, 1970. All genealogical in-formation and settlement and personal histories were gathered in Pemon, with the exception of some cases in which bilingual informants preferred to use Spanish for rapidity and ease of my comprehension (I had known Spanish from a prior visit to Venezuela).

I did not have any "principal" informant while in the field, and com-piled my information by detailed interviews with heads and members of some 30 or so settlements in the Uonken region. Much of my data, in-cluding detailed census materials, necessitated actual visits to the set-tlements concerned, and I undertook a comprehensive scheduling of visits to ensure that all settlements in my areal sample were covered. This meant that I saw the life of the region, not from any single vantage point but from multiple points in the social field.

It is often assumed by persons in our own culture that life in the tropics is necessarily harsh and physically discomforting. Such is seldom the case in the Gran Sabana of Venezuela, an area of unsurpassed physical beauty — to this day the valley of the Karuai River is the most beautiful place I have ever lived — and generally mild temperatures. While the rigors of travel on foot and paddling by canoe are physically exacting, there is always ample time spent around the fire in the evening drinking manioc beer and conversing about the day's events.

The list of those who helped teach me the trails and who accompanied me on them throughout the central part of the tribal territory is a long one, and I count many of these individuals as close friends. While my purposes in compiling my notebooks were not always directly intelligible to the Pemon, there was a general acceptance of the fact that I had come to learn the language and record history and happenings in the area. My measurements and concern with trade items sometimes aroused humorous responses on the part of my hosts, though the Pemon themselves spend time discussing trade and so my rather overprecise interest was tolerated. Likewise, the patience of my informants during genealogical interviewing was little short of phenomenal.

Interaction in the field was not confined to the Pemon, and included contacts with diamond miners (both Venezuelan and Brazilian), missionaries (Spanish and Italian), adventurers (some of them American), and the townspeople of Santa Elena, La Paragua, and other frontier settlements. My stays in these places were always brief, and they were mainly stepping-off points for journeys into Pemon settlements. I did not attempt detailed study of the relationships of Pemon with nonindigenous outsiders.

I was always addressed by the Pemon as "Tomas" or "Davi" and was not incorporated into kinship references by them, except sometimes in a joking manner. While I used address forms of kinship terms for some individuals, I was not incorporated into a specific family or living group (my mobility would have prevented this in any case) except temporarily, as a visitor. This did not prevent me from spending long stretches (in one case a month) with specific families and getting a close-up view of family life and the daily rounds of its members.

My return visit in June-July, 1975, was brief and directed at aspects of leadership and shamanism which were unclear to me after my earlier visit in 1970–71.

During my 1970–71 fieldwork I sometimes (about once in three months) exited from the field to Bolivar or Caracas to obtain food or to have equipment (tape recorder) repaired. I would estimate my total time "on the ground" with the Pemon at about twelve months during this fieldwork period.

Despite the isolation and feelings of anxiety over the quality of data-gathering which plague the neophyte anthropological fieldworker (for such I was in 1970), the hospitality and good will of the Pemon, and their kindness, made the task an enjoyable one; my time with the Pemon stands out in my mind in retrospect, not as a trial but as time spent among friends.

Fieldwork Specifics

Dates	Places	Topics
May-June, 1970	Uriman, Caroni River, and upstream Caroni to Avikara	word lists, settlement pattern survey
July, 1970	Paragua River drainage, La Paragua to Antabari River by canoe; overland to Uriman	document Pemon-Yekuana trading journey
August, 1970	Santa Elena; Yuruani River area; Peraitepui de Roraima	trade patterns; interviews with capitanes
September, 1970	Guacharaka mining camp, Caroni River	diamond mining: profits, prices, partnerships
October, 1970–May, 1971	Karuai River (Uonken region)	census, genealogies, Hallelujah and Chochiman ceremonies, household inventories of trade items, sorcery accusations, personal and settlement histories
June, 1971	Uriman	interviews with big traders
June, 1975	Uriman and upstream Caroni to San Miguel	interviews with capitanes, shamans, prophet; San Miguel religious movement; conflict histories
July, 1975	Karuai River (Uonken region)	census and settlement pattern update; interfamily conflicts, sorcery accusations

References Cited

Adams, Kathleen J.
1976   An Estate in Persons: Population Adaptation and the Premise of
         Equality among the Simple Societies of the Guianas. Paper
         presented at the annual meeting of the American Anthropological
         Association, November, Washington, D.C.
Adams, Richard N.
1970   *Crucifixion by Power: Essays on Guatemalan National Social
         Structure, 1944–1966.* Austin: University of Texas Press.
1975   *Energy and Structure: A Theory of Social Power.* Austin: Univer-
         sity of Texas Press.
Aguerrevere, S. E., et al.
1939   Exploracion de la Gran Sabana. *Revista de Fomento* 3 (19):
         501–735. Caracas: Ministerio de Fomento.
Armellada, R. P. Cesareo de
1943–44 *Gramatica y Diccionario de la Lengua Pemon (Arekuna,
         Taurepan, Kamarakoto).* Vol. I: *Gramatica;* vol. II: *Diccionario.*
         Caracas: C. A. Artes Graficas.
1949   Notas Historicas, Geograficas y Etnograficas in El Bajo Orinoco y
         El Alto Caroni (Gran Sabana). *Venezuela Misionera,* nos.
         130–131: 445–57.
1960   *Por la Venezuela Indigena de Ayer y de Hoy.* Vol. 1: *Siglos XVII y
         XVIII.* Caracas: Sociedad de Ciencias Naturales La Salle.
1964   *Tauron Panton: Cuentos y Leyendas de los Indios Pemon.*
         Caracas: Depto. de Publicaciones, Ministerio de Educacion.
1972   *Pemonton Taremuru: Invocaciones Magicas de los Indios Pemon.*
         Caracas: Universidad Catolica Andres Bello, Instituto de Investiga-
         ciones Historicas, Centro de Lenguas Indigenas.
1973   *Tauron Panton II: Asi Dice El Cuento.* Caracas: Universidad
         Catolica Andres Bello, Instituto de Investigaciones Historicas, Cen-
         tro de Lenguas Indigenas.
1977   *Fuero Indigena Venezolano.* Caracas: Universidad Catolica An-
         dres Bello, Instituto de Investigaciones Historicas.
Armellada, R. P. Cesareo de, and B. de Matallana
1942   Exploracion del Paragua. *Boletin de la Sociedad Venezolana de
         Ciencias Naturales* 53: 61–110.

Árvelo-Jimenez, Nelly
1971   Politics in a Tribal Society: A Study of the Ye'cuana Indians of Venezuela. Ithaca, N.Y.: Cornell University Latin American Dissertation Series, no. 31.
1972   An Analysis of Official Venezuelan Policy in Regard to the Indians. In W. Dostal, ed., *The Situation of the Indian in South America*, p. 31–42. Geneva: World Council of Churches.
1976–77 Entrevista con Carlos Figueroa. *Uno y Multiple* (Caracas) 1 (3): 38–39.
Basso, Ellen B.
1970   Xingu Carib Kinship Terminology and Marriage: Another View. *Southwestern Journal of Anthropology* 26 (4): 402–16.
Bodley, John H.
1975   *Victims of Progress*. Menlo Park, Calif.: Cummings Publishing Co.
Boletin Indigenista Venezolano, 1966. (B.I.V.)
Brett, William H.
1868   *The Indian Tribes of Guiana*. London: Bell and Daldy.
n.d.   *Mission Work in the Forests of Guiana*. London: Society for Promoting Christian Knowledge; New York: E. and J. B. Young.
Burridge, Kenelm
1967   Levi-Strauss and Myth. In Edmund Leach, ed., *The Structural Study of Myth and Totemism*, pp. 91–115. London: Tavistock.
1969a   *Tangu Traditions*. Oxford: Oxford University Press.
1969b   *New Heaven, New Earth: A Study of Millenarian Activities*. New York: Schocken Books.
Butt, Audrey J.
1956   Ritual Blowing. Taling—A Causation and Cure of Illness among the Akawaio. *Man* 56: 49–55.
1960   The Birth of a Religion. *Journal of the Royal Anthropological Institute* 90: 66–106.
1965–66 The Shaman's Legal Role. *Revista do Museu Paulista*, n.s., 16: 151–86.
Caulin, Fray Antonio
1966   *Historia de la Nueva Andalucia*. Vol. I: *Estudio Preliminar y Edicion Critica de Pablo Ojer, S.J.* Biblioteca de la Academia Nacional de la Historia, v. 81. Caracas: Fuentes para la Historia Colonial de Venezuela.
Clastres, Pierre
1977   *Society against the State: The Leader as Servant and the Humane Uses of Power among the Indians of the Americas*. New York: Urizen Books.
Colson, Audrey J. Butt
1971a   Hallelujah among the Patamona Indians. *Antropologica* (Caracas) 28: 25–58.
1971b   Comparative Studies of the Social Structure of Guiana Indians and the Problem of Acculturation. In Fco. M. Salzano, ed., *The Ongoing Evolution of Latin American Populations*, pp. 61–126. Springfield, Ill.: Charles C. Thomas.
1973   Inter-tribal Trade in the Guiana Highlands. *Antropologica* (Caracas) 34: 5–70.

Colson (continued)

1976   The Affinal Triangle: Some Interrelationships between Myth, Social Structure and Personal Anxiety among the Carib Speakers of the Guiana Region. Paper presented in the symposium "Social Time and Social Space in Lowland South American Societies," XLII International Congress of Americanists, September, Paris.

Colson, Elisabeth

1953   Social Control and Vengeance in Plateau Tonga Society. *Africa* 23 (3): 199–212.

1974   *Tradition and Contract: The Problem of Order.* Chicago: Aldine.

1977   Power at Large: Meditation on "The Symposium on Power." In Raymond D. Fogelson and Richard N. Adams, eds., *The Anthropology of Power*, pp. 375–86. New York: Academic Press.

Coppens, Walter

1971   Las Relaciones Comerciales de los Yekuana del Caura-Paragua. *Antropologica* (Caracas) 30: 28–59.

Conto, Cesar, and Emiliano Isaza

1895   *Diccionario Ortografico de Apellidos y de Nombres Propios de Personas.* 4th ed. London: Moffat and Paige.

Cultural Survival

1979   *Special Report: Brazil.* Cambridge, Mass.: Cultural Survival, Inc.

De Jouvenel, Bertrand

1957   *Sovereignty: An Inquiry into the Political Good.* Chicago: University of Chicago Press.

Dole, Gertrude E.

1964   Shamanism and Political Control among the Kuikuru. *Volkerkundliche Abhandlungen*, I: 53–62. Beitrage zur Volkerkunde Sudamerikas, Hannover: Niedersachsisches Landesmuseum Abteilung fur Volkerkunde Kommissionsverlag.

1966   Anarchy without Chaos: Alternatives to Political Authority among the Kuikuru. In Marc J. Swartz et al., *Political Anthropology*, pp. 73–87. Chicago: Aldine-Atherton.

Evans-Pritchard, E. E.

1964   *Social Anthropology and Other Essays.* Glencoe: Free Press.

Fock, N.

1971   Authority — Its Magico-Religious, Political, and Legal Agencies — among Caribs in Northern South America. Stuttgart: *Proceedings of 38th International Congress of Americanists* 3: 31–34.

Fortes, Meyer

1969   *Kinship and the Social Order.* Chicago: Aldine.

Geertz, Hildred, and Clifford Geertz

1975   *Kinship in Bali.* Chicago: University of Chicago Press.

Gibb, Cecil A.

1968   Leadership. In Gardner Lindzey et al., eds., *Handbook of Social Psychology* IV: 205–73. Cambridge, Mass.: Addison-Wesley.

Gillin, John P.

1936   The Barama River Caribs of British Guiana. *Papers of the Peabody Museum of American Archaeology and Ethnology, Harvard University* 14 (2): 1–274.

1948   Tribes of the Guianas. In Julian H. Steward, ed., *Handbook of South American Indians*, vol. III: *The Tropical Forest Tribes*, pp. 799–860. Washington, D.C.: USGPO.

Gluckman, Max
1965   *Politics, Law, and Ritual in Tribal Society.* Chicago: Aldine.
Goldman, Irving
1979   *The Cubeo: Indians of the Northwest Amazon.* 2nd ed. Urbana: University of Illinois Press.
Goodenough, Ward H.
1962   Kindred and Hamlet in Lakalai, New Britain. *Ethnology* 1 (1): 5–12.
1970   *Description and Comparison in Cultural Anthropology.* Chicago: Aldine.
Gulliver, P. H.
1955   *The Family Herds.* London: Routledge and Kegan Paul.
1971   *Neighbors and Networks.* Berkeley and Los Angeles: University of California Press.
Holdridge, D.
1931   Notes on an Exploratory Journey in Southeastern Venezuela. *Geographical Review* 21: 373–78.
Im Thurn, Everard F.
1883   *Among the Indians of Guiana.* London: Kegan Paul, Trench, and Co.
Kaplan, Joanna O.
1975   *The Piaroa.* Oxford: Clarendon Press.
Kirk, G. S.
1970   *Myth, Its Meaning and Functions in Ancient and Other Cultures.* Berkeley and Los Angeles: University of California Press.
Kloos, Peter
1971   *The Maroni River Caribs of Surinam.* Assen: Van Gorcum.
Koch-Grunberg, Theodor
1916–28 *Vom Roroima zum Orinoco.* 5 vols. Berlin/Stuttgart: Dietrich Reimer; Strecker und Stroder.
1953   Mitos e Lendas dos Indios Taulipang e Arekuna. *Revista do Museu Paulista*, n.s., 7: 9–202.
Kracke, Waud H.
1978   *Force and Persuasion.* Chicago: University of Chicago Press.
Layrisse, Miguel, and J. Wilbert
1966   *Indian Societies of Venezuela: Their Blood Group Types.* Instituto Caribe de Antropologia y Sociologia, Fundacion La Salle de Ciencias Naturales, Monograph 13. Caracas: Editorial Sucre.
Levi-Strauss, Claude
1963   *Structural Anthropology.* Trans. Claire Jacobsen and Brooke Grundfest Schoepf. Garden City, N.Y.: Anchor Books.
Loukotka, Cestmir
1968   *Classification of South American Indian Languages.* Los Angeles: UCLA Latin American Center Reference Series, vol. 7.
Lowie, Robert H.
1948   Some Aspects of Political Organization among the American Aborigines. *Journal of the Royal Anthropological Institute* 78 (1–2): 11–24.
Meggitt, Mervyn
1973   The Pattern of Leadership among the Mae Enga of New Guinea. In Ronald M. Berndt and Peter Lawrence, eds., *Politics in New Guinea*, pp. 191–206. Seattle: University of Washington Press.

Migliazza, Ernesto
1970   Map: Territorio de Roraima e Alto Orinoco: Populacao Indigena, 1970. Boa Vista.
Mitchell, William E.
1963   Theoretical Problems in the Concept of the Kindred. *American Anthropologist* 65: 343–54.
1965   The Kindred and Baby Bathing in Academe. *American Anthropologist* 67: 977–83.
Moore, Sally F.
1972   Legal Liability and Evolutionary Interpretation: Some Aspects of Strict Liability, Self-Help, and Collective Responsibility. In Max Gluckman, ed., *The Allocation of Responsibility*, pp. 51–107. Manchester: Manchester University Press.
Moron, Guillermo
1964   *A History of Venezuela*. Ed., and trans. John Street. London: George Allen and Unwin.
Mosonyi, Esteban E.
1972   The Situation of the Indian in Venezuela: Perspectives and Solutions. In W. Dostal, ed., *The Situation of the Indian in South America*, pp. 43–55. Geneva: World Council of Churches.
1975   *El Indigena Venezolano en Pos de su Liberacion Definitiva*. Caracas: Universidad Central de Venezuela, Facultad de Ciencias Economicas y Sociales, Division de Publicaciones.
Nadel, S. F.
1953   Social Control and Self-Regulation. *Social Forces* 31: 265–73.
Oberschall, Anthony
1973   *Social Conflict and Social Movements*. Englewood Cliffs, N.J.: Prentice-Hall.
Ojer, Pablo, S.J.
1966   Estudio Preliminar. In Fray Antonio Caulin, *Historia de la Nueva Andalucia*, I:i = ccxcii. Biblioteca de la Academia Nacional de la Historia, v. 81. Caracas: Fuentes para la Historia Colonial de Venezuela.
Ramos, Alcida R., and Kenneth I. Taylor
1979   *The Yanoama in Brazil, 1979*. Copenhagen: International Work Group for Indigenous Affairs, Document 37.
Rice, A. H.
1937   *Exploration en Guyane Bresilienne*. Paris: Société d'éditions geographiques, maritimes, et coloniales.
Roberts, Simon
1979   *Order and Dispute: An Introduction to Legal Anthropology*. New York: St. Martin's.
Roth, Walter Edmund
1924   An Introductory Study of the Arts, Crafts, and Customs of the Guiana Indians. In *38th Annual Report of the Bureau of American Ethnology*, pp. 25–745. Washington, D.C.: USGPO.
Sahlins, Marshall D.
1965   On the Sociology of Primitive Exchange. In M. Banton ed., *The Relevance of Models in Social Anthropology*, pp. 139–236. London: Tavistock.
1972   *Stone-Age Economics*. Chicago: Aldine.

Salazar, Ernesto
1977   An Indian Federation in Lowland Ecuador. Copenhagen: International Work Group for Indigenous Affairs, Document 28.
Schmidt, Richard
1933   Leadership. In Encyclopedia of Social Science, IX: 282–87. New York: Macmillan.
Schomburgk, Robert H.
1840   A Description of British Guiana. London: Simpkin, Marshall, and Co.
Schneider, David M.
1972   What Is Kinship All About? In Priscilla Reining, ed., Kinship Studies in the Morgan Centennial Year, pp. 32–63. Washington D.C.: Anthropological Society of Washington.
Sharp, R. Lauriston
1958   People without Politics. In Verne F. Ray, ed., Systems of Political Control and Bureaucracy in Human Societies. Seattle: University of Washington Press.
Simpson, George Gaylord
1940   Los Indios Kamarakotos: Tribu Caribe de la Guayana Venezolana. Revista de Fomento 3 (22–25): 201–660. Caracas: Ministerio de Fomento.
1944   A Carib (Kamarakoto) Myth from Venezuela. Journal of American Folklore 57 (3226): 263–79.
Stauder, Jack
1972   Anarchy and Ecology: Political Society among the Majangir. Southwestern Journal of Anthropology 28: 153–68.
Tate, G. H. H.
1930a   Notes on the Mt. Roraima Region. Geographical Review 20: 53–68.
1930b   Through Brazil to the Summit of Mt. Roraima. National Geographic Magazine 58: 585–605.
Thomas, David J.
1971   Pemon Kinship Terminology. Antropologica (Caracas) 30: 3–17.
1972   The Indigenous Trade System of Southeast Estado Bolivar, Venezuela. Antropologica (Caracas) 33: 3–37.
1973   Pemon Demography, Kinship and Trade. Ph.D. dissertation, University of Michigan, Ann Arbor.
1976   El Movimiento Religioso de San Miguel entre los Pemon. Antropologica (Caracas) 43:3–52.
1978   A Fair Deal: Customary Exchange Rates and Sahlins' Diplomacy of Primitive Trade. Paper presented in the session "New Studies in Economic Anthropology," annual meeting of American Anthropological Association, November, Los Angeles.
1979a   Sister's Daughter Marriage among the Pemon. Ethnology 18 (1): 61–70.
1979b   Ephemeral Frontiers: In Venezuela, the last of the independent diamond miners lead a rugged existence. Natural History 88 (10): 66–71.
Vila, Marco Aurelio
1951   Aspectos Geograficos del Estado Bolivar. Caracas: Imprenta Nacional.

Weber, Max
 1961 The Three Types of Legitimate Rule. In Amitai Etzioni, ed., *Complex Organizations: A Sociological Reader*, pp. 4–14. New York: Holt.
Whitten, Norman E., Jr.
 1976 *Sacha Runa: Ethnicity and Adaptation of Ecuadorian Jungle Quichua*. Urbana: University of Illinois Press.
 1978 *Amazonian Ecuador: An Ethnic Interface in Ecological, Social, and Ideological Perspectives*. Copenhagen: International Work Group for Indigenous Affairs, Document 34.
Yalman, Nur
 1962 The Structure of the Sinhalese Kindred: A Re-examination of the Dravidian Terminology. *American Anthropologist* 64: 548–75.
 1967 *Under the Bo Tree*. Berkeley and Los Angeles: University of California Press.

Index

99